Tom Cole was born in Engl[...]
Australia as a seventeen-year-o[...]
bush, droving, horsebreaking a[...]
in Queensland and the Northe[...]
brief period a linesman on the ....
Then he went buffalo shooting.

He describes himself as the only buffalo hunter alive who was an active horseback hunter, broke in his own shooting horses, held five hundred square miles of country and employed tribal Aborigines as his assistants. During these years before the war, crocodiles were a sideline. His experiences were the basis for the bestseller *Hell West and Crooked* and his collection of short stories *Spears and Smoke Signals*.

After the Second World War he earned a reputation as a crocodile hunter in New Guinea. Today he lives in the Sydney suburb of Lindfield. He has two daughters.

THE LAST PARADISE

TOM COLE

Angus&Robertson
An imprint of HarperCollins*Publishers*

An Angus & Robertson Publication

Angus&Robertson, an imprint of
HarperCollins*Publishers*
25 Ryde Road, Pymble, Sydney, NSW 2073, Australia
31 View Road, Glenfield, Auckland 10, New Zealand

First published in Australia by Random House Australia in 1990
This A&R Imprint Lives revised edition published in 1993
Reprinted in 1993

National Library of Australia
Cataloguing-in-Publication data:

Cole, Tom, 1906– .
    The last paradise.
    ISBN 0 207 17876 3.
    1. Cole, Tom, 1906– . Plantation owners – Papua New Guinea –
    Biography. 3. Coffee trade – Papua New Guinea.– 4. Hunters –
    Papua New Guinea – Biography. I. Title. (Series: Imprint lives).
338.17373092

Cover photograph of Tom Cole, courtesy of the author
Typeset by Dragonhill Publishing Services, Kew, Victoria
Printed in Australia by Griffin Paperbacks, Adelaide

9 8 7 6 5 4 3 2
97 96 95 94 93

CONTENTS

DEDICATION

MY PUBLISHERS asked me if I wanted to dedicate this book to some-one and after giving this very important matter some earnest consid-eration, I decided to create a precedent, as I've never heard of an author dedicating a book to himself.

And why not, may I ask? After all, it is the author who does all the bloody work – chained to a typewriter, sweating his guts out day and night, his only relaxation a bottle of whisky or rum (depending on the weather), shunned by his friends, except when they want a drink, and who then waste valuable time asking stupid questions like 'Why don't you get yourself a typist?' knowing full well that a typist, if she's efficient, costs the bloody earth, more than an impecunious author can afford to pay. And if she isn't, tho' compatible, she brings all construc-tive work to an end and costs more in the long run anyway.

Then there are publishers to put up with, a group who, unfortu-nately, no author can do without – and do they know their strength! Terrorising and beating authors into submission. Editors run them a close second, gleefully firing punctuations in with a scatter gun and wearing out blue pencils (or computer keys nowadays) faster than if they put them on a grindstone.

Battered and beaten, kicked from pillar to post, thoroughly cowed, he is then asked by his publisher, usually after enjoying a far more generous lunch than a P.B.A. could ever afford: 'Do you wish to dedi-cate this book to anyone?'

I can think of no more deserving recipient of this honour than:

THE POOR BLOODY AUTHOR

WHO HAS SO UNSELFISHLY GIVEN UP ALL OF HIS TIME,

MOST OF HIS FRIENDS,

AND SOME OF HIS BOOZE

(BECAUSE YOU HAVE TO BE SOBER NOW AND THEN).

ACKNOWLEDGEMENTS

I OWE a great debt to a number of people for advice and assistance during the writing of this book, including:

Tania Hilder, for typing the manuscript; Stuart Inder for invaluable help in organising the manuscript, and checking all manner of facts; and Laurie Oakes for many things – including editing and advice.

I would also like to thank my daughters, Kathryn and Gabrielle, for all their support and encouragement – and especially Gabrielle, for thinking up the title.

– Tom Cole
Sydney 1993

PROLOGUE

'YOU'LL PROBABLY be all right,' the District Commissioner had said. 'But watch your step just the same. There's nothing out there that won't eat you' – waving an arm towards the sullen, turbid river – 'malarial mosquitoes, man-eating crocodiles and the Goaribaris.' The Purari Delta is notable for at least three things: it is where the Reverend James Chalmers and the equally Reverend Oliver Tompkins ended up in the cooking pots of the Goaribari head-hunters; it has an annual average rainfall of something in excess of four yards; and it is chock-a-block with crocodiles. The latter being the reason I was there on a cold, wet and windy night. It was November 1951.

Sitting in the bows of two thirty-foot canoes that were lashed together for stability, a local tribesman holding a spotlight over my shoulder, I saw the reflected eyes of a very big crocodile under the leaning mangroves. Water was running off the brim of my hat and I cursed the rain as I pushed the safety catch of my rifle to the 'off' position. Eight muscular paddlers guided the canoes silently towards the unsuspecting saurian.

From the corner of one eye I noted my harpoon man, clad in a loincloth, standing like an ebony statue, tensed up, holding the shaft ready to drive it into the crocodile with all his strength, for the hide was very tough. A long rope was lashed to the harpoon, which was a length of hardened steel with a barbed point. If not harpooned immediately after it was shot, the croc could sink and be swept away in the current.

The canoes edged closer and leaves of a mangrove branch dripping rain brushed my face as I put the rifle to my shoulder. The crocodile moved its head, but it was not yet alarmed. I squeezed the trigger and the harpoon man drove a foot of steel into its back.

Then immediate pandemonium. The paddlers all tried to grab at the coiled rope at once. The canoes, now unguided, started to drift sideways and slid against a leaning mangrove. There was a swirl and, to my alarm, a tail thumped the canoe side. The crocodile was not dead. I shouted over the din to slacken the rope off, which they did, but somehow it got caught over the partly submerged stump of a broken branch no longer than a man's thumb. I handed my rifle to the harpoon man and went to clear the rope, putting one foot on the branch and bending over to release it. The other foot was on the canoes, which started to drift away. I gave a despairing shout and grabbed at an over-hanging mangrove limb that snapped off as I plunged into the water. Since I was wearing a knee-length raincoat and had buckled round my waist a belt carrying about thirty cartridges, I sank like a stone.

It is difficult, in retrospect, to assess one's feelings at moments like these. There is, of course, the overwhelming one of survival. That I was in a state of mortal terror there is no doubt. To be under water, weighed down and very close to a wounded crocodile is not a comforting experience – but looking back over a long span of years, the danger may not have been so very great. My bullet would have gone within a hair's breadth of the crocodile's brain and it would have been partially stunned. Just the same, I was in a situation and a state of mind that didn't lend itself to assessing matters dispassionately. The first law of nature was working overtime.

It seemed a long time to me before I surfaced, although in all proba-bility it was only a few seconds. Time can be extremely relative! I broke through the surface, gulped air and willing hands dragged me aboard. As I stood up, water pouring off me, the harpoon man, who was my boss boy, said: 'Oh, Taubada, me fella think you go finish!' And they all burst out laughing. I could have shot the bloody lot.

My diary records this incident happening on 21 November 1951.

ONE

A CROC SKIN HANDBAG

BEFORE THE war most of my life had been spent in western Queensland and the Northern Territory, mainly the latter, where I had done just about everything in the way of station life – droving, cattle work, brumby running, horse breaking and, during the last nine years up to the outbreak of war, buffalo shooting in Arnhem Land, which also embraced some random crocodile hunting as a sideline at the end of the buffalo season.

The country in which I hunted ran across from the Wildman River to the South Alligator River, an area of about 500 square miles, give or take 100 square miles. Boundaries were not surveyed, or very little else for that matter. For this I paid to the Northern Territory Administration a rental of a shilling a square mile per annum, plus a licence fee of one pound. I never did find out what that was for, perhaps it was just a bit extra they tacked on for luck.

A buffalo hunting season was a strenuous five or six months. My tally was never less than 1000 bulls, and in 1937, my best season ever, my total was something over 1700. Apart from one, or perhaps two trained shooters, the rest of my team would be skinners, up to their necks in blood and guts all day – not the most salubrious of occupations. When I turned to crocodile hunting for the last few weeks before the wet season broke, it was more of a relaxation after the monotony of skinning buffalo. Also, it was something they could participate in to a greater extent, because they were natural hunters and crocodile meat was one of their favourite foods.

For my part it was becoming increasingly interesting because of the financial return and after a couple of seasons, we swung into it very efficiently. Preparations were, of course, very important and involved the entire camp – men, women and children. The first task was to gather large quantities of bark, which was easily stripped from the large paperbark trees that skirted the swamps. As the name implies, paperbark consists of layer after layer of fine tissue paper-like material, which is not only very light but also extremely buoyant. Another advantage was its proximity to the lagoons and waterholes where the hunting took place.

The bark was lashed together with vines to form a rough raft which, when ready for launching, was about eight or ten feet long, three feet or so wide and perhaps a couple thick. A crazy looking vessel indeed to do battle with man-eating crocodiles!

Early in the morning before the slightest breeze ruffled the surface of the water, the hunter, perched precariously on his bark platform, would pole his way out to midstream and start thrashing the water with the harpoon shaft. Any crocodile disturbed below would immediately move along the lagoon bed, stirring the accumulated silt that would send up a line of bubbles. Where the bubbles stopped was where the crocodile stopped, and the hunter would then drive his harpoon straight down into the back of the unsuspecting creature, before quickly poling his way to the shore. All hands would then grab the rope that was lashed to the harpoon and with a great deal of enthusiasm and an incredible amount of noise, drag the creature to the bank where I would despatch it. Altogether it was a remarkable exhibition of the superb bushcraft of ancient hunters that never ceased to fascinate me.

Usually, after about an hour, a breeze sprang up ruffling the surface and then it was impossible to see the line of bubbles, so all operations were suspended. It was a primitive way to hunt and certainly effective up to a point; at that time, although I had vaguely heard of shooting at night with a spotlight, it had never occurred to me to try it.

In 1939 the sabre-rattling in Europe was beginning to be heard in

Darwin and troops began to arrive, very much a novelty in that outpost, but at the same time giving a very welcome boost to a fragile economy. The population of the town, black, white and brindle, was no more than 1000, and even then maybe you'd have to throw in a few dogs.

The Northern Territory became the 7th Military District. Because of my knowledge of the coast, I was roped in by the Intelligence Section. I became a Military Reporting Officer and was given a number: I was MRO 3. Until war broke out in September, my duties were fairly vague, but even then the military hierarchy seemed to have no illusions regarding the Japanese.

The Darwin pearling fleets were manned by Japanese and there is no doubt that these industrious little men made good use of the time they spent ashore replenishing their water supplies for, although the naval charts were accurate, the mapping of the hinterland up to that time had been very much a hit and miss affair. For example, on my map I moved the West Alligator River about ten miles and although my mapping effort may not have been precisely accurate, it was a hell of a lot closer to its correct position than previously.

Of several rivers and streams that emptied into the Arafura Sea, some were navigable but quite a few were not. To me it was all good, clean, harmless fun.

Then there was a kind of a vacuum when Mr Chamberlain declared that there would be peace in our time. But of course that didn't last long. Like a Creeping Death it seemed to become more and more inevitable. On 3 September I was at the Adelaide River Roadhouse run by my wild old friend Harry Gribbon. I often wondered why on earth he ever took a roadhouse on, unless it was because he could get his booze wholesale. Some surveyors were there and they were equipped with a wireless set. We all sat round silently as the Prime Minister, Robert Menzies, said, 'Fellow Australians, it is my melancholy duty to tell you that we are at war with Germany'.

My value as a Military Reporting Officer was gradually diminishing, particularly when the North Australian Observers Unit was formed. Also, by this time I was moving cattle south in partnership with another cattleman, Jack Guild. Previously, I had taken up a thousand square miles on the Barkly Tablelands, 400 miles to the south. It was agreed that when we got our cattle settled, he would run the place and I would enlist in the army. Of course, I could have joined up in the Territory, and was invited to do so, but it was going on for twenty-five years since I had seen a town bigger than Darwin and I fancied a couple of weeks among the flesh pots before placing my services at the disposal of my King and Country.

It was 25 May 1943, Empire Day, when I went into camp at Royal Park in Melbourne. The grass was white with frost, crackling under my feet. I was issued with a uniform, two blankets, a bag of straw and pneumonia. They slipped another bout of pneumonia in when I wasn't looking and put me in hospital. I hovered in a kind of fairyland for a week or so, and shortly afterwards I was discharged. I was past the flush of youth – there was no place in that army for weaklings like me. I spent the rest of the war in Sydney.

Sydney celebrated the war's end in style. The dust finally settled after years of stringent austerity, and most people were endeavouring to cope with unaccustomed indulgences, which they did not find too difficult except that everybody wanted everything at once and there just wasn't enough to go round. After the rigorous restraints of the war years, demand exceeded supply many times over, particularly in the area of luxury goods.

And so it was my good fortune that, with a modicum of inspiration, I was able to make a modest contribution towards easing the lot of at least a few people who were burdened with so much surplus money that it was running out of their ears and detrimentally affecting their health.

What really started me off was when, in an idle moment, I noticed a crocodile skin handbag displayed among many others in a shop window, priced at the then exorbitant figure of £12. I stood for a moment calculating the amount of leather involved in its manufacture – perhaps a little more than a square foot.

I was well aware that the international method of measuring and valuing crocodile skins was per inch across the belly and I also remembered quite clearly that a shipment of a couple of hundred skins averaged about twenty-two inches. The market price then was one shilling an inch. Taking a twenty-two inch skin as an example, I calculated that it would contain about fourteen to sixteen square feet of leather. Even being extremely conservative, and allowing for a few middlemen, there appeared to be substantial profits for someone – me for instance.

Suddenly I was lost in the past. My mind went back to those halcyon days of the Northern Territory where every man was his own destiny. The limitless plains, the galloping freedom of a good horse, blazing sunsets and, to quote Rudyard Kipling: 'Where the dawn comes up like thunder!'

A sudden blast on a horn by an impatient motorist in the stream of traffic behind me brought me back to earth. For the next few days I thought crocodiles and I dreamt crocodiles. My head was working like a tin of worms. I got in touch with an old mate, one Roy Edwards, who had a pearling fleet in Darwin that had been taken over by the Navy at the outbreak of war. They wrecked most of his luggers in a fairly workmanlike manner and, when the war business was tidied up, Roy got substantial compensation and successfully turned his talents into other channels. A couple of letters and we were in business – just like that.

It was a most rewarding enterprise. Roy would buy the skins and ship them to Sydney; when the shipping documents arrived I would arrange for a carrier to take them to a tannery; when the tanning process was completed they were delivered to a manufacturer and the manufacturer would happily post me a cheque. They were indeed salad days.

Then hunters found out about shooting at night with a spotlight. It was incredibly easy, but it was decimating too. With a powerful spotlight a crocodile can be approached to within a few feet. So can most other animals for that matter. Many motorists have had the experience of cattle or sheep transfixed in their headlights on country roads at night. Out west in kangaroo country, the creatures can be seen lying dead, hundreds of them that had been hit by cars mostly travelling at night. An animal does not associate a light with danger and, of course, animals – humans, too – cannot tell what is behind a powerful light.

As Northern Territory crocs were shot out, shipments of skins from Darwin started to taper off, and makers were clamouring for supplies, which I could not provide. My handbag makers were desperate, and I was even more desperate – crocodile skins were my life's blood.

My thoughts turned to New Guinea, and I got hold of my old cartoonist mate Eric Jolliffe. We got in touch with Ion Idriess, known to his friends as Jack, who was not only a successful author, but also had written at least two books on New Guinea. The number of people those two knew between them was astonishing. We did a pub crawl, a memorable pub crawl. It was the time of the year when most Australians in New Guinea took their leave, and we talked to Patrol Officers, we talked to oil drillers, we talked to trawler masters, coconut planters, rubber planters, and prospectors. The range of stories was incredible. Some said that they had been in the islands for years and never seen a crocodile, though, yes, they'd heard about them. One New Guinea veteran with an alcoholically-induced imagination claimed that they were often seen creeping through the streets of Port Moresby at night. When we left him he was seeing them in Martin Place.

About fourteen pubs later, give or take half a dozen, what I lacked in knowledge I made up for in enthusiasm. I decided to go to New Guinea and see for myself. My enthusiasm being strengthened considerably when I found that in order to encourage business ventures, all income tax had been waived.

It was seven o'clock in the evening, and in the limited area of the Sydney Airport departure lounge it was standing room only. I estimated that there were well over 200 people jammed into a space designed to accommodate half that number. There was no such thing as a bar at the airport in 1950. Consequently, everyone had taken the necessary precautionary measures to ensure that the leave-taking was conducted in the normal time-honoured fashion, which at the same time stimulated them sufficiently to generate enough decibels to float a battleship – or maybe sink one, whatever decibels do in vast quantities.

Air travel at that time, though by no means a novelty, was still comparatively limited. I had probably done more flying than most. Before the war I had experienced a few flights in private planes. I had flown in passenger planes down the west coast to Perth and across to Melbourne. I had flitted around the Queensland Gulf country, but by far the most interesting and certainly the most leisurely flight I had ever undertaken was by Lockheed Constellation to London, returning by flying boat. A steady five days by the 'Connie' and a stately ten by the seaplane, with the luxury of a bed every night both ways. Jet lag hadn't been invented, and although I didn't regard myself as a seasoned air traveller, I thought I knew what it was all about. But then, I had not flown to New Guinea before. It turned out to be quite an experience.

The aeroplane that I was about to join was a Qantas DC4 with a carrying capacity of about fifty plus a captain, first officer, radio officer and a couple of hostesses. Just on eight o'clock one of the ground staff walked around ringing a bell, calling on everyone to board. I understood we would be landing in Port Moresby at about sunrise.

I said goodbye to my wife, who was not only in a state of mortal terror at the thought of my going to New Guinea to hunt man-eating crocodiles, but also was a little bit pregnant. Eventually there was a final call to board the aircraft and we all drifted across the tarmac to the waiting DC4. Taking my seat beside a jovial fellow who was still clutching a bottle of beer, I buckled my seat belt and settled in for a long night. It didn't really turn out the way I expected.

Shortly after take-off, when we were given the all clear to release our seat belts, it quickly became apparent that the majority of passengers were one big, happy family. Everybody seemed to know everyone else and the hostesses were soon flat out serving drinks. My companion in the seat beside me was eyeing me off. He could see I was a 'new boy' and eventually he asked: 'Have you been to New Guinea before?'

I shook my head: 'No, this is my first visit.'

He nodded and I could see he was curious, trying to sum me up: 'What's your line – are you an oil man?' The Australasian Petroleum Company was up there in a fairly big way drilling for oil.

I put him out of his misery: 'No, I'm a crocodile hunter.'

This really shook him. 'A crocodile hunter – fair dinkum?' He prodded the man in front: 'Jim, this bloke's a bloody crocodile hunter!'

There was quite a racket going on and the hostesses were dashing from seat to seat with alcoholic refreshments. My companion was sufficiently impressed to insist on buying me a drink, which was all right by me, and soon most of the other passengers knew that I was a real live professional crocodile hunter – 'none of this weekend pot-shooting bullshit'.

Everybody was walking up and down the aisle buying. Others offered me drinks, and soon I had more than I could handle, or nearly more. I was plied with questions, most of which I couldn't answer. Where was I going? Were there many crocs in New Guinea? (That was something I wanted to know; none of them could tell me very much).

We landed at Brisbane, took off again, and flew all night, and drank all night. No one wanted to sleep, no one had any intention of sleeping. The hostesses never stopped. At about half past three in the morning one of them said to me: 'I hate these bloody New Guinea trips. I've never been on one yet when anyone slept. It's the only bloody run in the world where they never stop drinking.' She looked ready to drop.

We landed at Jacksons, the international airport that was named after John Jackson, a wartime Royal Australian Air Force hero who died in aerial combat with the Japanese. Most of us piled into a bus, some were met by friends and what I assumed to be company executives. Nearly all the passengers went straight off to sleep.

It was seven miles to town and the countryside bore no resemblance to what I had expected, having experienced other tropical countries in my travels. Except for the swarms of natives everywhere, it could have been part of Queensland. The trees were mainly a type of white gum and the grass was identical to what in Queensland is usually called kangaroo grass.

The road swung down towards a beach and here was a large native market that I was told was Koki Market. There were hundreds of natives and it was as colourful as it was noisy. I could not get much idea of what was on display, although I caught glimpses of fish strung on poles, some cooking pots and types of greens that I was unable to recognise. The bus slowed down and a couple of young fellows jumped on to the running board and gave the driver a handful of betel nut, presumably for their fare into town.

From here the road followed the beach, houses on the right-hand side overlooking the sea were all Queensland-style: built on high stilts, catching vagrant breezes and giving the occupants a pleasant view.

The cleanliness of the natives was very noticeable; most of the men wore white loincloths while the women favoured grass skirts, many of which were dyed in bright colours, that swung provocatively against their black satin skins as they walked, laughing and joking. They all looked clean and healthy.

I liked the place immediately and because of my unusual occupation I was something of a curiosity. There had never been any professional crocodile hunting before, which was very good news.

The town was smaller than I expected and apart from a few rusting hulks in the harbour, there was little to indicate that it had been a key enclave during the war. At the end of the war I guessed that the whole place had been redeveloped with ex-army and navy surplus. Almost everyone had some kind of wartime vehicle, most people seemed to have a jeep, including the Administration officers.

There had been huge disposal sales of surplus army material, a lot of the stuff going for the proverbial song. One man bought a telephone line for £10 and when he rolled it up had twenty tons of copper wire, which was at a premium in Australia. Another who thought he was bidding for a five-ton truck found himself with a brand-new tank bristling with machine guns and a dozen cases of .5 ammunition.

Among other things, Port Moresby was notable for the number of clubs in relation to the size of the town and the population – it supported six clubs with ease, in addition to two hotels. The Public Service, which was the predominant sector, had two. The oil company Oil Search had one, there was a golf club where playing golf was regarded as a disadvantage, and an RSL Club on Ela Beach where the art of fighting was not lost. The Papua Club was a stronghold of planters whose competence and dedication put them in world class. True, it was in the tropics and not very far from the equator and I don't think that anyone died of thirst, but judging by the desperation with which they threw themselves into their only form of relaxation, it must have been something that was uppermost in their minds.

At the clubs and hotels, all drinks were served by European barmen and barmaids. The indigenous people, although employed, were not allowed to handle drinks or pour them, which mystified me. I assumed that there was some reason for it, but never found out why. They washed glasses, cleaned up, carried trays of drinks to the lounge areas, but pouring drinks was against the law.

Before the First World War, New Guinea, which comprised New Guinea, New Ireland, New Britain and adjacent islands, had been German territory and was ceded to Australia as a Mandated Territory by the League of Nations and was governed from Rabaul.

Following the Second World War it was found expedient for New Guinea and Papua (an Australian territory) to be combined and governed from Port Moresby, and the region was proclaimed the Territory of Papua and New Guinea. This was done largely with the object of co-ordinating self-government some time in the future.

Papua New Guinea was governed from Canberra through an Administrator, Mr J. K. Murray, an agricultural academic who, because of his amiable disposition towards the natives, was contemptuously referred to as 'Kanaka Jack'. I found him a very good bloke, very much a gentleman, but he appeared to be quite unsuited to the job.

The lingua franca on the Papua side of the territory was known as Police Motu, which I immediately set about learning. Apart from a white man being known as 'Taubada' and a white women always called 'Sinabada', it was not used exclusively in Port Moresby but would be essential if working among natives. It was the dialect of the Motuan people, a fairly large group whose villages were scattered up and down the coast from the capital.

The Motuan people were blue water sailors centuries before the white man arrived. Their huge, seagoing lakatois, hewn out of solid logs with stone axes, rigged with the spectacular crab claw sails, beat into the south-east trade winds year after year loaded with mother of pearl, tortoise shell, and clay cooking pots, which they traded with their coastal neighbours. Although they probably avoided the head-hunting villages of the Purari Delta, they sailed as far west as the Fly River. The biggest of their villages was Hanuabada. In their language Hanua means village and Bada means big. It was just above this marine village that sat on stumps in the tidal waters of Port Moresby's harbour where the Administration buildings and Government House were built, and it was from here that the first native people were recruited, so it was logical to adopt their dialect as a means of communication.

For administrative purposes, the country was divided into districts, which were controlled by District Officers, later upgraded (although in name only) to District Commissioners. Each DO, as he was known then, had an Assistant District Officer (ADO) with, depending on the size of the district, Patrol Officers and Cadet Patrol Officers (POs and CPOs). At this time the DOs were nearly all prewar men and very dedicated. Nearly all the incoming Officers and Cadets were the product of the Australian School of Pacific Administration (ASOPA) where they underwent a rigorous training period. When they went out into the field, they had completed courses covering law, surveying, advanced first aid, and general administration, among others, and they took their oaths to serve faithfully and well.

The country and adjacent islands were divided into twelve districts which – because of the rapidly expanding oil exploration, mining and agriculture, the opening up of what was previously designated 'uncontrolled territory' – soon became too unwieldy for effective administration and so were gradually subdivided.

The life of an Administration officer in one of these outposts was one which, in addition to all the things he learned at ASOPA, whether he be a lowly Cadet or District Commissioner, required a great deal of courage, lots of stamina, plenty of resilience, an abundance of patience and, perhaps above all, a great sense of humour. Before the Second World War, field officers were not supposed to marry until they reached the rank of DO, although a few did risk the wrath of their superior officers and take the plunge. After the war this was greatly relaxed and consequently it was not uncommon to find women on some of the outstations. Most of them led lonely lives when their husbands were on patrol for weeks on end.

Their only form of transport was 'shanks pony'. With a line of carriers they doggedly walked through fever-ridden, leech-infested jungle in blazing tropical heat or drenching rain, climbing mountain ranges in swirling mists and icy winds. And they died, too. They died under a hail of arrows, they died from massive axe wounds, they died of the dreaded malaria fever. And they kept their oaths.

Although Australia was only just over the horizon, this was another world, entirely different to the one I had known – the climate, the terrain, the indigenous population and the adventurers who were blazing new trails and reshaping the lives of these Stone Age people.

Here one of the world's last frontiers was being broken down and for them nothing would ever be the same again. Roads were blasted from mountainsides, jungles were bulldozed flat for airstrips. A war of unimaginable ferocity had been and gone, leaving scars and wounds that would take a long time to heal. Drills relentlessly bored their way deep into the earth in a frantic search for oil, copper and gold. The natives stood and watched all these activities with a mixture of awe and wonder, and they learnt to drive tractors and motor vehicles, and drink the white man's booze (although when I arrived, they weren't permitted to do it legally). And they were told that in the not very distant future they would be governing their own country. They were not sure that they liked that idea, it sounded a bit frightening, but anyway that was 'by and by'.

I had to make a start somewhere and it seemed to me that the logical place was one of the clubs. I was already being regarded as something of a curiosity, there was a lot of interest in my unusual occupation. There were a few vessels plying the coast, most of which I was given to understand were ex-army vessels with perhaps a forty-ton capacity, referred to as 'K' boats, most of their names beginning with a 'K'.

I talked to the captain of a copra carrier, explaining to him that I was hoping to be able to go for a cruise along the coast to have a look at the possibilities of crocodile hunting. He unhesitatingly offered me a passage. 'It might be a bit rough,' he explained.

That didn't take any thinking about and on a Monday morning we left the placid calm of the harbour, turning into a strong south-easter. It was heavy going, and the seas were breaking over the wheelhouse where I stayed beside the captain. We reached Redscar, a monolithic headland which, once rounded, gave us a slightly improved passage. Soon after, we turned into Galley Reach and anchored in calm waters just off a village called Manu Manu.

The anchor had hardly hit bottom before we were surrounded by outrigger canoes, skilfully manoeuvred by grass-skirted villagers clamouring to trade fish, fruit and vegetables for tobacco. The fruit was limited to bananas and paw paws and the vegetables, with the exception of what appeared to be a variety of Chinese cabbage, were unknown to me. After a good deal of jabbering, and shrieks of laughter at the captain's attempt to bargain with a very limited knowledge of Motu, we got an enormous bunch of beautiful bananas and some nice fish. He pointed out that if the fish's eyes were not sunken, you could be sure they were fresh, something I have frequently confirmed since.

The next morning we were on our way at the crack of dawn, and an hour and a half later tied up at a plantation jetty with a background of tall rubber trees. A couple of blasts on the boat's siren quickly brought an old army blitz truck loaded with plantation workers.

The driver was Trevor Ward, managing the plantation for his father, who had retired to Australia. I introduced myself and we sat talking on bales of rubber. I explained my purpose in coming to the country, and his interest was immediate. Why not leave the ship, he suggested, and stay with him? That, needless to say, I was happy to do. After the boat left and the stores were loaded on to the truck, we drove to his house where I met his extremely attractive wife, Peggy.

Plantation life in Papua New Guinea was very pleasant and orderly. The house was roomy, sitting on stilts about eight feet off the ground and completely surrounded by wide verandahs so that it caught every precious breeze. There were three servants, clad in spotless loincloths called ramis, gliding silently about their tasks. The house was run with a quiet efficiency.

Trevor was fascinated with the idea of crocodile hunting and assured me that there were plenty in Galley Reach. But he had never heard of anyone wanting to hunt them, except for sport or to kill them when they became a danger to plantation workers or stock. Most plantations kept a few head of cattle and some saddle horses.

His enthusiasm was so great that he asked his wife to arrange dinner early and in the meantime, after listening carefully to my description of the procedure, suggested we go down to the jetty and get things ready. He very quickly got a grasp of the general requirements and, with his boss boy and a couple of others, we got into his truck and went down to the river. There were a number of canoes secured along the bank. They appeared pretty flimsy and most of them were half full of water, but when a couple of the biggest were bailed out, they rode quite high. I estimated them to be at least twenty-five feet long. Talking rapidly in Motu, Trevor asked who owned them, then turned to me and said, 'They belong to a couple of my blokes. I'll fix them up with a few sticks of tobacco. We'll lash a couple of the biggest together and deck them over with bark, which will make them stable – you'll be surprised at what they'll carry'. I nodded, he was in his own territory and he certainly knew what he was doing. He fired a string of instructions in Motu again, after which we got back into the truck and returned to the house where we stretched out on a couple of squatter chairs on the verandah and repaired our wasted tissues with a few Scotches.

I was fully equipped – my rifle being a .25 calibre high velocity Mauser action in perfect condition. I had a powerful spotlight and a heavy-duty battery, a couple of harpoons and about fifty feet of half-inch rope attached to one of them. I had also brought a bag of salt for curing the skins.

Over dinner I told Trevor that crocodiles were found at night mostly under the mangroves, with just the top half of the jaw showing above the water, usually resting on the mud. When a strong light was shone on them, the reflection of their eyes was quite intense. They could be approached to within a few feet, but silence was important – the slightest sound of voices and they would immediately submerge.

Peggy anxiously asked if it was very dangerous and I confidently assured her that there was no risk unless someone did something particularly stupid. Then, flashing me a smile, she said: 'Well, you take care of my husband – he's the only one I've got.'

Just before dark we drove down to the jetty. Two of the biggest canoes had been lashed firmly together using vines. They were separated by about four feet, with a decking of bark laid on top also secured with vines, which Trevor assured me were as strong as ropes. I was quite impressed with the efficiency of it all.

There was another man there who I hadn't seen yet – the Plantation Assistant, a young fellow from Queensland who was anxious to join in the fun, and Trevor introduced me to Barry Black.

A large group of plantation workers had gathered at the jetty, most of them carrying paddles and all of them jabbering excitedly. After a good deal of arguing and pleading, Trevor's boss boy and four others were selected and we pushed off. We paddled out into the main stream, keeping about 300 or 400 yards off the mangroves. Someone had thoughtfully provided two empty cases, so I sat on one and Trevor took the other. It was now dark enough for the light to be effective. I switched it on and began sweeping the bank. Very soon I picked up the reflected eyes of a fairly big croc, which I judged to be about ten feet long. Signalling silence, I handed the light to Trevor, who gave a low whistle of amazement and handed it back. I explained that the crocodile was only visible to someone looking straight along the beam. Barry then took the light and after that it was passed round to the crew one by one. I judged that we were about 400 yards away and handing the light to Trevor, told him to point it over my right shoulder and keep it firmly focused on the reflected eyes.

Conditions were perfect – it was a beautiful night with a gentle breeze, and where the crocodile was lying was clear of mangroves. The canoes glided towards the target, Trevor was doing a perfect job, and as we got closer the head became more recognisable. It was obvious that where the croc was lying was very shallow, which meant the harpoon would not be needed. The canoes glided closer and at a range of about twelve feet I pressed the trigger. The reptile gave the merest shudder as the bullet smashed into its skull.

It was a clean kill. Trevor said, 'You really had me scared, Tom. I thought you were never going to fire, but I'll say this, you certainly made it look easy!' The entire crew excitedly jumped into the black, slimy mud to drag the dead crocodile aboard. We pushed off into deeper water and I realised then that the native canoes were perfect for this kind of operation. They were easily manoeuvred, sliding over the mud comfortably, and their weight carrying ability was better than I first thought. The crew sat along the side dangling their legs in the water to wash off the stinking mud, then took up their paddles and we were once more on our way, everyone's enthusiasm at fever pitch.

Very soon I picked up a second croc with the spotlight, killing it as easily as the first. Then, when we were out in deep water again, I handed my rifle to Trevor. 'Have a go,' I said. 'You'll be okay.' He was delighted. We cruised along for a couple of miles before I spotted another one and as I was swinging the light round, I saw yet another. This was not unusual. A male and a female will often be alongside one another. I told Trevor: 'There's two there, about a hundred yards apart, but we'll only get one this time. We may pick the other fellow up later. I think the one furthest away is the bigger so we'd better take a wide sweep around. If the one this side gets a smell of us, he could startle the other.' We came around, the paddlers doing a good job, and I stood up behind Trevor holding the light. I had told him that he was to fire when I tapped him on the shoulder – and not before. The craft, now gently propelled, glided closer. I could sense that Trevor was getting strung up. There were no obstructions, because the tide was dropping fast and most of the crocodile's head was out of the water. It was a big one. I tapped Trevor on the shoulder and he pressed the trigger, the detonation reverberating across the water. It was a clean kill. I laughed. 'Simple wasn't it?' For a second or so he didn't reply – I thought he was getting his breath back – then: 'I thought that bloody tap was never coming, but you're right. It certainly is simple.' Then reflectively: 'When you were explaining it over dinner tonight you made it sound so easy I didn't really believe you.'

When the crocodile was dragged aboard, I noted that we had about a foot of freeboard – say a couple more crocs. We travelled about half a mile and turning around a mangrove point and we spotted one that I guessed was about eight or nine feet. Barry's rifle was an ex-army .303, which had been partially stripped down and was quite effective.

He took his seat while I kept the light steady over his shoulder and as we glided up I gave him a tap. It was a clean kill and when it was pulled aboard, Trevor remarked that we were getting close to our limit.

The tide had now turned and we crossed to the other side of the estuary and shortly after picked up the eyes of a big fellow lying in a thicket of young mangroves, half out of the water. It looked an awkward shot so I told Trevor I would take it.

We weaved around for a while until I got a fairly good sight. It was further away than I would have liked, but I killed it cleanly. It was the biggest of the four and, while it was easy enough to drag over the slimy mud, it took a fair bit of juggling to get it aboard. Every time the crew tried to lift the beast, they would sink further in the mud, all of which they thought was hilarious. Eventually they got it aboard, laughing heartily while they cleaned the mud from themselves.

Trevor said, 'I think we've got our limit, Tom'. I glanced at the freeboard and agreed. We headed for home, and pulled into the plantation wharf shortly after midnight. Canoes were unloaded and we walked up to the house. We had a couple of nightcaps and I said the crocodiles had better be skinned early in the morning. Putrefaction set in quickly in that climate.

We were up at dawn. A fresh pot of tea was standing on a side table and after a hastily swallowed cup, we made our way down to the wharf. There was plenty of labour available, I had already learned that what Trevor referred to as 'the labour line' amounted to more than 200 workers, most of whom were rubber tappers.

After the skinning was completed and the skins were salted, rolled up and stacked in a corner of the shed, we went back to the house for breakfast. Later Trevor took me for a drive round the 1000-acre plantation. It was beautifully laid out, the trees planted with symmetrical precision using an equilateral triangle so that no matter what direction one looked they formed a perfect line. There seemed to be swarms of tappers all over the place busily collecting the sap, called latex. The tapping was done with a special knife, the bark being scraped away, which allowed the milky latex to drip into a small cup that was attached to the tree with a wire holder. The full cups were collected, emptied into cans, and the latex was carted to a factory where it was coagulated, dried in a smoke house, and baled up. The tappers and factory workers seemed a happy lot, laughing, joking and singing as they went about their tasks.

Over lunch I gave Peggy and Trevor a rundown on the business side of crocodile skins and the various steps and stages before they got to their final destination – the customer. I told them of my early experiences in the Northern Territory and how the business had developed and about my anxiety when the Territory skins started to taper off. I was extremely grateful to both of them for their hospitality and Trevor's interest and assistance, which to me, being very much a new chum, was overwhelming. I was in another world and it was a period of initiation that was invaluable. I was anxious to express my appreciation in some practical way and wasn't quite sure how to go about it. I decided to take the bull by the horns.

He laughed: 'Don't think for one moment, Tom, that I'm too proud to pick up a quid. Sure, my old man owns this place and I'm working my way into shares, but – as he frequently tells me – he came up the hard way and anything I get I've got to work for.'

I felt better after that and also made a mental note to get a nice crocodile skin handbag made for Peggy.

That night there was the usual bunch of plantation hands down at the wharf, their enthusiasm stimulated not only by the novelty of hunting with a spotlight but also by the thought of the crocodile meat. The boss boy, Igo, walked over and engaged Trevor in conversation, which I judged to be of some importance. I had been furiously studying the Motu dialect and caught the word for crocodile, which was 'huwala', and 'bada heria', which meant very big. Trevor turned to me. 'They know of a big crocodile that lives up a creek towards the coast. If it's as big as they say, we'll be flat out carrying it.'

I pondered for a moment. 'What do you think? Should we lash another canoe on?'

'No, I don't think so, it would take too long. If we can't carry it we can tow it behind. When these fellows get worked up about anything a story loses nothing in the telling.' I thought they weren't much different from our Aborigines.

We headed down the estuary and made good time, and an hour or so later we turned into a creek lined with Nipa palm, the overhanging fronds from each bank touching. Now we had the current against us and it was hard pulling. After a while, Igo spoke rapidly to the crew and they pulled in to the bank for a rest. Soon after they resumed paddling I saw a fairly big crocodile, but it did not seem to be anything special. Igo, after a brief look, shook his head and grunted 'Las'. I knew what that word meant and told Trevor: 'We'll pick him up on the way back, he'll still be there.'

We paddled on and about a quarter of an hour later I picked up the eyes of a monster, not in at the bank but swimming strongly towards us. I cursed silently as I handed the light to Trevor. He handed it back and whistled in amazement. The crocodile was about 200 yards away, making a wake like a battleship. The light went the rounds of the crew who whispered excitedly: 'Bada heria!' It was a big one, right enough. I turned the craft into the bank opposite to the side he was following, keeping the light on him until he swam out of sight.

'What do we do now?' asked Trevor.

I pointed out that we knew which way the croc had gone. 'He'll pull into the bank sooner or later so best we stay here for a while,' I said. 'I would think that it will be sooner than later.'

The crew took the opportunity to roll cigarettes. With few exceptions they were compulsive smokers, which they alternated with chewing beetle nut, a combination that would shrivel anybody's tastebuds. After half an hour we resumed the hunt. It was now one o'clock. We hadn't gone far, perhaps a mile, when we saw our prey lying peacefully on the mud, maybe dreaming of some alluring female crocodile.

I would like to be able to relate an exciting and dramatic story of how I killed the monster, of an heroic struggle with a mighty saurian, but unfortunately I can't. The simple truth is, I shot the poor bugger when he was asleep. The titanic struggle was trying to get him on to the canoes. Looking at him lying quietly in the mud, I reckoned he would be between fifteen and eighteen feet long and weigh maybe three-quarters of a ton.

Imagine our almost enthusiastic crew up to their bellies in stinking, slimy, black, bottomless mud struggling with an enormous member of the lizard family weighing nearly a ton, grunting, groaning and panting in their endeavours to lift him on to our canoes at two o'clock in the morning. You would probably say: 'Impossible!' You would be dead right, too, and it didn't take us very long to find that out either.

There was only one way to get him home and that was to tow him behind the canoes. Using the harpoon rope, for which up to now we'd had no use, we lashed his head to one of the poles holding the canoes together. It was heavy paddling. We arrived just before daybreak.

It was now getting towards neap tides, the low tides, which were the best time for shooting because of the mudbanks being more exposed. After our efforts last night, we took a night off; everyone was weary.

Trevor had been telling me about the Purari Delta, which sounded pretty exciting. It was about 100 miles across and probably about fifty back to where the Purari River came crashing down from the Highlands country thousands of feet above. It was a mass of waterways and islands, and was lousy with crocodiles. The District Headquarters was at Kikori and apart from the outstation, there was only a trade store half a mile away, a sawmill at a place called Romilly Sound and an outstation at Beara where the ADO in charge was a man named 'Speed' Graham. The oil company, APC, was out there somewhere, too.

The Number One Kiap, as Trevor called him, was something of a living legend. 'Clarrie' Healy was a contemporary of Jack Hides, Ivan Champion, Jim Taylor, John Black, and Jim O'Malley – most of whom could 'strip their sleeves and show their scars'. Some still had arrowheads embedded in their bodies. Healy had quite a reputation as a crack shot and another claim to fame was a remarkable ability to demolish a bottle of rum. It seemed I might have a soul mate out there in the Purari Delta, and a profitable one at that. Profitable soul mates are very rare. Trevor had been out there a number of times recruiting labour. I knew him well enough by now to be sure that he was not given to exaggerating. But even allowing for a little extra colour, it still seemed like a crocodile hunter's dream.

Villages were scattered throughout and each one was controlled by a village policeman, who were selected in consultation with the District Officer and the villagers. These two men were, in most cases, the village chief and his offsider. There had always been a recognised kind of hierarchy among themselves with their traditional chiefs.

The villages were visited regularly by an ADO or an experienced PO and nearly always accompanied by a cadet gaining field experience. They held courts and settled disputes. Most tribal matters of a minor nature were dealt with by the village policeman.

Each village had a Rest House that was set aside for the exclusive use of District Services officers when on patrol or for travellers, recruiters, prospectors and, I thought to myself, crocodile hunters, which Trevor confirmed. 'So you'll have no accommodation problems,' he said, 'and if you need a cook the village policeman will arrange that, too, although most people take their own. I always travel with a cook and my personal boy.' It sounded better and better.

From then on my thoughts were completely dominated by the delta and the next morning at breakfast I asked when the next boat was due. 'A couple of days I'd think,' he said. 'There's no set schedule.' I had to get back to Moresby to get myself organised.

Trevor told me: 'You won't have any trouble with canoes out there. Make sure you've got plenty of tobacco, it's the best currency you can have. Money's important but tobacco more so. Take a hundred quid in shillings.' In New Guinea, shillings were called marks.

He went on to tell me an amusing story of Clarrie Healy in his younger days shortly after he joined District Services. As a child, Healy lost the sight of an eye in an accident and had to have a glass eye fitted. When he first became a Patrol Officer, he was given a gang of prisoners and ordered to build an aerodrome. His gang was split up, with some felling trees, some dragging the fallen timber, some digging drains, and he was having great difficulty keeping them all working. As soon as he left one gang to supervise another, they would stop work; running backwards and forwards between them was not only frustrat-

22

ing but also exhausting. Healy came up with a bright idea. He called the tree felling gang together, paced off an area that he considered was a fair day's work, and solemnly took his glass eye out and placed it on a log. Then he told them to get on with the job because he was watching them. The ploy certainly produced results – for a while. But one day the trees did not seem to be crashing to the ground with such regularity and he went back to the gang to see why the slow-down had occurred. It was very simple – one of them had come up with the bright idea of covering Clarrie's glass eye with a filthy sweat rag!

Trevor said: 'Bear in mind that the Kiap, wherever you are, is about two jumps ahead of Jesus Christ. The missionaries are mostly all right, but the Popey's are the best of that lot.'

'What's a Popey?' I innocently enquired.

'They're Catholics – take 'em a bottle of rum and you've got a friend for life. There are forty-seven different varieties of missionary – you've only got to kick a hollow log and one jumps out of each end.'

Trevor looked thoughtful: 'You know, Tom, it just occurred to me – the missionaries will do anything for a quid, they've got some of the best plantations in the country, they've got sawmills, trade stores, shipping – you name it they've got it. There's a saying in New Guinea about the missionaries – 'They came to do good and they did bloody well!' We both laughed.

'There's no reason why you couldn't recruit some of them – get 'em croc hunting. Quite a few of them go out shooting wild pigs, pigeons and so forth. Some of 'em are very good shots.'

Two days later I said goodbye to the Wards, but it was by no means the last I saw of them, and from time to time a case of crocodile skins would arrive in Moresby with a consignment of rubber from the Ward plantation.

TWO

1000 BULLETS, PLEASE

THE CREW let the lines go and we chugged down Galley Reach at a steady eight knots. I asked the skipper what the weather was like outside. His reply was not very reassuring: 'Bloody terrible! Even the cockroaches were seasick!' It was something like an eight-hour run, I reckoned I could put up with eight hours of intense discomfort and although I didn't expect to be seasick, it was touch and go at times. It was nearly dark when we tied up at the wharf.

I took a room at the Papua Hotel, 'the Top Pub' as the locals called it. All business houses, Government offices and the Post Office opened at eight o'clock so I was able to make an early start. I went to the Post Office first. Among my mail was a letter from Johnson's, the skin buyers, offering ten shillings an inch across the belly for crocodile skins and one shilling a foot for pythons. I wasn't interested in the snake skins, but worked out that I could pay shooters about one shilling and sixpence an inch for dry salted croc skins. I had already found out that freight and handling were going to be fairly expensive.

The bloke in the wholesale division of Burns Philp was startled when I gave him an initial order for five tons of salt. He asked if I'd made a mistake – he couldn't possibly imagine what anyone in that country would want with five tons. I assured him I hadn't and told him that it was for curing crocodile skins, which shook him even more. When I asked for 1000 rounds of ammunition, which they could not supply, minor shock waves ran through Port Moresby's leading business house. Before I had completed my shopping, the manager turned up, apparently curious to look at this strange character who was buying salt by the ton and wanted enough ammunition to start a war. A man of massive proportions, he introduced himself as Eddy Frame and seemed quite a good bloke. He said that there was plenty of ammo around at some of the army disposals dumps. 'See Warren Murphy,' he said, 'He'll be at the pub I expect.'

At the Top Pub someone looked at their watch and said Murphy would be most likely at the RSL Club. There, a short walk away, the club manager pointed him out to me; he was sitting on the lawn with a couple of others under a huge umbrella. I walked over and introduced myself. Murphy called to one of the club stewards, ordered me a drink, and I told him what I wanted. He shook his head: 'I could let you have a few hundred miles of copper telephone wire, a dozen or so jeeps, twenty or thirty blitz wagons or fifty radiator cores. Copper's more in my line.'

One of the others said: 'What about Jack Bourke? – I saw one of his trucks go past this morning loaded with shells of some sort. He'd be sure to have some ammo.'

After a somewhat prolonged lunch – Murphy insisted he was in the chair – he took me out to Jack Bourke's yard, which was about ten acres of just about everything that was ever used in the Pacific war: bombers to barrels of nuts and bolts. There was a group of natives busy chopping up aeroplanes – I was surprised how easy it appeared to be – and feeding the pieces into a furnace. Another group was flattening brass shell cases with sledge hammers. After some preliminary introductions, Warren told Bourke what I was after.

He pointed over to the other side of the yard: 'There's a whole stack over there. Help yourself.'

I walked over to where there were several cases. Some were broken open; they hadn't been there long by the look of them. I went back to Bourke and asked how much he wanted per case. He scratched his head and after a while said, 'How about a fiver?' which was cheap enough. He told a couple of boys to throw two cases in the back of Warren's ute while we yarned. He asked if I used an army rifle, but I explained that I had a .270 calibre Mauser action weapon that was chambered to take a .303 shell case I necked down to take the .270 slug. I reduced the load slightly, which gave me a cartridge with a flat trajectory and something like a 3000-foot per second muzzle velocity. I had the slugs and loading equipment, which was compact and efficient. He was a bit of a gun buff and knew what I was talking about. We rounded the day off at the Ela Beach RSL, which I didn't mind in the least.

Two days later I walked up the gangway of Steamships Trading Company's MV *Doma*. As the beat of the diesels increased, the lines were let go and she swung into the stream, weaving her way through assorted shipping to head for Kikori in the Purari Delta – real crocodile country.

Captain John Stitt and I had already met. He showed me my cabin just below the bridge, alongside his own, and in the best traditions of a South Sea Islands skipper, indicated a bottle of rum in a locker alongside my bunk. 'It's all part of the deal,' he said. The bottle seemed rather lonely so I topped it up with a few I had brought with me. They were reinforced, of course, with a couple of cases in the hold.

Our first port of call was Kairuku, which we left as soon as the cargo was discharged. Kerema was next and we stayed the night, departing before daylight so that we could reach Kikori in one day. We turned into the delta and I spent most of the time hanging over the rail, admiring crocodiles sunning themselves on the mudbanks. As we approached the Government station, a few blasts on the ship's siren assured us a welcome.

Looking from the wheelhouse while we were berthing, I could see a series of thatched houses on stilts looking neat and cool among a profusion of the ubiquitous coconut palm. The ground sloped up from the river and sitting on the highest eminence dominating the scene was a house of more substantial proportions, not far from which was a flagpole with an Australian flag flying proudly. Undoubtedly it was the District Officer's residence.

As soon as the lines were secured, the first up the gangway was Clarrie Healy, demanding to see 'this crocodile hunter'. As I was the only one he didn't know, I was soon identified.

He was about five feet eight and moved with a quick, springy step; lean and bronzed, he was all whipcord and wire. We shook hands and went to my cabin with Captain Stitt. Healy wanted to know all about crocodile shooting with a spotlight. Predictably, the news of my activities hadn't taken long to travel.

I opened a bottle of rum while explaining to him how it was done. He obviously found the simplicity of it all quite extraordinary and kept saying: 'Do you mean to tell me that you can get that close to them?' I told him that if you're so inclined and the wind is the right way, you could pat 'em on the head. He looked my rifle over with the eye of an expert and remarked on the ammunition. I explained the conversion process. Then he said: 'Look, Tom, you're welcome to stay with me. We'll get some canoes and get a team together. I've got plenty of good labour going to waste in the calaboose here, and they need some exercise. There's enough crocodiles here to last you the rest of your life.' I doubted that, but didn't say so.

I asked the captain when he was sailing: 'Tomorrow sometime.' It looked like a torrid evening was coming up.

At sundown I heard the Last Post being sounded on a bugle and, looking out of a porthole, saw the flag being ceremoniously lowered, and a detachment of police presenting arms. It all looked very impressive – sort of far-flung outpost of the Empire stuff. I opened another bottle of rum.

The conversation was all crocodiles – everybody had a story and before long the cabin was chock-a-block with crocodiles, tied up, strung up, dead and alive, every which way. It would be difficult to think of any other business that generated such enthusiasm. Every now and then I added a little fuel to the flames, but the fire didn't need much stoking.

Sometime during the early hours, the party petered out and I was more than pleased to get some sleep. The next morning the DO turned up with some boys who collected my cargo and stacked it in a shed by the wharf, and everything of a personal nature was taken up to the house, where I met Healy's wife. As with the Wards, the servants looked smart in their spotless ramis and went about their work with the same quiet efficiency. Clarrie and I went down to the wharf where a Government work boat was tied up with two police boys standing by.

It seemed very efficient, forty feet overall with four bunks, a neat galley and everything very shipshape. Powered with a six-cylinder diesel, she looked a good seaworthy craft. Clarrie said, 'We'll go up river and get some canoes. Bring some tobacco, that's all you'll need'.

With one of the policemen at the wheel, we headed upstream. The current was running strongly, but the launch made light work of it and half an hour later we pulled into a village, the screw churning up the mud at a flimsy looking wharf as the motor reversed. Before the boat was secured, two village policemen appeared, their badges of office around their necks. The DO climbed cautiously on to the wharf and the two village officials came smartly to attention and saluted, which Healy returned. Speaking rapidly in Motu, he explained what we wanted. We were soon surrounded by about half the village, chattering unceasingly. One of the policemen turned and addressed them in their own dialect and Clarrie said, 'There's plenty of competition, we can take our pick of the canoes'.

The policeman turned to us and said they were going to bring some to the jetty for our inspection so we stepped back on to the launch and sat down in the cabin.

Clarrie said: 'The villages throughout the delta have almost nothing in the way of an economy that could generate any sort of an income. They live on coconuts, sago, fish and crabs, which seems to keep them fairly healthy, although there's a fair bit of grilli, a skin disease, among them. They like crocodile meat when they can get it, but catching crocs is a bit beyond them. Whatever you bring into the area in the way of employment, which I realise won't be very much, is very welcome. As you probably know, wages are one pound a month plus rations.'

By now we were surrounded by canoes and clamouring owners, so I left everything to Healy; I was far too inexperienced to attempt to negotiate and was grateful to him for handling everything. We ended up with two canoes that I thought were about thirty-five to forty feet long. They were secured to bollards and with two villagers in the canoes to steer them, we towed them to Kikori.

We made fast time, as the current was with us. After we tied up, Clarrie told one of the policemen to get the station carpenter, to whom he fired off a string of instructions in Motu. I had already explained the decking arrangement. A gang of prisoners carried some planking down and they were soon hammering away, the carpenter acting in an advisory capacity.

We then went to the office where I met his ADO, Eric Flower, who in addition to his field duties also held Magisterial office. There were twenty or thirty natives lounging about and eight or ten police. When I asked what was happening, he was a bit vague: 'Oh, the same old thing, a bit of spearing, a bit of rooting, tribal fighting, it goes on all the time, nothing serious. The calaboose is just about full at the moment. I don't need the labour.'

Justice seemed fairly flexible, seemingly governed by the labour requirements on the station. We went from Healy's office to the house where his wife offered us a cup of tea. He looked at me and said: 'I think we might settle for something else.' Not wanting to spoil his day, I nodded and said, 'Anything is okay by me'.

He took me to a room off the verandah where he had a small bar set up and half a dozen guns in racks. Picking out an American Savage 30.30, he asked me what I thought of it. I knew it by reputation as a good rifle with a rotary magazine that held five cartridges. Judging by the size of the cartridges, they carried a heavy load. It was well balanced and obviously had a flat trajectory. At the range that we would be shooting, the bullet would come out the other side.

We then talked of the market and general demand for skins, which

I told him was insatiable. He said that he had heard of a market, but didn't know much about it and never thought about skinning the few crocodiles that he shot from time to time. When the news filtered through to the delta that some bloke was shooting them at night with a spotlight by the dozen in Galley Reach (a reasonably normal exaggeration), he immediately became interested. News of this kind spreads at something like the speed of light. Activities of that description were not likely to interfere with his official duties. If anything, his diligence in patrolling the Purari Delta would be intensified.

It was getting on towards sundown. Healy told his wife that we would be going out shooting and that we would have our dinner when we got back. She nodded, I expect she was used to those kind of decisions. He then called for a policeman, who arrived at the double, stopping at the foot of the verandah steps, coming to attention and saluting smartly. Clarrie told him: 'I want six calaboose with baras.' Saluting again, he turned and headed for the jail. I didn't know whether prisoners took their paddles to jail with them but whatever – I had no doubt there would be six of His Majesty's compulsory guests at the wharf very shortly – all equipped with paddles. And so it turned out.

In the 'gun room' we had a final couple of drinks 'to steady our nerves', as the DO said. I was beginning to understand what one of my favourite poets meant when he exhorted adventurous Englishmen: 'Go take up the white man's burden.'

Just after sundown we went down to the river where fifty or so natives had gathered to watch proceedings. Any event, no matter how ordinary, seemed to attract crowds. The local people didn't have very much to do beyond tending their gardens and fishing – subsistence, that was all, and always dozens of piccaninnies, youths and girls. There were mission schools but they were attended in a very desultory fashion. Children were there at first from curiosity, going back to their villages when boredom overcame the initial interest.

The policeman, a corporal I noted, had the prisoners lined up, each one with a paddle. As we stepped on to the wharf, they all came to attention and saluted smartly. Rudyard Kipling would have loved it.

The two canoes looked quite seaworthy with the sawn timber decking and an additional luxury of two canvas folding chairs, used when out on patrol, Healy told me. The canoes were wider than the ones we had used in Galley Reach and consequently would carry more. Everything was very much up-market; the DO saw to that, of course. The policeman had a box.

As we went up river, it was fascinating to watch the precision and rhythm of the paddlers singing in time to the paddle strokes, not unlike the Australian Aboriginal corroboree songs. They crossed and re-crossed the river, taking advantage of favourable eddies in the bends and shallows. The current in the main stream was running strongly.

We dropped off the two villagers. It was quite dark now and Clarrie consulted the corporal. From what I could gather, the policeman was urging him to go further upstream. Whatever was worked out, I was happy to tag along and listen to the experts.

Clarrie turned to me and said that the corporal knew of a place where there was a big old man croc.

'Well, let's go and have a look at him,' I said. 'I expect we'll get some more on the way back.' He assured me we would and off we went, the paddlers worked up about the latest 'hard labour' extension to their sentences.

It was tough work going against the stream, but we were carrying our particular burden in reasonable comfort, and it didn't surprise me when Healy spoke to the corporal who produced a haversack from the box he was sitting on and handed it over. Clinking sounds proclaimed its contents and very soon the night air was heavily scented with one of the more popular by-products of the sugar industry.

We travelled upstream for an hour before we sighted the one we were after. Clarrie saw the croc first, as he was holding the light, and was almost speechless when he saw the intensity of the reflection. The light was handed round – to the corporal first and then the crew. Their excitement was predictable; I felt a bit like the original discoverer of

Halley's Comet. The corporal had decided to be our harpoon man and was practising imaginary thrusts until the DO told him to sit down. As we got closer, I said that perhaps it would be better if we approached from upstream. It didn't appear to be an ideal place, and by the look of it the bank was a bit steep, indicating that it fell away into deep water. We were about fifty yards off the bank when we came up level with him. It didn't seem too bad and judging by the way the current eddied, it wasn't running as fast as I first thought. We went another hundred yards and I signalled to turn into the bank. We were brushing the mangroves as we came back with the current. I was sitting comfortably in the patrol chair and shot a cartridge into the breech of my rifle. Clarrie was holding the light over my shoulder, the corporal was on my right with the harpoon poised, and the paddlers had perfect control of the canoes. They knew instinctively what to do, gently turning in towards the banks. I already had my rifle pressed firmly into my shoulder. I could see now that he was a big fellow right enough – about ten or twelve feet.

I pressed the trigger, and it was a clean kill. As he started to slide back into the water, the corporal drove the harpoon with unerring aim, hitting right in the centre of the skull, undoubtedly the thickest, hardest, most solid piece of bone in a crocodile's entire body. The dead creature hesitated momentarily then continued its slide into the water and disappeared with scarcely a bubble. The corporal looked at the bent harpoon and shattered shaft in amazement and in his best, recently-acquired English exclaimed: 'Jesus, bloody buggery!'

The body swung around in the current and suddenly a couple of feet of the tail broke the surface. Two of the prisoners immediately jumped overboard and grabbed at it, but the water was deep and they started to drift away until they got caught up in mangroves. The corporal shouted at the other prisoners to help the two in the water who were struggling to hang on to the tail in the strong current.

Clarrie said: 'I hope it's dead.' I was sure of that, I knew I'd hit it fairly. The other four prisoners slid into the water, swam downstream and grabbed the hind legs, but it was a big croc and the pull of the current was very powerful. They tried to work it towards the bank where they could get some sort of a foothold.

There were only two paddlers in the canoe now and we were all hanging on to the mangroves, edging our way towards the others in the water. It was pitch black, of course, and everybody except Clarrie and I was shouting advice. I was trying to keep the spotlight focused on them, but light rain was starting to fall and the mangrove branches, now dripping water, were in the way most of the time. We dared not let the branches go or we'd be swept away. Eventually I threw the harpoon rope towards the group in the water and they quickly tied it around the crocodile's middle. Soon we had it alongside and the prisoners clambered back into the canoes. We started to drift downstream, but nobody cared much – the entire crew were regaling themselves with what had happened, all laughing heartily at what they regarded as the most hilarious moments. The corporal called them to order and spoke to the DO who then turned to me and, indicating the crocodile said, 'We're going to find a place where we can pull in comfortably and bring this fellow aboard'.

We went down river for a while until we came to a place where there wasn't much current and a fairly firm, sandy bottom. It wasn't much trouble loading the dead reptile, though awkward and slippery.

Now everything had settled down, we got on to the subject of shooting at night with a spotlight and, like Trevor Ward, Clarrie could not get over how simple it was – how close it was possible to get.

'The way it looks to me, you'll have this place cleaned out in no time.' I didn't agree with him entirely and recalled his earlier remarks to the effect that I'd be here forever and a day.

He looked at the croc lying peacefully on the decking and asked: 'What will he measure, Tom?' I said about about fourteen feet, which turned out to be not far out. I was more concerned with the belly width and thought that it would be somewhere between fifty and sixty inches. He then said: 'I am beginning to understand a bit about all the bullshit that's talked about crocodiles; I've seen this fellow two or three times when I've been cruising up and down the river and I've always reckoned he was about twenty feet.' I agreed with him: 'They all look tremendous in the water, especially when they're ploughing along, leaving a wake like the *Queen Mary* – there are plenty of stories of crocs forty feet and more, but they just don't exist. Maybe they did 5000 years ago, but I've seen quite a few and the biggest I've ever seen I shot in the Victoria River in Australia. It was eighteen foot nine and I can tell you, it was a bloody monster.'

I didn't have to invite Clarrie to have a shot – he took his seat in my chair and just grinned at me. I had no doubt that he was there for the rest of the night, which I didn't mind in the least. I knew that I had another happy hunter and I certainly didn't intend doing anything to discourage that. He shot six and we tied up at the wharf at half past ten. He told the corporal what to do and we walked up to the house. The cook and his offsider were asleep on the kitchen floor, but they soon had a meal prepared and after a couple of nightcaps we went to bed.

The next morning I was up shortly after daybreak, watching the flag being raised and Reveille being sounded. Healy joined me and the houseboy brought breakfast in. I said that we'd have to get the crocodiles skinned before it got hot so he told one of the servants to call the corporal. When we finished our tea, the corporal was waiting at the foot of the steps. Clarrie fired off a string of instructions and we walked down to the jetty. A bunch of prisoners was not long arriving and after all the saluting was done with, I handed out half a dozen knives and showed them how and where the initial cuts were made to get the maximum out of the skin.

The scale pattern of a crocodile skin varies from being rounded along the sides to a square shape on the belly, developing to oblong along the tail. The square pattern of the belly area is the most highly regarded. Because of this, the skinning process is started along the back, the initial cuts being made each side of the very pronounced horny ridge. This ridge is raised and knobbly and is a bony formation.

It is not connected with any part of the creature's skeleton and is known as a floating dorsal.

With such enthusiastic labour, it did not take very long to complete the skinning. I measured them up, the largest was fifty-two and the smallest nineteen inches. I was able to tell the DO that they totalled 212 inches. They were then salted down and stacked away in the cargo shed at the wharf.

At breakfast, Clarrie regaled his wife with our previous night's work and how we nearly lost the big one. He said, 'If it hadn't been for those two fellows jumping in and hanging on to its tail, we would have lost it. They are due for release, but I might keep them a bit longer, they're too good to turn out bush'.

I told Clarrie that at one shilling and sixpence an inch he had made £16. His eyes lit up at that news, it was nearly a week's salary. His wife said, 'The delta will *really* get patrolled now'.

After breakfast I walked to the office with Clarrie. Eric Flower, the ADO, told a native clerk to start the motor that ran the radio transmitter, which in turn passed the order down the line to a police constable. When the engine came to life, Flower picked up a mike, gave the Kikori call sign and said: 'Moresby, do you read me?' After getting an affirmative answer, he announced that he had three signals, the term for a telegram. There didn't seem to be any confidentiality; anyone with an ordinary radio set, provided they knew the frequency, could hear it. There were weather reports and some Government business and, when all that was dealt with, we listened to various other stations as they came in one by one. There was nothing of any interest except shipping movements and I noted that the *Doma* was at Daru and was expected back at Kikori in four days.

Halfway through the morning, a boy appeared with morning tea. Clarrie asked Eric Flower if he had any court that morning. The ADO, with a mouthful of cake, nodded.

'Two or three,' he said. 'Nothing serious: some bloke chopped up his wife, a couple of rooting cases.'

He turned to me and said: 'It's illegal here, you know – adultery is a crime in this country. They can screw as much as they like until they're married, but once they are married, there's a law against it – except with their husbands, of course.'

'Is it actually a law – on the statute book?' They both nodded.

'What about us?' I asked. They both laughed: 'No, no, not us.'

'One law for the rich and one for the poor – it that it?'

'Well, yes, I suppose you could say that – thank God,' said Eric, with some feeling.

Clarrie explained: 'It's one of their laws. There are quite a few of them that have been embodied in the native statute book by request.'

Before we went back to the house for lunch, he told the ADO to get *Kestral* checked and fuelled up. Turning to me he said: 'We'll take the launch tonight. After all, I'm working for a strong firm – and underpaid at that.' We had an early meal this time and before we went down to the jetty I opened a case of rum. 'In case of snake bite,' I explained to his wife, 'or some unexpected natural disaster such as earthquakes or hurricanes.' We went to the 'gun room' to first test its strength and purity as a precautionary measure. She seemed to understand.

At the jetty there was a sergeant in charge of the launch and another fellow who was first mate or something. The engine was running and the canoes were secured. We had the same corporal in charge and as far as I could see, the same prisoners as the night before, all wearing fairly clean ramis stamped all over with big broad arrows. I expect they had got themselves freshly geared up for their new and exciting duties.

We headed upstream again, the DO taking charge of the spotlight. I could see that there wasn't going to be much for me to do. He was playing the light on the bank and at regular intervals would tell me, 'There's one, there's another', until he realised he was missing out on his share of the rum.

We travelled about ten miles and then turned the launch into the bank and anchored. We transferred to the canoes. Clarrie told the sergeant to take the launch out into midstream and keep level with the canoes, which, because of our spotlighting, he would have no difficulty doing.

We cast off and this time Clarrie took the right-hand chair that had been adopted for the shooting seat. I was quite happy about this. His enthusiasm was important to me. We hadn't gone far when he shot the first one, about ten feet in length. Soon he had two more and was enjoying himself hugely. Another one fifteen minutes later brought the tally to four. The crew were equally excited. Being in this jail certainly had compensations, the meat being important. The next croc was quite big and I was marvelling at the seemingly inexhaustible supply, although I knew that shooting at this rate would probably deplete the area for quite a while. I wasn't sure what the replacement rate was or to what extent they moved around. I knew they took a long time to reach maturity. The next one was also big and – because we didn't have much freeboard – Clarrie decided we'd better transfer most of them to the launch. That proved to be too awkward a job, but there was plenty of rope, so we tied them together in pairs and slid them overboard for the launch to tow.

There was no shooting the next evening. Once a month the DO would invite to dinner his staff and perhaps other Europeans who may have been on the station. Tonight was the night. Clarrie's PO was out on a Census Patrol with a cadet officer so there was only Eric Flower, his wife and myself as guests.

Clarrie was determined to hold the conversation to crocodile hunting, but he was fighting a losing battle and after a while gave up. The main topic was a recent decision of the Administrator's to change the title of District Officer to District Commissioner. An Assistant District Officer would become a District Officer, Patrol Officers and Cadet Patrol Officers would remain the same. It seemed it was a prestige change only – District Commissioner sounded better than District Officer – as there was no increase in salary.

The conversation drifted to the early development of established authority, a subject on which both Clarrie and Eric were particularly well informed. They related how the Queensland Government Agent stationed at Thursday Island, Mr H. Chester, in 1883 was instructed by his superiors in Brisbane to raise the Union Jack at Port Moresby, claiming New Guinea for the Crown. But this piece of colonial effrontery was quickly knocked on the head – the damned cheek of them! It was repudiated and done properly the following year by Commander Erskine, Commodore of the Royal Navy's Australian station, who, after a volley of musket fire, proclaimed it a 'protectorate' on behalf of Queen Victoria, at the same time telling her brand-new subjects: '...always keep in mind that the Queen guards and watches over you, looks upon you as Her children and will not allow anyone to harm you, and will soon send Her trusted Officers to carry out Her gracious wishes in the establishment of this protectorate.' This speech was translated by the Reverend James Chalmers. The Goaribari tribesmen may have had this piece of sanctimonious cant in mind fifteen years or so later when they cut off his head and ate him.

'It's quite a story,' Eric said. 'It went on for years.'

Clarrie, who was half-asleep, piped up and said: 'He disagreed with something that ate him.'

The party broke up after that quip.

Quite a lot was known about British New Guinea, as it was first called, long before Queensland's impudent attempt to annex it.

The region had been graced by such characters as D'Albertis, an aria-singing Italian, who had sailed nearly 600 miles up the Fly River. With him was an engineer named Lawrence Hargrave, who was one of the first men to fly, although in an engineless box kite. Captain Moresby, named after his father Admiral Sir Fairfax Moresby, who gave his name to what became the capital, surveyed much of the coastline. There was Rev Chalmers, described by his friend Robert Louis Stevenson as '...a big stout man, wild looking, with the energy of a volcano and just as likely to erupt'. 'Chinese' Morrison got himself liberally punctured with arrows and nearly died of blood poisoning on behalf of the Melbourne *Age* newspaper. There were prospectors, Bird of Paradise hunters and blackbirders shanghaiing labour for Queensland's canefields.

Chalmers arrived in 1877. The London Missionary Society already had one representative in Port Moresby, the Reverend W. G. Lawes. Chalmers's task was to further extend the 'Word of the Lord', which he carried out with dedication and enthusiasm, travelling in the LMS schooner *Niue*. By 1901 he was at Daru, an island off the mouth of the Fly River. Just before Easter that year he sailed forth, taking with him an up and coming young 'God botherer', the Reverend Oliver Tompkins, who was 'learning the trade'.

It was Easter Sunday when they anchored off Samo, one of the larger villages on Goaribari Island. Chalmers had been in New Guinea for twenty-five years and no one knew more about the coastal natives. He was well aware that the Goaribaris were among the cruellest, most savage head-hunting cannibals in the entire Pacific. In their raids they showed no mercy whatever to man, woman or child.

There was no good reason for his visit, even less for him to have left his ship. The nature of the people was such that it was a piece of suicidal insanity for which no historian, or anyone else, has ever suggested an explanation other than that he believed it needed to be done. Chalmers's crew came from Kiwai Island, his captain was a Thursday Islander.

The little ship was soon surrounded by canoes. The people were well aware of its identity and some came aboard, inviting Chalmers ashore. No doubt because it was Easter Sunday and he was concerned with his devotions, he promised to go to the village on the Monday.

Next day, Rev Tompkins decided to go along, too, despite attempts by Chalmers to talk him out of it. Tompkins no doubt assumed that the experienced Chalmers would not have ventured ashore if there was any likelihood of violence. God must have been busy that day with other business. So Chalmers and Tompkins, with a Kiwai chief and nine Kiwai mission students, went ashore. It was established later that the entire party was enticed into the men's Dubu House, which would be equivalent to a clubhouse, but dark and forbidding with no openings for windows. When they were seated and a friendly atmosphere established, they were attacked from behind with stone clubs. The Kiwai chief managed to kill one assailant before he was felled by several Goaribaris. The twelve bodies were immediately beheaded, cut up and eaten with sago, every village on that dank mud island participating.

The captain of the *Niue* could clearly hear the massacre taking place and probably to some extent may have expected it. When a number of canoes put out from the shore, he wasted no time getting the anchor up and heading for Port Moresby.

When the news was brought to Sir George Le Hunte, the Lieutenant Governor, he was horrified. He had formed a genuine affection for the priest, had a great admiration for him, and frequently sought his advice, particularly on matters relating to natives.

It was still the days of gunboat diplomacy – something the Goaribaris were not familiar with. They were about to pay a very heavy price for their meal. The Government steam yacht *Merrie England* sailed from Port Moresby, Le Hunte himself in command of the expedition. There were six Europeans and thirty-six constables, all armed. They anchored off Goaribari Island just as the sun was rising. When the smoke of the rifles had drifted away, the population of that mud island had been substantially reduced.

But that was by no means the end of the matter. The Lieutenant Governor wanted the return of the skulls, which he knew were taking pride of place among several hundred others. The Goaribaris had one very big Dubu House where trophies were kept. This house was guarded day and night by two men known as 'The Keepers of the Heads'.

Once again the *Merrie England* sailed for Goaribari Island and again anchored off Samo village. Le Hunte sent a pinnace ashore with armed constables under orders to bring back the chief and the heads of the two missionaries. They returned with the chief, who had one head only, which he said was that of Chalmers. Whatever explanation he gave to Le Hunte is not recorded, but the Lieutenant Governor returned to Moresby. Although satisfied that he had the head of Chalmers, (one wonders how he determined this), Le Hunte reported that '...they still have an unpurged offence to account for'.

Early in 1904, Le Hunte went on leave and, as was normal, the Chief Justice Mr C. S. Robinson was sworn in. Given his legal training and lofty position, he might have been expected to take a balanced approach. But Christopher Robinson was the son of an archdeacon and it has been suggested that this had some influence on his feeling and attitude towards the killing of Chalmers and Tompkins. Be that as it may, the arrest of the killers and the recovery of Tompkins's head became an overriding consideration with him.

For a third time *Merrie England* sailed for Goaribari Island. Robinson was on board with a police party and when they dropped anchor at Samo, the villagers were justifiably suspicious. However, some of them paddled out to the ship, under the impression that the murders of the missionaries and the Kiwai Islanders had been paid for; 'payback' was something they understood very well.

They were enticed aboard with displays of trinkets and beads – this was regarded later as a treacherous action on the part of Robinson. A Goaribari informer on board pointed out a man who had axed Chalmers and he was seized by the police. What happened after this has never been clear, but it confirmed the islanders' earlier suspicion that their visitors were not overflowing with the milk of human kindness. Those in the canoes fitted arrows to their bows, a policeman shot one who was aiming at Robinson, and then everyone started firing their rifles, including the administrator. It was a one-sided battle. There were no casualties on board *Merrie England*.

The number of natives killed was never really established: the estimates varied from eight to fifty, the latter from an eyewitness aboard *Merrie England*. Nearly 300 shots were fired, a figure that could be calculated with reasonable accuracy as most of the shell cases would have been easily recovered. One thing is sure – the police on board would have entered into the shooting with great enthusiasm.

Whatever Judge Robinson felt about his foray is not recorded, but when the news reached the Australian Government, the reaction was one of predictable horror. After all, it was three years since Chalmers and Tompkins and their crew had been slaughtered. Although a lot of people were uneasy about the way Le Hunte sailed in and turned his guns on the village, it was largely nullified by the horrific stories of the cannibalism. What Robinson did was punish someone twice for the same crime – not cricket, sir!

There was a tremendous uproar, with missionaries leading the way. The pressure was considerable and this led to calls for a Royal Commission; Robinson was instructed to return to Australia to face the enquiry. By now, completely overwhelmed by the turn events had taken, it was more than he could stand. In the early hours of the morning of 20 June 1904, the Acting Administrator walked out of The Residency to the foot of the flagpole and shot himself.

The royal commission proceeded. The final opinion attributed the shooting to 'overzeal and want of judgement' rather than anything approaching 'conscious or wilful departure from the absolutely straight path befitting the high office he held'. It seems a most peculiar and clumsily worded expression of opinion from such an august body as My Lords Commissioners. After all, Christopher Robinson was the Chief Justice.

Sir George Le Hunte retired and was succeeded by Captain R. F. Barton, who took up the crusade where Robinson had left off but with more success. He got Tompkins's skull back and, in 1909, the Goaribaris delivered a bundle of bones, which they said were the remains of the two missionaries. Some doubt has been expressed that they were the right bones, but I believed they were. In returning them the tribesmen were more concerned with their own fortunes rather than any feelings of remorse or repentance.

Nearly all primitive people are governed by superstition: dreams are regarded as particularly important, and even minor tribal misfortunes are often related to some form of occultism. Missionaries have been encouraged to think that they were making substantial progress when interest was displayed in stories such as the 'Resurrection' and parables like 'The Loaves and the Fishes', which bore some similarity to their 'cargo cult' beliefs. Things like that they understood.

I hunted crocodiles extensively in the Goaribari area and got to know the natives very well. The men were excellent workers. They took me through their Dubu House where, in spite of missionaries' endeavours to have them destroyed, there were still rows of skulls, decorated and painted, all with elongated noses attached.

Chalmers, Tompkins and the Kiwai Islanders were killed by the fathers of my hosts only fifty years previously, and there were some old men – children at the time – who declared that they had sat at the feast. Of course, as is their fashion, the story had been told and retold a thousand times. Sitting in that gloomy, dark Dubu House, with the two men who were 'The Keepers of the Heads', chattering children in the background, skulls grinning down, they told me how the village had been cursed.

To kill Chalmers and Tompkins had been a great mistake – every misfortune that had overtaken them since then was blamed on it. The white man's puri-puri (magic) had been too strong. Not only Samo village had suffered for it, but also the entire Goaribari tribe, because they had all partaken of the feast.

'And the Kiwais, is their puri-puri strong, too?' I asked.

'No, not the Kiwais,' came the reply, somewhat contemptuously. 'Goaribari puri-puri stronger than Kiwai.'

'What about Tamate's God?' I asked. Chalmers was known to the natives as 'Tamate'.

'Yes, Tamate's God made the puri-puri.'

I asked them if they went to church, but they seemed a bit horrified at the idea, probably thinking they'd all be struck dead or something. There was a church on the main island, although I'd never seen it. They said that some of the piccaninnies went; they liked the sing-sing.

I shot crocs around the Goaribari area for a fortnight. Crocodiles were far more plentiful than I ever imagined, mostly big ones, fifteen and sixteen feet long. My Goaribari crewmen loved it. The biggest croc I had ever shot was eighteen feet six inches. I was anxious to shoot a twenty-footer and was sure that if I was ever going to, it would be here.

One morning soon after I heard the beat of a diesel motor. Healy presently arrived in the *Kestral* with mail, and told me that he had shot ninety-five crocodiles. He said that he had an ADO, 'Speed' Graham, over on the other side of the Purari Delta at a place called Beara, who wanted to shoot crocodiles, too. Would I go over and give him a start? No problem; I packed up and went back to Kikori that afternoon.

There were a few matters occupying my mind. First and foremost was my family. My wife was now very pregnant and I would have to get back to Sydney soon. But I had better get Speed Graham started up.

Clarrie said that he'd take me over to Beara: the outstation was due for a visit. Early the next morning we headed off, arriving at about mid-day. It was similar to Kikori, but on a smaller scale, with thatched buildings surrounded by neat, well-tended gardens. A group of prisoners were cutting grass with long steel blades called 'sarifs'. There were several acres of beautifully kept lawn. The sarifs intrigued me: they were swung with remarkable efficiency.

Speed Graham was an experienced ADO who had joined the service before the war. I could see that he knew all about running a Government station. We had lunch with Speed and his lovely wife, Ruth, and their young son before Clarrie returned to Kikori. Then Speed and I settled down to discussing crocodile shooting.

There would be no problems with labour or canoes, in fact the canoe situation was better than at Kikori. Being an outstation, it didn't rate a launch but had two big canoes and an outboard motor. As for labour, it was out there swinging sarifs with regular monotony.

I had already been giving some thought to outboards and was glad of an opportunity to try one out. Not that I had any doubt as to their suitability or efficiency, it was just that I hadn't had any experience with them. We set off at sundown with a policeman and four prisoners, all of whom were equipped with paddles – they all seemed to have them. I asked Speed about this and he explained that when they were sentenced, their relatives usually brought a canoe and left it at the station so that when they finished their time they could paddle back to their village.

Turning upstream, before long we were beyond the tidal limits and dense jungle took over from the mangroves. The outboard was struggling a bit against the current; I made a mental note that more power was needed. Speed said one word to the policeman – 'Bara', which was the word for paddle – and with a rapid flow of Motu, which obviously wasn't complimentary, they all took up their paddles, shrieking with laughter in which the policeman joined. I looked at Speed who said: 'The cop just told them what a bunch of useless shitheads they were.' The relationship between prisoners and guards seemed an unusual and friendly one, probably unparalleled, and it appeared to work, too.

As soon as it got dark I switched on the spotlight and almost immediately picked up a fair sized crocodile on a sandbank, half out of the water and perfectly positioned. We stopped the motor and paddled quietly over; I could not have wished for an easier shot. Suitably impressed, the crew dragged the beast aboard with the usual excited chattering that I had come to expect – background effects. Less than a quarter of a mile further on I shot another just as easily and a little bigger. When it was pulled aboard I told Speed to take over the shooting. He had a Government-issue .303 and, of course, plenty of ammunition. As I expected, he took to it like the proverbial duck to water.

It was a beautiful night, although the mosquitoes were bad, but there was no getting away from them. We cruised upstream, Speed explaining that further on we would turn into a creek that would take us into a fairly big channel, which would take us back to Beara. 'We should see a good few crocs.'

We came around a bend and suddenly I saw one of the most amazing sights I have ever seen. At first I couldn't quite understand what I was looking at; we were some distance away and it seemed quite uncanny – a diaphanous, shimmering cloud suspended over water and below it a perfect reflection. It was about twenty feet across – a mass of throbbing luminosity.

I turned to Speed: 'What on earth is that?'

'Fireflies.'

As we came closer the intensity of light increased and when we drew level I could see literally millions of flickering fireflies gathered on a tree that was leaning over the water. The pulsating light was caused by the quivering wings of millions and millions of the insects, creating one of nature's fairylands.

'What magic,' I whispered to Speed – it didn't seem quite right to talk aloud – 'a scintillation of fireflies.'

It was one o'clock in the morning when we got back to the station; we had nine crocodiles.

At sunrise I went through the skinning routine with a bunch of prisoners whose only fault was an excess of enthusiasm that the prospects of a feed of crocodile meat had generated. When they were salted down, I told Speed that he had made about £20. Ruth was delighted, especially as they were due for leave at the end of the year. I wasn't sure what his salary was – probably about £10 a week, which I later found to be almost spot on.

That afternoon a canoe arrived at the wharf. It was quite big and equipped with an awning. A white man was sitting in the bow but to me he seemed to be rather well dressed for delta country. Speed, peering over the verandah, called to his wife, 'George has just arrived, dear'. Up to her arms in flour, she replied, 'Oh, bother'. Turning to me, he said, 'It's a missionary neighbour of ours, not a bad bloke'.

He seemed very active for a man of the cloth as he clambered on to the wharf. I saw one of his paddlers hand a rifle to him, which surprised me. One doesn't associate firearms with clergymen. I saw him slide back the bolt of the firearm, extract a cartridge, slip it into his pocket and hand it back.

'He's keen on shooting, he's probably been potting crocs.'

I thought to myself, 'I'd better put a stop to that'. I couldn't have people going around indiscriminately shooting crocs and no doubt leaving them to rot. Divining my thoughts he said, 'You could probably rope him in, Tom; he'd be more than happy to make a quid'.

I recalled the remark that they came to do good and did bloody well. I was happy to make my contribution, providing it worked both ways. He walked to the house and the ADO greeted him at the foot of the steps. They shook hands and I heard the missionary say, 'I believe you've got a crocodile hunter here who's buying skins'.

I suppose I shouldn't have been surprised. I knew enough about the so-called bush telegraph to realise that my activities would be well known by now, if only by reason of the nature of my operations. The two men came up onto the verandah and I was introduced.

'I shot a croc coming along this morning, I've got him in the canoe.'

I tried to stop looking surprised, and asked, 'How long ago was it shot?' 'About an hour,' he replied, 'why?'

I explained that putrefaction set in quickly in that climate and that the first signs were scales lifting. He assured me that it had been under the awning and also covered with bushes. I was quite impressed; he seemed to be a very practical bloke.

The mission station where he lived was about ten miles away and he had come over to find out about 'this crocodile shooting bloke', and also a couple of his flock who were in the Beara calaboose.

A houseboy brought a tray on to the verandah and Ruth joined us. The missionary asked the ADO about the prisoners, as they were due out in about a fortnight. 'But,' Speed said, 'you can take them back now if you like, my jail is a bit overloaded.'

George Carrington seemed quite pleased to hear this and said: 'I was hoping you'd let me take them back. That fellow who chopped his wife will be a good preacher and I can promise that he won't do it again, it was only one of those domestic spats. Her leg's okay now and she has asked me when he's coming back.'

Speed said: 'Yes, if he hadn't used an axe, I wouldn't have put him inside; I'd have let him go with a caution.'

We finished our tea and I showed the missionary how the crocodile should be skinned. It was twenty odd inches wide, and he was quite excited when he found out how much it was worth. He then questioned me closely about the shooting method, the spotlight, how close he could get with a light at night. He was very surprised when I explained that a hunter could get up to within a few feet and obviously a bit sceptical; I was sure he didn't believe it. It was Speed who suggested that we go to his mission tomorrow and have a night's shooting together, but he somewhat regretfully pointed out that it was Sunday so we settled for Monday. With that he left.

That night we did a short cruise down towards the coast and shot six crocs. On Sunday night, we, or rather Speed, shot eleven. As he said, 'The better the day, the better the deed'.

On Monday Speed said that we would get away early as he had some official business to do at a sawmill, which he explained wasn't far out of our way. I hadn't heard of the sawmill before, but it was at the head of Romilly Sound and the sawmiller's name was Charlie Chambers.

We pulled into the sawmill wharf, where there were huge stacks of sawn timber waiting for the next boat. Chambers, who was checking the lumber, gave Speed a wave and went on with his work. We climbed up a ladder and he walked over and shook hands.

He said to me, 'I s'pose you're the crocodile man'. I nodded, I would have been disappointed if he hadn't known about me.

From my limited experience of sawmills, this seemed to be a fairly big operation. Logs were stacked over a wide area, several acres, and tethered to the bank were huge rafts of logs waiting to be pulled ashore. There were large stacks of sawn timber on the wharf, ready for transportation to Port Moresby where postwar development had created an insatiable demand for timber.

We went to the house where I met his wife May, who was just as interested in crocodile hunting as everybody else. We yarned for a while and then a bell rang announcing the midday meal. We took our places at the table as one of the houseboys came in from the kitchen carrying the biggest dish of mud crabs I had ever seen in my life. I suspect that they were anticipating my astonishment, as they were all smiling. One mud crab per person would be a generous meal anywhere, but at least twenty between four people was an outsized lunch. May said: 'Don't bother with the bodies, it's too messy, eat the big claws, there's some more out in the kitchen.' For the next half hour we steadily munched our way through delicious mud crabs.

Charlie said, 'The delta is lousy with them. I buy them from the local natives – ten for one stick of tobacco is the going rate. They bring them in by the canoe load; that meal we've just got through probably cost three sticks of tobacco. Actually, I feed my labour line on them'.

I looked at Speed – I hadn't tasted or seen a crab until today – and thought he'd been neglecting his obligations as a host. He must have guessed what was going through my mind.

'We've been living on them until I couldn't look a crab in the face, although I think I'm back to normal now.'

I didn't think it was possible to get sick of them, but, as I found out later, it was.

After we had yarned for a while, Chambers said, 'I wouldn't mind coming out shooting with you fellows', to which Speed said, 'Well, it's okay by me', and looked at me. I thought it was a good idea, I could see another croc hunter. 'You're as welcome as the flowers in whatever month they bloom.'

As I expected, he had an army .303 – everybody seemed to have one.

He said: 'My labour line can have some croc meat as a change from mud crabs.' I couldn't imagine anyone preferring croc meat to juicy mud crabs but, as they say, there's no accounting for taste.

It was only five or six miles from the sawmill to the mission and George, who would have heard our motor, was at the wharf waiting. He asked if we would like a couple of extra paddlers. The Beara canoes were about forty or fifty feet long and now that we had the sawmiller, the weight was building up. I said it was a good idea, we were struggling going upstream and were certain to get crocodiles, how many and how big no one knew. He yelled out 'Mero!' and half a dozen young, budding missionaries quickly appeared, all of them clutching paddles. He pointed to a couple of brawny, cheerful looking characters and said, 'Oi mi', and with that they leapt aboard.

Everyone was obviously familiar with the delta except me so I kept out of it, and after a brief discussion we left. It didn't seem to matter which way we went, crocs were everywhere.

I intended to take a back seat and settle for the spotlighting job, and I worked out the shooting in order of seniority. Speed owned the canoes so he could have the first couple of shots; Charlie would be next and when he had shot a couple the missionary could have a go. Chambers had brought a bottle of rum, which was enough for the three of us.

It didn't take the ADO long to shoot a couple. Then it was Charlie's turn and it took him a little longer, which was nothing to do with his shooting, it was just that they were a bit further apart.

The missionary then took his seat and very soon shot his first one in a very competent manner. He got the second one just before we reached his wharf. He clambered up on to the jetty in a somewhat bemused state, his boy carried the crocodiles and we left him. Charlie shot one more and Speed got a couple before we tied up at Beara.

I now had three more hunters, five altogether with Healy and Ward. I could see that it was going to develop into a fairly big operation. There were several big rivers to the west – the Fly, the biggest on this side of the island, was something like a hundred miles across at the mouth, then on the New Guinea side there was the Ramu and the mighty Sepik.

But getting back to Sydney was starting to worry me, my approaching family was a real concern. The next morning I explained the situation to Speed: I had to get back to Australia very soon. Ruth said, 'You could probably get a lift to Moresby in an APC plane'.

This was the first time I'd heard the oil company mentioned. I knew they were drilling somewhere in the delta, but had no idea where.

Speed said, 'That's a good idea; they're only four- or five-hour run from here'. After a brief discussion, Speed said that he'd run me across to the oil camp the next morning.

After an early breakfast, I made my farewells to Ruth. We were soon on our way, accompanied by a police sergeant and a couple of prisoners, presumably in case we broke down and paddlers were required.

We reached the oil camp at midday. It seemed to be an enormous operation out in the jungle and swamps. It was like a small town with a dozen or so buildings for accommodation, long store sheds, trucks and bulldozers, a ship tied up at the wharf and a small seaplane swinging at anchor. And towering over everything was a huge drilling rig.

We tied up at the wharf and Speed and I made our way to the administration building. The men inside, poring over what appeared to be graphs, greeted us jovially. I was introduced and someone said, 'I suppose you're the crocodile bloke'. I endeavoured to nod casually. Just then a siren sounded, the signal for the midday break. Speed was well known. From time to time he had minor official duties to do with the native labour.

We walked over to a big mess hall and twenty or thirty men trooped in. I guessed that counting those working on the drilling rig – it was never left unattended day or night – there would be thirty or forty Europeans, together with hundreds of natives. There were several bungalows, and obviously some workers had brought their wives with them.

There were two or three big tractors and several tipper trucks, probably used when the hillside was torn away to level off the area. Surrounding it all was a wall of dense, green jungle.

We took our place at a long table, where there was a profusion of food – oil men were well looked after – as well as a number of natives hovering around to serve the hungry drillers.

The talk was mostly directed at me, as there were some enthusiastic prospective crocodile hunters here. I was flat out answering their questions, and it looked like my croc hunting team was about to be substantially increased.

There were three or four APC aluminium dinghies with no restrictions whatever on their use by any of the men. In fact, anything that was of a recreational nature was welcomed. I imagined the boredom became fairly intense after a while. Speed and I were seated together and during a brief lull in the conversation I gave him a nudge: 'What about me getting to Moresby?' He nodded: 'You'll be all right.'

Although I was confident that I would get away, I couldn't help feeling a bit strung up. My wife was due to have the baby in August and I was starting to worry, imagining all sorts of catastrophes. Then he said to me: 'I s'pose you'll go out tonight?' There was no getting out of it – half the camp wanted to go shooting and although my heart wouldn't have been in it, it was certainly better than sitting in the camp.

Speed then turned to one of the men we had met in the office and said, 'Tom wants a lift to Moresby, Bob, I s'pose he'll be all right?' Bob was busy tackling an enormous steak and he had no intention of letting it escape. He just nodded and when the last of it had disappeared he said, 'You'll be okay, she's going back empty, the driver's up at the boss's place'. It all seemed so simple and straightforward; I was sure I had no worries in that direction.

I had no heart for the shooting that night and I could see that Speed wasn't too keen either – he had settled in at the club house. In any case I couldn't have stood a night of idleness and with half the camp rearing to go crocodile shooting there was no getting out of it.

We took the two biggest dinghies. Speed took five men and I took four. That was one night of which I have no record, but I seem to recall that we got about nine or ten crocs between us. I didn't care much but I had a whole bunch of new shooters, a pretty boozy mob they were, too. It was a miracle they hit any, but one thing impressed me: although they were all solid drinkers, they all treated the firearms properly and with respect; they weren't by any means foolish in that regard.

THREE

RIFLES, SALT AND A BABY

THE NEXT morning I was up at dawn and watched as the little seaplane was towed up to the jetty. I was already packed – there wasn't much to pack – and had left my rifle with Speed who, in his usual efficient manner, said he would look after everything such as packing and shipping the skins in one of the oil company's boats. I would have to arrange storage in Port Moresby; everything was piling up a bit.

I was soon clambering in beside the pilot. A launch did a couple of runs down the river in case of logs or, as the pilot said, crocodiles. We were quickly airborne and it was then that I realised the immensity of the Purari Delta. I looked at the altimeter and saw that we were cruising at 2000 feet. Down below was an impressive sight, I estimated that there was something like 50,000 square miles of mangroves intersected with creeks and channels and, I hoped, seething with crocodiles. We were doing about 150 knots and in what seemed like a few minutes we passed Kerema, then the island of Kairuku. Galley Reach was next and I had no difficulty recognising a tiny doll's house that was the Ward homestead. Shortly after we landed at Moresby's Jackson's Airport – the little plane was amphibious.

I spent the rest of the day, between drinks, arranging storage for the skins, which turned out a lot easier than I expected. Ivan Hoggard, the oil company's recruiter, told me: 'Leave it to me – I've got plenty of space out at the compound and it will be something for the boys to do while they're waiting for transport.' So far no one had mentioned anything as sordid as freight charges or rental.

The next day I boarded a Qantas DC4 and settled into my seat. There was no distinction in those days between first or tourist class and looking over the passengers I reckoned we were all somewhere in between. Beside me I had for a travelling companion a quite substantial lady who I had previously been informed was a German Lutheran missionary whose knowledge of English was as limited as mine was of German – there were no conversational problems.

Darkness closed in just before we passed over Newcastle and soon Sydney came into view. I have never ceased to wonder at the magnificent grandeur of that city at night from several thousand feet. It has an ethereal beauty that is a long way from the real thing – coming back to earth.

Kathleen was there to meet me. She had put on a fair amount of weight and was glowing with rude good health and pregnancy. It was quite a long drive from the airport to Strathfield where we lived and under the circumstances we agreed that it was better she drove. Kathleen was an extremely competent and careful driver. I was, too, but in a slightly different category.

It was a pleasant change to be home after the last four months of living in all sorts of strange places and crocodile hunting half the night. I had not realised how peaceful our little flat was. I was sure that I could put up with a month or so without any undue strain.

Apart from periodic visits to the hospital to check on junior's progress, my time was was largely taken up inspecting outboard motors, high-powered rifles, ordering large quantities of salt and ammunition, and having discussions with prospective skin buyers as well as my old friends at Ace Tannery in the outer suburb of St Marys, who were the only people who understood the rather specialised process of tanning crocodile skins. It was owned by three brothers named Broomham and over the last few years we had become good friends.

In the meantime, in Port Moresby, Ivan Hoggard had not been idle. One morning a large envelope arrived in the mail containing shipping documents for seven cases of crocodile skins and judging by the measurements shown, they were very large cases, too. I realised that I would soon be producing more crocodile skins than my friends at the tannery could handle or, for that matter, the manufacturer. After a lot of thought, numerous letters, a number of phone calls and telegrams I found that Singapore, one of the world's great clearing houses, had an insatiable market for crocodile skins. I was assured that there was no limit. Finance? I tentatively asked. No trouble whatever!

Then on 16 August the most beautiful baby in the world was born, a girl. I was told that the baby was to be called Kathryn. The following week was somewhat euphoric. I got myself back to earth and took my new family home from hospital to where a spare room suitably decorated and equipped was ready and waiting. The next few weeks passed quickly and although I was completely enraptured by our latest production, the stern necessities of life kept my feet on the ground.

By the middle of September I was winging my way back to Port Moresby. There was plenty to do – a sizable stack of crocodile skins had accumulated and were starting to encroach on the oil company's space. I did not want to strain their benevolence unduly, bearing in mind the free shipping space and aeroplane travel. I had no trouble finding alternative storage.

Although I was anxious to get back to the Purari Delta, where the real action was, there were several other matters claiming my attention, not the least of which were a few prospective hunters. Mostly they came to the pub looking for me and over a couple of drinks it wasn't difficult to sort them out. Two of them were entirely unsuitable and would have quickly got themselves into trouble. I was able to discourage them by simply exaggerating, making it appear so dangerous that I almost scared myself; another, an ex-Patrol Officer named Roy Edwards, I was sure would be outstanding. Edwards was an interesting man and one of the most competent bushmen I have known.

We left Port Moresby on MV *Doma*. I had a great deal of cargo that included two outboard motors, which were going to make life in those mangrove swamps a lot easier. Two days later we arrived at Kikori and were enthusiastically greeted by Clarrie Healy who was now a District Commissioner, his enthusiasm visibly increasing when I presented him with a cheque for £200, the proceeds of the skins he had shipped to Port Moresby.

The next few days were spent inspecting canoes, and Roy Edwards being fluent in Motu was a tower of strength. I bought two thirty-footers that matched up very well. Roy got a couple about the same size after a lot of haggling. We borrowed the station carpenter and soon had them joined and decked over.

The next day we headed to the Goaribari area, where I renewed my acquaintance with my head-hunter friends of Samo Village. Edwards was well known from his Patrol Officer days and was obviously well thought of. He joked freely with the village policemen, asking them if they had eaten anyone lately. They threw their hands up in horror – how could Taubada think of such a thing? Paraphrasing Shakespeare, Roy said: 'Methinks the gentlemen protesteth too much.'

Afterwards, when we had tidied up the rest house to our satisfaction, he said: 'It'll be a long time before cannibalism is entirely eliminated. In District Services we always knew that it was still going on, limited certainly, but still being practised for sure.'

We got everything shipshape for the coming evening's hunting after which Roy said with a smile, 'Let's walk over to the Dubu House, I bet I can pick out the odd fresh head'.

'How can you tell?' I asked curiously.

He laughed: 'They smell different.'

Although it was a revolting subject, I had to laugh. When I walked through the Dubu House before I didn't look too hard at them, they all looked the same to me. Some were painted and nearly all of them had elongated wooden noses attached, a few of them elaborately carved. I was told that after the bodies were eaten, the heads were put in a tidal salt creek where they would soon be cleaned up. I once put a crocodile head in and it came out quite clean and white.

We clambered up a ladder at the entrance and, bending low through the doorway, we went inside, standing for a minute or so to get used to the dark interior. One of the 'Keepers of the Heads' spoke rapidly to Roy in Motu; he seemed to be the one in charge. The other man was sitting on a woven mat pounding away at something with a pestle and mortar. All the heads were on one side, the top row about six feet up.

Roy joked with the two men as he walked casually along, glancing at the skulls from time to time. Some were hanging from the rafters, suspended by plaited lawyer vine. I tried to count every head, but it was too difficult; I was sure that there were somewhere between eighty and a hundred. I knew that at one stage the missionaries had tried to get the people to destroy them, but they weren't very successful. Then the Administration stepped in and declared that they could keep them.

Suddenly Roy pointed to a skull on the top row and turning to me he said, 'I bet that head hasn't been there too long'. It didn't look different to any of the others to me. He reached up and took it down, giving it to me to hold. The man with us was starting to look decidedly uneasy, and when Roy reached up again and took the one beside it, he cried out, 'Taubada, Taubada!' The man working with the pestle and mortar joined us.

I started to feel uneasy myself. Edwards completely disregarded them and with a half smile smelt the skulls one after another. Then he shook them and there was a dull rattle that I assumed was the dried out brain. He handed one of the heads to me, it had a sour kind of smell, not unlike the carcase of a buffalo or crocodile that has been out in the tropical sun for some time and completely dried out. He then gave me the other one; there did seem to be a difference, but it could have been my imagination, I wasn't really sure.

The two men were quite alarmed now and burst out in a torrent of Motu, which they addressed to Roy, who smiled easily. Waving one of the skulls, he spoke briefly, to which they vigorously replied, 'Las, las, las!' Then, holding the head that I thought was the newer one close to the older man's face and smiling wickedly, he spoke at some length, very little of which I could follow. They started to smile and then both started to laugh uproariously, at the same time disclaiming volubly, 'Las, las!' The four of us then sat down on the mats that were strewn over the floor and, with the head in the middle and a great deal of banter, Roy started to ply them with questions. It seemed quite hilarious and I was sorry that I couldn't follow it.

I suppose joking with head-hunting cannibals about one of their victims may not have been most people's idea of entertainment, but when one is living and working in such a place it is surprising how easy it is to absorb the atmosphere and understand it.

Before the beginning of time it had been their way of life. Then the white man arrived, told them that they musn't go around killing people and eating them, and substituted tuberculosis, venereal disease and a few other things as well as liquor, tobacco, flour, tea and sugar, which decimated them far more effectively but not as spectacularly.

Old customs die hard, especially with primitive people. With the heads in the background, one could visualise the old warriors recounting with nostalgia the battles they fought in the past, and the feasts afterwards. The stories would have lost nothing in the telling. Catching an unwary villager who was a traditional enemy was a very short step back in time. It was easy to believe.

The Samo Rest House was a short distance from the main village, which was normal. There was lots of room and, being thatched and fairly open, it was quite cool. The toilet, or 'small house' as it was known, was on stilts positioned over the water, a very rickety affair that swayed perilously. There was a separate cookhouse, also thatched, with a thick caked mud floor that was the fireplace and a substantial stack of firewood close by. We had our own cook from Kikori whose specialty seemed to be stews. There was a reasonable supply of fish from the villagers, but vegetables were scarce, mainly, I assumed, because this part of the delta was under water at the time of the spring tides, which was once a month.

There were plenty of bananas, which came in by canoe; huge bunches costing only a few sticks of tobacco. From time to time flights of duck went over, but usually too high for my gun. Sometimes I would bring down the odd Torres Strait pigeon, another of nature's remarkable phenomena.

There were dense colonies of them in the mangroves, countless thousands, and at first light they would leave for their feeding grounds. In the evening, as sundown approached, they would return. For an hour or so there would be a continuous stream, perhaps half a mile wide, returning to their camping grounds. These colonies were quite remarkable and from a distance gave the appearance of an enormous, snow-white, fluttering mass, the reflection in the water doubling the effect.

I anticipated that Edwards would take to crocodile hunting naturally and would require minimal preliminary tuition. We were going out in my canoes. I had already given the motors a trial spin and was looking forward to a good, solid workout this evening.

Just after sundown we pulled out into the stream, Roy observing that it looked like rain. Bearing in mind that the annual average rainfall was something in the vicinity of 150 to 160 inches, he wasn't scoring any points as a prophet. We had raincoats but the natives never seemed to worry about any form of protection; being in the tropics it wasn't cold and, of course, they grew up with it. Quite frequently I noted that if they were wearing European clothes they would discard them when it started to rain, roll them up and cover them with palm folds or bark and put them back on when the rain stopped.

I gave Roy the spotlight and very soon he picked up the eyes of a crocodile. I switched the motors off, we quietly paddled up and I shot him very easily. He was astonished at the ease of the operation, as I expected, and when we pulled it aboard it looked about nine feet. I started the motors again, asking Roy to take the shooting seat as I picked up the spotlight. A mile further on I sighted a reflection that must have been half a mile away and I knew it was a whopper. This was confirmed as we got closer and I steered the canoes over to the opposite bank. We were travelling upstream and I wanted to get above him and come back with the current, because when I cut the motors it would be easier to manoeuvre travelling downstream, which was running fairly slowly. Everything went according to plan and as we approached I could hear the whispered remarks of the crew, 'Bada heria'. We came in at an angle. I didn't think it necessary to give Roy the customary signal when to shoot. I was confident he would handle the situation efficiently, and so it turned out. He fired, his bullet going straight into the centre of its skull. He turned to me with a satisfied smile as the reverberations of his rifle died away.

It was a big fellow right enough, all of fifteen feet and it took the six of us to get it aboard. By now it was drizzling rain so we put our raincoats on, I started the motor and we pushed on upstream. We cruised another two miles, came round a bend and there was one on a shelving bank half out of the water, every bit as big as the last one. There was no time for any fancy manoeuvring; I quickly cut the motors, the paddlers got into action and as we closed in, the croc started to slide back into the water. It didn't seem to be alarmed, and I thought that it was probably curious to find out what was approaching. It never found out – as we glided up Roy blew the top of its skull off, fragments flying through the rain that now was starting to come down heavily. Again we had to help to get it aboard and when that was done we were liberally caked with mud and very wet. I grabbed the spotlight and shone it on my watch – it was midnight and still furiously raining.

I said to Roy, 'I think we should turn back. We'll probably pick something up on the way, and the weather won't get any better'. He nodded as I peered at him, water pouring off his hat. All in all it wasn't a bad night's work even if we didn't get any more. I started the outboards and we headed back. I had the light, but I didn't really look for more crocodiles; just made sure that we kept in midstream and didn't hit any logs.

During the night the rain continued but at dawn it had cleared. We started to skin the night's booty as the sun came up in an almost clear sky. There were plenty of recruits for the job, most of whom were familiar with the procedure from my previous visit.

The skins were salted down and we went back to the Rest House for a breakfast of stewed something. Roy said he thought it was cassowary, which our cook confirmed. He had bought a portion of a thigh from one of the villagers for a couple of sticks of tobacco.

In the meantime I had been doing some thinking. I could see that a few things were piling up. I knew Roy was going to be a top hunter; he had everything going for him – he was familiar with the country, he was fluent in Motu, and he got on well with the people. There was no point in me staying around.

I explained that I should go around the traps – Beara, the Mission, the sawmill and the drilling camp. There should be quite a few skins to be shipped out, one way and another. He was disappointed that I was leaving so soon – apart from having company there was the advantage of the outboards. I stayed another night and we got seven.

The next day I got away at daylight and headed for Beara. Speed and Ruth Graham were pleased to see me, particularly Speed. He had about forty skins and said that the missionary had also been shooting – he had run into him one night over at Romilly Sound. I asked him about Chambers and he said that he'd come over and borrowed a bag of salt, which was very reassuring. That afternoon I measured his skins, which worked out at £69. I stayed the night and set off the next morning. The missionary had fifteen and the sawmill blokes had another twenty. Charlie and May pressed me to stay the night and they didn't have to work too hard on that.

The next day I went to the oil drilling camp. As I approached their jetty, I could see the usual group of natives standing around. As soon as they saw who it was, they immediately started calling out, 'Huwala taubada, huwala taubada!' (Crocodile man, crocodile man!) I was really becoming known.

I received a very hearty welcome and there were about sixty skins for me. It seemed that the first burst of enthusiasm had resolved itself into four regular hunters, one of whom had been transferred to Port Moresby. I was also told that the drill had just about reached its limit and as it was unlikely that oil would be found, a move to another site to the west was imminent. However, they would be staying in the coastal area – crocodile country that hadn't been shot before.

It was now the end of October and the wet season was building up; the rain was increasing in severity. Hunting for this season was almost at an end. I had plenty to think about: it was becoming clear that I had to have some kind of organisation in Moresby as next year would see a lot of skins coming in.

After squaring up with the hunters, I made my way to the office and asked it I could get a message to the District Commissioner at Kikori. This was no trouble: I was handed the mike and told to go ahead. After a few 'Wana calling Kikori, Wana calling Kikori' I got a quick response. Eric Flower came on, 'Go ahead Wana, we read you'. I announced who I was and asked for the District Commissioner, who soon came on air. I asked him how many skins he had. 'About thirty in hand but we've sent a case of thirty into Moresby.' We chatted for a while and I told him that I would be going into Moresby, probably on the APC plane. He agreed that because of the approaching wet season, hunting was just about coming to a standstill. I explained that after I made some arrangements in town for receiving skins and shipping them out, I would be going to Sydney until after the wet season. I reckoned I would be back about March or April.

The next day I climbed into the little float plane, took my seat beside the pilot and we took off for Port Moresby. As we flew over swamp and jungle, I reflected on my good fortune.

Despite its proximity to Australia, New Guinea was, in reality, a very remote and primitive country that was heavily populated with people not far removed from a prehistoric era, in fact in some parts not at all removed. In a brief five months I had successfully established a business that could certainly be described as unusual. After my years in the Northern Territory, although it differed somewhat, I found no difficulty fitting in to the way of life and I had quickly made a lot of friends. It was all tremendously rewarding. We landed in Moresby and taxied to the oil company wharf and after the little plane was secured, I walked across to one of the sheds and found someone I knew. When I asked if there were any skins for me, he laughed and said: 'There's skins in cases, there's skins in bags and there's just skins; I got no idea how many, but you'd better get them out of here – the boss was complaining about the smell the other day.'

He indicated a corner of the building and I looked them over. There were 150 skins altogether, and whatever the manager thought, I liked the smell. It didn't take long to arrange storage space and someone to take care of the shipping. A few days later I was on way back to Australia and my family.

Kathleen was at the airport to meet me, holding our beautiful baby daughter Kathryn who, after one brief look at me, went back to her teddy bear. At home there was a pile of mail of varying importance ranging from a few accounts to a couple of substantial cheques that enabled me to go out the next day and buy a new Holden sedan.

When the excitement had subsided, I went to the tannery at St Marys (another smell I liked) that processed my skins. Time passed quickly and Christmas arrived; our home was festooned with balloons, decorations and toys. January galloped past and February disappeared when I wasn't looking. I realised that I would have to start planning my return as the wet season in New Guinea ranged from about December to the end of March. In the delta it rained day and night over that period, and after that it was mainly afternoon and night – it could hardly be called the dry season. At the end of the first week in April we went out to the airport and while saying our goodbyes, I gave Kathryn a new teddy bear, which generated more affection when I left than when I'd arrived a few months previously.

I boarded the flight and we were soon airborne. By now I was getting to know quite a few people and I was better prepared for a rugged night, which really got into gear after we left Brisbane. Port Moresby hove into sight at sunrise, we landed and disembarked – there was no such thing as Customs, they just hadn't got round to it. Ivan Hoggard was at the airport to meet me.

'There aren't many skins in hand,' he said – I didn't expect many anyway – 'but there are a few prospective hunters who will be happy to see you.' He asked me how the flight was and I was able to assure him that it easily maintained its reputation for gallons per mile and ruggedness. He took me to the hotel, where I crashed for a few hours.

On surfacing, I was waylaid by one of the men Ivan had mentioned, Bluey Wynn, from Woodlark Island, near the Trobriand group. After we'd had a talk I borrowed an army jeep and after sundown we went to Waigani Swamp, just outside the town, where I was able to show him some small crocodiles with a spotlight. The swamp was smothered with water lilies and reeds, and it was too difficult to give a shooting demonstration. However, he seemed to grasp the idea fairly well – after all, it wasn't that difficult. The next day he got himself set up, placing an order with Burns Philp for a ton of salt, and a spotlight and battery charger, items I had suggested they stock.

Then a couple more recruits turned up who were rearing to go – Alan Johnson and Harry Holt. Carpenters by trade, they had built quite a good dinghy about ten feet in length and equipped it with an outboard motor. After some discussion, it was decided that they would go out to the Fly River. I said that I would go along to start them off. The coastal ship *Doma* was due in Port Moresby in about a week and on its next trip would be going to Daru, an island off the mouth of the Fly. I had no doubt that from there we would be able to make some arrangements to get up the river.

The *Doma* came into port and Captain John Stitt didn't have to tell me what the weather was like. From the comfort of a squatter's chair on the lawn of the RSL Club on Ela Beach, the sea pounding the reef at Basilisk Passage was very visible. Four days later we headed into it.

It was an uncomfortable two days to Daru. A Civil Aviation boat was at the wharf; it pulled out to let us in and then tied up alongside *Doma*. The 'CA 70' was renewing buoys for the Catalina flying boats, which did a weekly run from Port Moresby to Kairuku, Kerema and Lake Murray. Captain Jim Dwyer, a jovial character, came aboard for refreshments, settling down under an awning with John Stitt, and me and my two crocodile hunters. Shortly after we were joined by some of the Daru residents, the doctor and his wife, a Patrol Officer and a couple of others.

The day passed pleasantly until his first mate told Stitt that the cook had disappeared. Some of his friends had turned up and after generously loading their canoes with as much food from the galley as they could comfortably carry, joined them and headed for parts unknown.

These sort of incidents were, I was finding out, a part of New Guinea life and there wasn't much that could be done about it, except that another cook had to be found. Two crew boys who unhesitatingly declared that they knew of a very good cook on the island were sent off to recruit this gifted culinary artist, thereby escaping the more exacting work of unloading the cargo.

Then Jim Dwyer suggested that we take a day off and go fishing at Bramble Cay. I had no idea where this cay was, but had no doubt that it would be interesting, especially when the Daru people all thought it was a marvellous idea.

'We'll go in CA 70,' Dwyer announced, 'and we'd best load up with the booze tonight because we'll leave early tomorrow morning.'

I asked about this fishing paradise and was told it was a sandy atoll in the Coral Sea, in Queensland waters. 'Almost due east of here,' Stitt said, 'just about where the Barrier Reef peters out.'

By sundown the *Doma* cargo had been unloaded, the hatch covers were back in place and the two crew members who had been cook-hunting appeared with a genial character who started to give an impressive rundown on his abilities – until cut short by the captain. Everything was back to normal.

At sunrise the next morning we climbed over the bulwarks on to CA 70 and headed for Bramble Cay. The wind had dropped and the sea was quite moderate, it was all very pleasant. About mid-afternoon the cay lighthouse was sighted, but it was some time before the little island could be seen. It was only a few feet above sea level, had not a single tree, and millions of seabirds, some species of tern, I thought, shrieking and wheeling over it as we dropped anchor just before sundown in the lee. The crew quickly had fishing lines out while we settled down to do some forward planning.

The next morning I went ashore with John Stitt. Several of the crew came with us, each one carrying either a bucket or a sizable billycan. It was nesting time and Bramble Cay was a breeding ground for tens of thousands of tern. They laid a solitary, brown, mottled egg; there was no sign of any nest, just a single egg on bare ground. There were hundreds and hundreds of them, just a few feet apart and sometimes closer; one had to watch to avoid stepping on them. There were also little chicks that would scuttle away at our approach, attempting to hide in a tuft of grass or low bush. The boys with the billycans were busy collecting eggs and in no time had them full. For the rest of the day we fished and it was the most prolific fishing that I have ever experienced. We caught mainly red emperor and spanish mackerel, a great fighter that would test anyone, and a magnificent table fish. There were other species that I couldn't recognise.

The following morning we headed back – our timing had been pretty good, the south-easter was just starting up again. It usually blew for five or six days then eased up for a day or so, and now we had it behind us. We made good time and tied up at Daru in the early afternoon. The spoils were divided, we took a copra sack full of fish and a bucket of eggs, which the captain tested in a bucket of fresh water. About two-thirds of them refused to float so presumably they were fresh. He called the cook, who came up on deck beaming, and asked him if he could make sponge cake. John was particularly partial to sponge cake.

'Oh, Taubada...' he started off, about to go into raptures over his sponge cake making abilities. He was cut short in midstream, given two dozen eggs and told to get back to the galley and make a sponge cake. John observing as he left, 'He will probably eat the eggs and breathe on the flour'.

Promptly at four o'clock the bell sounded for afternoon tea, the cook's offsider appeared with a tray loaded with a teapot, cups and accessories, and then the cook himself arrived bearing a dish with the biggest sponge cake I'd ever seen, a large carving knife beside it. He placed it on the table beaming proudly then stood back waiting for someone to cut it, ready to modestly accept the accolades.

John peered at it and observed that it was a funny looking sponge cake, which was the same thing I was thinking. The first mate took the carving knife and cut a generous slice, picked it up, his eyes almost popping out of his head; in fact, all our eyes were doing the same. One thing was certain, the cook hadn't eaten any of the eggs because every one could be counted – they were hard boiled.

Early the next morning I was on the bridge having a cup of tea. A small cargo boat about fifty feet long had squeezed into the wharf and was busy unloading copra. The *Doma* captain and I watched as the little ship's boom swung out and two crew members expertly tipped bulging sacks from the sling. A white man clad only in shoes, shorts and a battered sun-helmet stood tallying the bags. John Stitt said: 'That's John Stocks, he'll take you fellows up the river, he's got a plantation on Mibu Island. I'll be taking his copra into Moresby; when he's finished unloading he'll come aboard and you can talk to him.' An hour or so later the planter boarded *Doma* and joined us on the bridge and Stitt introduced me. He smiled as we shook hands, 'You're the crocodile man I suppose'.

Johnson and Holt joined us, Stocks was enthusiastic and helpful. The Fly River was, he thought, about sixty miles across at the mouth and scattered through the estuary were twenty or thirty islands, the biggest being Kiwai. Crocodiles? 'Lousy with 'em,' he observed laconically.

My hunters' dinghy and cargo was stacked on the wharf and the latter was transferred to Stocks's boat, the *Bonney*. He intended getting away early the next morning, and the dinghy would be towed. Just after sunrise we made our farewells and with the dinghy tied on behind we headed for Mibu. It didn't take long to find out that towing it was a failure; it kept filling with water. After this happened a couple of times, Stocks lashed it onto the port side and there were no more delays.

It was getting rough, the south-easter building up again. We slipped through a passage between an island and the mainland that gave us some shelter. I asked Stocks how far his plantation was. He said, 'Not far, just round the corner', referring to a headland that marked the entrance to the river, 'about twenty-five miles'.

This was the mighty Fly River, which wound its way from the clouded cordillera of the island's backbone, thundering through formidable gorges, pounding rapids and jungle fastnesses for hundreds of miles, finally emptying itself serenely into the Coral Sea. Here its mouth spread sixty miles from the southernmost point to its northern extremity.

Our boat passed through the passage, turned north and entered the mouth of the river. We now had a following sea and the tide was with us as well. We passed several huge, seagoing canoes that must have been hewn from tremendous logs. They were loaded with bags of copra on their way to Daru. They had double outriggers, and the sails were patched and tattered, but they rode the seas remarkably well and every one was crowded with people.

Two men were struggling with an enormous paddle, which acted as the rudder; they were obviously good seamen. We tied up at the Mibu wharf. A crowd of plantation workers was waiting and immediately started unloading. John took us up to his house, which was built of bush material. The walls were of woven palm and the roof was heavily thatched and very cool. A pretty, dark-skinned girl greeted John. I thought that perhaps she was a half-caste, but couldn't be sure; a lot of the Papuan girls were very light skinned, or maybe she was a Thursday Islander, but whatever, she was damned attractive.

John took us out on to the verandah and the girl brought a tray with drinks. She smiled shyly at John as she poured his drink first and he smiled back. I was sure then that her duties extended beyond the kitchen, which in this country, and many others, of course, was normal. A Biblical quotation came to mind: 'Man cannot live by bread alone.' The connotations of which seem to be frequently misinterpreted. After lunch we repaired to the verandah again, which, as it is everywhere in the tropics, was the leisure area.

Stocks was a tower of strength as he was very familiar with the area. He told us that the Fly estuary could get very rough at this time of the year, the south-easter reaching gale force velocity at times, but there were a lot of islands most of which gave protection. He said that he would take us to Dawarri Island, where there was a good rest house. He knew the native policeman stationed there.

The following morning we left for the island; it was only a half-hour run from Mibu. The village policemen and the policeman, accompanied by a crowd of villagers, came down to the beach to meet us. John Stocks explained the purpose of our visit, which was greeted with enthusiasm. The village policeman rolled his eyes and threw his arms in the air, going into a long convoluted rigmarole, which boiled down to pretty well what we already knew.

The cargo was unloaded and Stocks left. I had already arranged with him to come back the next day and pick me up. I reckoned that by then my two recruits would have the hang of it. I could see Johnson was an old hand in the bush and I had no doubt Holt was no new chum. After the cargo was carried to the Rest House and stacked away, the all-important matter of a cook had to be settled, for which job there was no shortage of applicants. Harry Holt took over the process of elimination, finally settling for the son of the village policeman, which was sensible, there being nothing like having a friend at court.

There was still five or six hours of daylight left so we decided to put it to good use and have a cruise around the islands to get an idea of the geography. I took my rifle but didn't bother with a cartridge belt, not expecting to be doing any serious shooting; anyway there were a few rounds in the magazine. This turned out to be a significant mistake.

Accompanied by two villagers we set off. We turned north between two islands and sighted a crocodile just sliding into the water. I fired a random shot that predictably missed. Further on I saw another on a bank several feet above the level of the stream. I waved to Harry, who was steering to bring us closer to the bank, and he slowed down as we approached, the current holding the little dinghy almost stationary. I had a good sight and fired and the creature shuddered as the bullet struck. It then started to thrash around and I knew I had not killed it. I jerked the breech open to slip another cartridge into the chamber, glancing at the magazine. There were no more bullets – I had fired my last shot. Cursing myself for such carelessness, I called to Harry to bring the boat closer to shore. At the same time I undid the rope that was used to secure it. Although partially stunned, the crocodile, about a ten-footer I judged, was writhing around on the bank and getting closer to the water. As soon as the dinghy grated on the sand and came to a stop, I jumped out, ran up the bank and grabbed it by the tail, calling to the others to follow. It was starting to come good now. Alan and Harry were just behind me: 'You fellows hang on to its tail and I'll get the rope around its jaws.'

I quickly fashioned a loop and with a long stick I managed to secure its jaws. I then took a couple of hitches around its neck and I had it under control. We paused for a breather and to assess the situation. I could see that there was no way we could kill it: I had no cartridges and we didn't even have an axe or a tomahawk. We couldn't kill it with a stick, we wouldn't even give it a headache, apart from the one it already had, with half its skull blown off. I thought that if we could get it into the dinghy we could get it back to the camp, but that wasn't going to be easy – it was about the same length as the little craft.

Johnson and Holt looked at it dubiously. I said, 'We'll get it into the dinghy, the rope's long enough to fasten it so that it can't move'.

Alan scratched his head and said, 'There's five of us – do you think there's enough room for us and the crocodile, too?'

'Yes, sure,' I told them, 'the tail part will slide under the seats; I'll tie it so that it can't move.'

Harry said, 'I dunno, I'm not sure we want it that bad', then with a laugh, 'I'm a bit paranoid about being bitten by a crocodile'.

I suppose it was some kind of insanity, but by then I was determined to get it back to the camp and was quite sure we could do it. 'Well, let's give it a go. I promise I won't let it bite you,' I said.

We had no trouble getting the creature down the bank; as it was heading towards the water, it did its best to help. But getting it into the boat was another kettle of fish – it stopped helping, and I soon found out that we weren't going to tuck its tail under the seat either. We eventually got most of it on the boat, but its head was hanging over the bow. We lashed the tail onto the seats and then pulled its head back – it looked a bit top-heavy, giving the appearance of an enormous figurehead.

We pushed out into deep water, started the motor and headed back to the camp. Arriving at the village was quite sensational. I ran up to the Rest House to get my camera as I was anxious to get a photograph. I was sure no one would believe the story, but when I got back they had unloaded it and it was lying beside the dinghy. I was quite disappointed, it would have made a terrific photo.

Just before sundown we pushed the dinghy out into the stream to do some serious hunting. The tide was just turning and a cool breeze was beating up from the sea. The sun was settling in the west, wedges of geese were honking their way upstream and Torres Strait pigeons were heading back to their camping grounds. As I anticipated, the two men quickly got the idea and we had a very encouraging night's shooting with crocodiles on board and crocodiles towed. I suggested they would be better off hiring some canoes.

The next morning Stocks arrived early to pick me up. I gave the village policemen half a pound of tobacco each and they assured me that they would look after the two men. From there we went straight to Daru, expecting to catch the flying boat, but there had been a medical emergency and it had been and gone.

Storekeeper Lennie Luff had shot himself and the plane had been sent out a day early to take him to hospital. It appeared to be a case of attempted suicide because he was shot in the head. I thought it would be difficult to shoot oneself in the head accidentally. Anyway, whatever the truth, he was seriously wounded, although not unconscious all the time, drifting from incoherent babbling to intelligent remarks. When he was being carried along the jetty to the flying boat, in one of his lucid moments he said to the first aid man who accompanied the stretcher, 'When we get to Moresby please tell the doctor that I'm allergic to seafood'. As is sometimes the case, his health had suddenly become a matter of concern, or maybe he just wanted to die in comfort. However, he survived, his wife maintained that it did him a lot of good: '…should have done it years ago,' she said, 'he's been quite amiable ever since.'

I got a lift in a copra boat to Kikori, from where I planned to take the seaplane to Port Moresby, feeling a little guilty for missing the Christmas of 1950 with my family. But there had been some pressure from a new contact that I had made in Singapore – Ott & Company, who were anxious to take all the skins that I could produce – there was no limit to what they would accept. They also requested that I give particular attention to the skinning and curing. Their standards were more demanding than most buyers but their offer was a point or so better, too. Consequently, I had been contacting my hunters and giving them a pep talk. It was now late January 1951.

The flying boat was due to arrive some time on Sunday morning and I was packed and ready fairly early, with my gear on the wharf near the mooring. By midday I was becoming anxious and because it was Sunday there was no normal radio communication. A peculiar haze had developed and we were all wondering what had caused it. It seemed to have drifted across from the east; the sun looked more like the moon. Healy was also concerned at the non-arrival of the flying boat and eventually decided to call Moresby. It was then that we received the shattering news – Mount Lamington in the Northern District had erupted. The blast had wiped out the Government station at Higatura, killing the entire population, which, with the Anglican Mission, was thirty-five people, including the District Commissioner and his son. The toll of native deaths was expected to be in the thousands. Kikori was asked to stay off the air until further notice.

This was a tragedy of massive proportions. Healy told me that the District Commissioner was Cecil Cowley, who was married and had two children. We tuned in to Radio Australia and heard more details. The announcer said that the whole side of Mt Lamington had been blown out, and everyone within a radius of eight miles had been killed. A number of villages had been engulfed and the death toll was estimated at 4000 to 6000.

The next day I was fortunate to get a seat on a Mission plane to Port Moresby where the only topic of conversation was the eruption. The District Commissioner's wife and daughter had been visiting friends, relatives of one of the Sangara Plantation assistant managers, but the Territory's Director of Native Labour, W. R. Humphries, who had been visiting the district, was among the dead. The toll had stabilised at 3500; the exact number would never be known.

After some weeks back in Sydney, I started to give some thought to heading back north. For some time I had been trying to talk my wife into coming up for a visit, but she had not shown any great enthusiasm. I thought that perhaps some of the stories I had frequently related to admiring audiences, stories of man-eating crocodiles with a few head-hunting cannibals thrown in, had not done anything to induce a desire to see the country. Eventually, I persuaded her to come on the *Bulolo*, which would reach Moresby at the end of June. She would spend ten days ashore while it continued around the islands and rejoin it on its return. There was no difficulty arranging for the baby to be looked after by my wife's sister Madge, who doted on her.

I returned in April and a couple of days later I was greeted with the startling information that a lion tamer was looking for me. I had a fairly wide circle of friends, some of whom could claim to be slightly unusual, but there were no lion tamers among them. It sounded interesting but at the same time I couldn't help wondering what such a professional could possibly want with me. I decided to let nature take its course. If it was true, the logical place to catch up with an exponent of lion taming would unquestionably be a bar.

Shortly after, at the Bottom Pub in the appropriately named Snake Pit, oil man John Gordon introduced us. His name was Thompson, 'Call me Tiger', he said, presumably because he was a lion tamer. He was a passenger on a ship from Japan, where he had been delivering, as he put it, 'a crate of lions'. And did I have any crocodiles? He told me that most Japanese cities of any size had a zoo – they were a predominant and popular feature of the Japanese entertainment scene. He explained that he ran a very profitable wild animal business, specialising in training lions. He was hoping to get some crocodiles for which, he assured me, there was an insatiable demand in Japan.

Thompson was a most entertaining character. He had been in Japan for a month or so teaching the Japanese to train lions. We drank a fairly substantial lunch, John Gordon left us to go back to whatever he was supposed to be doing, and Tiger Thompson and I went down to the ship that he thought would be sailing later in the afternoon. We went to his cabin, summoned a steward and ordered drinks; we were joined by a couple of passengers and a young officer. Tiger was obviously popular. He introduced me as a famous crocodile hunter, which I thought was piling it on a bit.

Thompson was a great raconteur, telling a story with a lively sense of humour. The officer left saying that he had to get back up on deck, the ship would be sailing soon. Some more passengers joined us and drinks were pouring into the cabin like the Niagara Falls. The stories of the Japanese learning to be lion tamers were hilarious. Suddenly I felt the beat of the engines increase, I looked across at Tiger and then glanced out of a porthole and saw Paga Point go past – the ship had sailed, we were on our way to Australia! Everybody started laughing except me. They all thought it was a great joke, but Australia was the last place I wanted to go, with nothing except what I stood up in.

Tiger said, 'I'd better go up and see the captain, he's not a bad bloke'. I thought maybe he wasn't, but it might depend on the circumstances. We all went up on deck and although we were inside the reef that ran for five or six miles offshore, there was a howling south-easter blowing and a heavy sea running.

Tiger came down from the bridge looking serious. 'The captain has signalled the harbour master. I think the Customs launch will come out and take you off.'

I said, 'Should I go up and apologise to the captain?'

'No, for Christ's sake don't go near him; talk about a man smoking at the arse, there's streaks of blue flame coming out!' Then, 'What are you like on a rope ladder?' I looked over the side at the heaving sea, it seemed a hell of a long way down.

'Nothing to it,' I said bravely, 'but if there's any of that whisky left, I could do with a slug.'

He went down to his cabin as two seamen appeared carrying a large bundle, which they dropped on deck – a rope ladder. Tiger came back with half a bottle of whisky and a glass. Glancing at the rope ladder, he handed me the glass and said, 'Say when'. Words almost failed me, but he stopped halfway.

We were now close to Basilisk Passage, a break in the reef through which all shipping passed, and we had almost stopped. I could see the Customs launch bouncing its way towards us. I swallowed the whisky and felt much better. The rope ladder was dropped over the side as the ship swung around so that I would be going over on the lee side, which didn't seem much different to me. I had another shot of whisky and started to feel astonishingly confident. The Customs launch came alongside; harbour master George Evans gave me an encouraging wave. I shook hands with Tiger and climbed over the side. It didn't seem too bad at all. As I got down towards the bottom rung, I glanced over my shoulder at the launch bouncing off the ship's side, heavy fenders protecting it. I was on the bottom rung and Evans called, 'Jump'. It was easy.

The motor quickened and as we gained speed I looked up and waved to my erstwhile lion tamer friend. The captain was leaning through a window on the bridge shouting something that I could not hear. Whatever it was it wouldn't have been complimentary. As we ploughed back to the Moresby wharf I couldn't help wondering what a live crocodile was worth – I never did find out.

FOUR

ERROL FLYNN WAS HERE

THERE WAS now more work to do than ever before. I secured an office in Hunter Street and storage space in Lawes Road. I flew out to the Purari Delta, called on Clarrie Healy and spent a few days with Roy Edwards. The oil company had moved further west to the Bamu River. I returned to Moresby and bought a thirty-foot launch from Hornibrooks, who had been building an airstrip on Fisherman's Island off Port Moresby and had no further use for it.

Then, in the first week in May, an interesting letter arrived from Charles Chauvel, the well known film producer, offering me a part in a film he was about to make called *Jedda*. I had been recommended to him by a John Julian, who I had never heard of, and a Miss Molly O'Neil who, to my everlasting regret, was also a complete stranger.

Chauvel's reference to Errol Flynn was interesting and although it is not strictly accurate that '…it is not wise to say too much about this in New Guinea', he certainly didn't leave with an unblemished record. Chauvel made, among many others, a film called *The Wake of the Bounty* and it was in this movie that Flynn first appeared and caught the eye of a Hollywood talent scout; the rest, of course, is history.

Flynn, the son of a professor, was born in Tasmania and first sailed into Port Moresby on his own yacht, *Sirocco*, which was wrecked on a reef shortly after his arrival. At the time he was accompanied by a local barmaid and although he was known to be a competent sailor and the weather was favourable, he came to grief. There were several theories as to the cause of the accident, none of which varied greatly. This

77

CHARLES CHAUVEL
PRODUCTIONS
LIMITED

PRUDENTIAL BUILDING, 39 MARTIN PLACE, SYDNEY, AUSTRALIA . . . PHONE BW 2861

30th April, 1952.

Mr. T.E. Cole,
Box 27,
PORT MORESBY, PAPUA.

Dear Mr. Cole,

One of my Directors, Mr. John Julian, of Yass
and Miss Molly O'Neil have spoken to me of you in reference to
my forthcoming film production, "Jedda".

They have mentioned that you could prove a very
strong possibility for the role of McMann, the station man in the
story and that you would also no doubt be able to conduct operations in connection with the securing of crocodiles.

This is all of great interest to me and I hope
that I am not presuming too much in writing this letter to you,
but as I found one of my outstanding film leads in New Guinea in
the past it might be possible for me to repeat this success.
The film "find" which I allude to is that of Errol Flynn.   I
believe it is not wise to say too much about this in New Guinea
where Flynn evidently cut such a dash.

I fail to see how I can make a deal with you
without you coming to Sydney for an interview to enable me to
sum up your possibilities for a screen role in "Jedda" as apart
from any assistance you could give regarding the crocodiles.
Failing the part of the station man, there is another good role
in that of the police patrol officer.

If we could come to a deal you would be required
with us for a period of from three to four months, commencing from
the latter part of next month.

BRINGING THE NORTHERN TERRITORY TO THE SCREENS OF THE WORLD

I should be leaving for the Northern Territory about two weeks from to-day, on about May, 12th so that if you are interested it would be necessary for you to try and make a trip down to see me as quickly as possible.

I am most interested in meeting you with a view to your playing a role in and assisting with the producing of "Jedda" and hope that you will be able to make the trip.

Please wire me if you can come down.

Awaiting your reply.

Yours sincerely,

(CHARLES CHAUVEL)

P.S. The role of the cattle man (station owner) would carry a salary of £25 per week for a period of five weeks and you would be required if chosen, to attend at the studio again for a further two weeks in November at the same salary. A separate arrangement would have to be entered into regarding the securing of crocodiles.

incident may have been the origin of the saying 'In like Flynn'. He must have had some affection for the boat because it was the name he gave to several boats he owned during his years in Hollywood.

There were quite a few people who had clear memories of him, particularly those from whom he borrowed money. After he hit the big time some wrote to him with a gentle reminder of his indebtedness and although they always got a reply, it was not exactly what they hoped for. He sent them autographed photographs, one of which I saw.

There were numerous stories, some of which were amusing but few that reflected any credit. He left Port Moresby by boat which, in those days, was the only means of travel, cautiously boarding it shortly before it sailed. Burns Philp, the principal business house, heard the alarming news and sent a fast runner to the ship with his outstanding account. Flynn, keeping the courier until the last moment, penned a brief reply:

If you are prepared to forget this account,
I am,
Yours faithfully,
Errol Flynn.

But the story I like best of all is of the occasion when the first film in which he starred came to Wau, a goldmining town where he had been well known as a recruiter of labour.

All the locals flocked to the open-air theatre to see the first film made in America by the local boy who had made good. One can imagine the expectant hush when thrown on to the silver screen was:

CAPTAIN BLOOD

ADAPTED FROM THE NOVEL BY

RAFAEL SABATINI

STARRING

*** ERROL FLYNN ***

DIRECTED BY SO-AND-SO

FILM PLAY BY SO-AND-SO

PHOTOGRAPHY BY SO-AND-SO.

...And so on – until the local dentist could stand it no longer. He jumped to his feet and shouted, 'And teeth by Ween, and not bloody well paid for yet either'.

I did not have to give Chauvel's letter a great deal of thought and I replied to him a few days later:

P.O. Box 27
Port Moresby

Mr Charles Chauvel
Charles Chauvel Productions
Martin Place
Sydney

Dear Mr Chauvel,

Thank you for your letter of April 30th, the contents of which gave me some surprise, mainly perhaps because I am unable to place either Mr Julian or Miss O'Neil. However, it is with some regret that I am unable to accept your offer because of my commitments here. As you are obviously aware, I am engaged in crocodile hunting, which has developed into a business of fairly substantial proportions with a number of hunters who are largely dependant on me, as I am the only buyer and exporter of crocodile skins in the country. And apart from the fact that, in my opinion at least, there is some doubt that you could repeat your previous success and discover another Errol Flynn, I am sure you will not take offence when I explain that while perhaps the remuneration you offer is quite generous, it would barely be sufficient to keep me in rum beyond about Tuesday dinnertime.

Thanking you,
Yours sincerely,
Tom Cole.

The boat that I had bought from Hornibrooks needed some work and I was able to use the Papua Yacht Club slip, being a member, where it received a good clean down and a couple of coats of paint. I had a compass fitted that my good friend the harbour master cheerfully swung for me, still chuckling over the lion tamer incident. After a few more refinements, like a comfortable bunk and the installation of a toilet, I loaded up with a month's supplies, christened her *Seabird*, and left with one Kiwai Islander as first mate.

The first day was a comfortable run to Galley Reach where I called on my friends the Wards. From there I headed for Kairuku, pulling into the wharf in time to see Ron Slaughter's copra boat leave with a brand-new fibreglass dinghy (a novelty in those days), one end securely tied to the wharf, the other end just as efficiently fastened to the cargo boat, whose powerful Ruston engine had no difficulty pulling it apart somewhere about the middle. 'They told me that they were unbreakable,' wailed Ron, 'but they hadn't tried them out in this country!' I did my best to console him and left the next day with a hangover.

As I headed for Kerema, schools of dolphins joined me, playing round the bows. I ran a line out and caught red emperor, trevally and kingfish, reeling it in when I had as much as the two of us could eat. At Kerema I caught another hangover – medium size – courtesy of District Officer Jim McLennan and his wife. They hadn't seen anyone for a while, and were most generous and entertaining hosts.

The next day I had more dolphins for company and came dangerously close to a family of huge whales before quickly changing course. I turned into the Purari Delta quite pleased with my navigational abilities. On the way up to Kikori I shot three crocodiles. I made fast at the wharf just before sundown, very satisfied with my performance.

I spent a day with the Healys and headed across to where Clarrie told me Roy Edwards was off hunting. A blinding storm came up as we weaved our way through the channels, but I was now familiar enough with the waterways for it not to worry me. Roy was doing well; I told him he could have my canoes, as I had come to the conclusion that I had more than enough on my plate and didn't expect to be doing much hunting in the future.

I called on Charlie Chambers and spent a night with Speed Graham and his wife, who were just back after his recent leave in Australia. What I wanted to do most was catch up with my old oil drilling friends, who had moved across to the Bamu River. A few cases of skins had been arriving in Moresby on the company boats and I thought it was a good idea to 'show the flag'.

Apart from the storm that we had experienced a few days previously, we had enjoyed good weather and because I wasn't bound by time, I could afford to lay up if we struck severe conditions, although the south-easter ran to a fairly predictable pattern. It was starting to beat up again when we turned into the delta. When we left for the oil drilling camp, I calculated that it would be easing off. We cruised down Romilly Sound towards the coast and as we approached the open sea, the swell gradually built up; it was still a bit dirty outside and as we'd be turning westward, the boat would be heading into an uncomfortable beam sea. I turned towards a small island and anchored in its lee.

Lying peacefully in the tranquil shelter, I turned on my radio in an endeavour to find out what was happening in the great big outside world – civilisation. The first station I came to was a broadcast of the Commonwealth Parliament – the governors of our country were in full throat. A gentleman with a slightly less than cultured accent was explaining to a colleague, at least I presume he was a colleague, that he wouldn't know whether his backside was punched, bored or eaten out with white ants. I would liked to have heard some devastating reply to this witticism, but unfortunately it was completely lost in the uproar that followed. The next station I tried produced a discussion on Jack the Ripper, which was quite boring; eventually I found some pleasant music and settled down to reflect on my good fortune. I had been in Papua for two and a half years and looking back to my first few days, I realised that Lady Luck had smiled very generously on me and had continued to do so.

Coming to Papua as a complete stranger and establishing myself in business in such a short time seemed quite remarkable. The hospitality everywhere had been exceptionally generous: people like the Wards accepting me unhesitatingly; the generosity of the oil company, the use of their seaplane, ships and storage; the advantages of the village rest houses and the friendly cooperation of the villagers; then people like the Chambers, the District Services officers such as Healy and Speed Graham.

My wife, too, had made a tremendous contribution in that she had never raised the slightest objection to my leaving her at what was undoubtedly a critical time, when we were just starting a family. I have no doubt she realised that I would have not only been very unhappy in a city environment, but also unbearable and would probably have sunk without trace anyway. It was a profitable business, too. I was blessed many times over – and also beginning to take a liking to the very pleasant way of life: cruising along the coast, interspersed with social calls.

It was with some trepidation that I first sailed out of Port Moresby in my new boat, but it was something that had always held a great deal of attraction for me. From time to time I had taken the wheel on the odd coastal boat, and reading a chart never presented any difficulties. I had bought the necessary charts for this trip and had a set of parallel rulers and dividers. I was rarely out of sight of land and had no intention of taking any risks or travelling at night.

The next morning, as soon as daylight broke I was anxiously scanning the horizon. A light mist was curling in from the sea, although it would disperse by sunrise. My offsider got the anchor up as I started the engine, and we headed down the estuary. The sea was well down, just steady rollers sweeping in from the south. I turned south-west, gave my bosun a course, and went below and stretched out on my bunk to prepare myself for some constructive thinking.

Cruising along at a steady eight knots, I happily thought what a wonderful way to enjoy life and at the same time go about my business. There was no pressure on me to head out into bad weather – an extra day here and there would make no difference. In fact, skins would be steadily piling up all over the place. Two lines were trailing over the stern and when I turned into the Bamu River I had four nice fish.

The next morning it was something of a relief not to have to worry about the state of the sea for a few days, as we were about to undertake a comfortable cruise up river to the oil drilling camp, which was, I estimated, about forty miles away. The tide was rising as we up anchored and headed upstream – no worries, or not immediately visible.

I got the primus stove going and was in the process of preparing a pot of tea when it happened – nothing dramatic, just a gentle simple mishap. I felt the boat heel over; a big floating log had suddenly appeared and my Kiwai helmsman spun the wheel to avoid it, then another and he turned again and this time the boat slid gently on to a sandbank.

I quickly put the engine into full astern for a few minutes, but that just spewed up a great swirl of mud. It didn't seem too bad; we were well settled and on an even keel. The tide appeared to be rising, but as it was meeting the oncoming stream, it was doing so slowly. We might be stuck for an hour or so – I couldn't be sure, but there didn't seem to be anything to worry about. We were close to the bank and I could see some natives who appeared to be gathering betel nut. I went below and stretched out on my bunk with a book, and my bosun waded ashore and returned with a bunch of bananas and yams. He seemed uneasy about something, padding about the deck muttering to himself, occasionally calling to the people on the bank.

Then suddenly I heard it. I leapt from my bunk – it was a most uncanny sound – and went on deck. The Kiwai was jabbering excitedly, pointing up river. Then I saw it: a great wall of water thundering towards us. I knew immediately what it was – a tidal bore. I had vaguely heard of it from seamen who, of course, never let a few facts spoil a good story. The way I recalled their tales, it spelt complete destruction for a little vessel like mine. I quickly stripped down to my underpants, as I had no doubt my boat would be reduced to matchwood. From the corner of my eye I saw the group of natives on the bank reclining under the palms, placidly chewing away. I briefly thought of making a dash for the bank, but abandoned the idea of floundering through the mud and probably being engulfed. Cruising the Papuan coast suddenly became some sort of insanity – I must have been out of my mind when I bought the boat. The wall of water was now only yards away. As the wave hit, it picked my little boat up and gently floated it off the sandbank – we were saved.

Apart from a tremendous feeling of relief, there was also an overwhelming one of foolishness. I felt that nature had deliberately played a huge joke on me. I was reasonably furious, but tried to console myself with the thought that had I been further up the river where it was much narrower, I may not have got off so lightly. My enthusiasm for cruising the tropic waters of Papua was considerably diminished as I restarted the motor.

We went on up river and just before sundown I sighted the oil rig towering above the surrounding jungle. The company had not wasted any time establishing its latest camp: there were several comfortable looking cottages on the side of a hill and the usual conglomeration of administration buildings and quarters at a lower level. A huge bulldozer was parked close to the wharf where we tied up. I was greeted by two men who were fishing nearby, and seemed quite happy to abandon their sporting activities when I came ashore, suggesting that we go up to their club – oil companies didn't do things by halves; looking after their staff always had a high priority.

They told me that there were quite a lot of crocodile skins stacked away in one of the sheds, but there hadn't been much hunting lately as the river was pretty well shot out. A launch was expected from Port Moresby and when that arrived they would be able to go further afield.

The next morning I checked the skins: there was nearly 100 between four hunters, who I paid after the measuring was completed. They seemed quite happy with that and said they would pack them and send them into Port Moresby on the next company boat.

The next day I headed for the Fly River, which turned out to be much better for business. Johnson and Holt had a couple of hundred crocodile skins, Tom Holland had more than three hundred and John Stocks had nearly fifty.

When I got that all tidied up, I asked Stocks if he'd arrange the shipping. We came to a good working arrangement and early the next morning I headed for Daru to send some telegrams. I note in my diary that I got stuck on a sandbank at the mouth of the Fly for three hours. The mouth of the Fly was far too wide to be 'bore' country so I was quite safe and by now feeling quite blasé about such details.

At Daru I sent some telegrams. Sandy Bray, who had been crocodile hunting with Tom Holland, was at the wharf hoping for a boat to take him to Port Moresby. I thought that perhaps he would take *Seabird* in and I could catch the flying boat tomorrow. He jumped at it and the next day I got the last seat and was back in town by early afternoon, wading through an accumulation of mail.

I was much in demand. Would I come out to Abau and Robinson River? And the Sepik River over in New Guinea – they were up to their knees in crocodiles over there. A missionary somewhere up the Ramu River was desperate. And John Stitt was in town. I caught up with him in the Snake Pit, and as he was leaving at six o'clock the next morning for Robinson River, I ordered my fare for the passage – a case of whisky; he'd gone off rum, he explained.

Meanwhile, the *Bulolo* arrived in June and by some miracle of organisation I was there to meet it. Kathleen was at first slightly stunned in a country teeming with people of a different colour and speaking a language she couldn't understand.

My good friends Colin and Joan Sefton had previously asked me to bring her to Koitaki, and so, after a couple of days, we drove up the range to the rubber plantation. We drove around the plantation and watched the tappers collecting the latex; saw it being coagulated, smoked and dried.

Koitaki had a club where the planters regularly gathered, with well laid out tennis courts. The social life of rubber planters seemed to be far more onerous than their plantation duties, but at an altitude of 1500 feet the Sogeri Plateau was a pleasant change from the steamy heat of the coast.

After two or three days we returned to Port Moresby and settled in at the Top Pub, where Kath met a wide range of characters found only in places like Port Moresby. I think she was slightly bewildered.

On our second day, Tom Henderson and his wife Toby, from Sangara Plantation, came to town. I knew Tom from previous visits, although I had never met his wife, a lively and entertaining lady. Kathleen and Toby had an immediate rapport, I was pleased to see.

At dinner the next day, Tom Henderson asked if we would like to visit Sangara. I immediately and enthusiastically took up the offer before Kath had a chance to demur – mainly because I had a good idea that volcanoes were something she wasn't exactly overboard about. He told us that Tony Taylor, the vulcanologist, was also staying at the plantation and that he had an aeroplane standing by. 'I daresay you'd have no difficulty getting a ride with him, he goes up almost every day,' Tom said.

The Hendersons went back the next day and as I had some skin shipments to deal with, I planned to follow a couple of days later. We boarded a tri-motored Drover the following day and headed for Popondetta, which was District Headquarters now that Higatura had been wiped out. As we circled the airstrip, the devastation was clearly visible. Everything in the path of the monstrous blast had been destroyed.

Tom Henderson met us for the short drive to Sangara, where we were made welcome by Tom's wife Toby, after which we were introduced to vulcanologist Tony Taylor, a delightful and charming man.

At the time the Mt Lamington activity started, the Administrator, Colonel Murray, was on leave in Australia and, as was normal, the Chief Justice, 'Monty' Phillips, had been sworn in as his deputy. Monty had been in Rabaul in 1937 where, by coincidence, he was also Deputy Administrator when Vulcan and Matupi blew. Consequently he regarded himself as something of an expert on volcanoes.

The vulcanologist's headquarters were in Rabaul, but after visiting

Higatura the Deputy Administrator decided there was no immediate danger and didn't call for Taylor. He had no idea of the severity of the build up in activity.

On the Saturday night the sky was lit up with glowing clouds, and earth tremors were continuous. Some time after ten o'clock on Sunday morning the side of the mountain blew out with a shattering roar.

An enormous black cloud rolled down on Higatura and the surrounding countryside, and a blanket of red-hot ash covered an area eight miles out from the base of the mountain. There were no survivors inside this area. A priest, the Reverend D. J. Taylor, was found walking to Mongi Mission and suffering from appalling burns. He died shortly after. His entire family – wife and four children – died in their house.

Of all the buildings at Higatura, only one remained intact and that had been lifted off its stumps by the blast and settled about twenty yards away. Some houses were a pile of wreckage while others had been blasted off the ridge into gullies nearby. It was not possible to locate or identify all the European casualties. But for a change of wind the death toll would have been higher.

Tony Taylor was a dedicated vulcanologist and in simple terms explained to us that the Mt Lamington was a very rare type of volcano known as a 'glowing cloud' and further activity could be expected, which was the reason why he was keeping a close watch on it.

Taylor's Dragon aeroplane was standing by at the Popondetta airstrip and he invited us to join him the following morning. I took up the offer with enthusiasm; Kathleen declined.

At five o'clock next morning I was at the airstrip. The pilot was tinkering with the aircraft and after some reluctant cloud cleared we climbed in and took off. The boundaries of the devasted areas were sharply defined. It was a grey no-man's-land, in the centre of untouched flourishing jungle. I noticed one extraordinary feature: the banks of the creeks that wound down from the mountain were lined with dead trees for fifty yards on each side after they entered the jungle. Tony explained that following the eruption, the streams were trapped under a blanket of red-hot ash, but the water finally burst through as a boiling flood that killed everything it touched. The trees and vegetation on the banks had been boiled. Lamington, with one side blown out, was an awesome sight. Steam and cloud rose eerily from the crater. When nature gets going, atom bombs are in the minor league.

It was now close to the time of the *Bulolo*'s return and Tom Henderson was in touch by radio. The day before she was due to dock in Moresby we said goodbye to these charming people and climbed aboard the Drover again. The next day Kath joined the ship, and, with the new friends she had made, we waved her goodbye.

We got away early and Arona Plantation was the first port of call. Next day we reached Abau, at the estuary of Robinson River, the biggest coconut plantation in Papua. It was managed by Rolf Cambridge for Burns Philp, which owned just about everything else in the islands. Rolf was a great bloke with a distinguished record: he was one of that elite group known as Coastwatchers, who worked behind the Japanese lines in New Guinea during the Second World War. They were dedicated and courageous men who lived off the land, moving like wraiths in the night. Using portable transmitters, they sent invaluable information on troop and shipping movements to Allied headquarters.

For those who were unfortunate enough to get caught, there was no mercy – they were immediately and ceremonially beheaded. In their peculiar way the Japanese believed that by executing them in this fashion they were honouring their enemies. There were two schools of thought about this, as the Japanese found out at the war crimes trials. There was nothing ceremonial about the hempen rope that was slipped around their necks when they mounted the gallows.

The *Doma* left for Samarai, Stitt saying he'd be back in a couple of days. I initiated two men into the subtleties of crocodile hunting and settled down to be entertained by Rolf; it seemed life in the islands, even during the Depression years, was very pleasant and comfortable. With air travel and refrigeration it became even better.

I returned to Port Moresby and arranged a flight with Gibbes Sepik

Airways to Madang on the other side of New Guinea. I flew out of Moresby early one morning and as the plane was fully loaded and there were no other passengers, I took my seat beside the pilot. The plane was a single-engine Norseman, a high-wing monoplane; a real work-horse that could lift nearly 2000 pounds from sea level.

We climbed steadily to 7000 feet and just before midday the brand-new town of Goroka came into sight. Goroka was 5000 feet above sea level and enjoyed one of the most beautiful climates I have ever experienced. After the enervating heat of the coast, it was a joy to breathe the mountain air. Although only six degrees south of the equator, it was a land of eternal spring.

The Norseman had to do a couple of quick flights to outstations and I was grounded for the rest of the afternoon. This was no hardship – it didn't take long to find a couple of acquaintances and, as is the fashion in most remote places, before long I had met almost the entire European population, about twenty I guess.

As sundown approached the temperature dropped quite sharply and most of my acquaintances produced a pullover – something I didn't own, not in New Guinea anyway. The next morning our departure was delayed by a heavy ground mist that swirled over the airfield, very effectively obscuring the country and, more importantly, the surrounding mountains. My pilot observing that there were old pilots and there were bold pilots, but there were no old bold pilots.

The cargo for the next leg of the journey was mobile – recruits going to the coast to work on a coconut plantation; the Highlands supplied most of the coastal labour force. As soon as the fog cleared the plane was loaded with the most murderous looking individuals I had ever laid eyes on. They had already been equipped with machetes for cutting grass and scrub by the recruiter, who was in the business of supplying plantation labour.

When the fog cleared loading started, the recruits were lined up and one of the ground staff called their names from a load sheet and they climbed in and took their seat. Apart from the normal regulation issue of clothes, blankets and mosquito nets supplied by the recruiter, they also carried huge 'bilums', woven string bags, into which was packed an extraordinary range of personal effects. Then there were bundles of bows and deadly looking arrows; one even had a mewing kitten. The plane was almost completely surrounded by wailing relatives who had come to farewell them and who, judging by the crying and distress they exhibited, didn't expect to ever see them again. As they took their seats and one of the ground staff made sure that their seat belts were secured, the door was slammed and locked, and Roy said, 'Let's go'.

We climbed in and took our seats; the smell wafting through from the 'cargo' was overpowering. I put a handkerchief to my nose, it was clear that the Highlands climate was not conducive to hygiene. The pilot smiled at my discomfort and adjusted some vents as he warmed the motor up before take off. We flew straight towards the Bismarck Ranges and as we got closer a narrow opening appeared through which the Bena River cascaded – we were in the Bena Gap, the sheer walls each side towered above us and disappeared into cloud.

As we flew it seemed at times that the wingtips of the sturdy Norseman were brushing the limestone cliff face. We broke through the cloud and from there, as the pilot said, it was downhill all the way. Through breaks in the cloud I could see the deep blue of the sea and scattered islands, and soon the little town of Madang came into sight. After a couple of circuits the plane landed without drama on an airstrip of crushed coral. I wangled a lift into town on one of the airline trucks, which left me at the only hotel in town, on the edge of the harbour.

Built around a series of lagoons, Madang was the most beautiful town I had ever seen, and probably one of the loveliest in the Pacific region. During the Second World War it had been in Japanese hands and when the tide turned the town had taken a severe hammering from Allied guns and bombers. The harbour was littered with Japanese hulks, battered, beached and rusting; the older concrete buildings were pitted and bullet scarred.

My concern was to get to the Sepik River, where I recalled 'they were up to their knees in crocodiles'. I made some enquiries and was told, 'See Shanghai Brown'. I thought to myself, 'He sounds like the kind of bloke I'm looking for'. I was dead right, too. I found him at the wharf loading his ship, the *Thetis*.

A tall, angular bloke with a very pronounced British accent, he told me that I was as welcome as the flowers in May. He was a labour recruiter for the Bulolo Gold Dredging Company, which owned the ship, and his job was to return native labour to their villages after they had finished their time, then pick up another load, sign them on and take them to Lae from where they would be transported to the Bulolo goldfield. During the war he had held the rank of Lieutenant Commander in the Australian Navy and knew the Pacific like the palm of his hand.

We left at first light the following morning and in the late afternoon tied up at Bogia, where twenty or so of his 'finish time', as they were known, left the ship. Shanghai was well known and a number of natives noisily insisted on being signed on for work at the mine; he explained that he would pick them up and sign them on when he returned.

Leaving early the next morning we sailed between the mainland and Manum Island, where an active volcano belched smoke and flame like an angry god. The next evening we turned into the Sepik River just after sundown and dropped anchor a few miles upstream.

Shanghai Brown was one of that small but interesting group that is found only in places like the islands. That evening, relaxing on deck with a cool drink, a breeze blowing in off the sea, at peace with the world, he gave me a brief thumbnail sketch of his more recent career.

He was married to a part Chinese girl and they had two daughters. The elder girl was married to a Swiss engineer and lived in Switzerland. The other, who was very much younger, was with her mother and lived in Hong Kong, which surprised me. I thought that there was a story there, but didn't pursue it; if he wanted to tell me no doubt he would in the fullness of time, although he did say, 'I must get them down some time'. He went into his cabin and after rummaging round for a while, came back with a photograph of his elder daughter, who I judged would have been in her early twenties. She was beautiful.

We turned to the subject of crocodiles, which was closer to my heart. He had already given me a partial picture of prospects on the river; what he had told me as well as what I had already gleaned from other quarters was astonishing.

He explained that crocodiles were an integral part of native life and legends. He drew my attention to the numerous canoes that were plying the river. Nearly all of them had a carved crocodile figurehead; some were elaborate and realistic, with the standard of carving very high indeed. Some of the canoes were enormous and would have come from huge logs. The bigger ones were propelled by as many as a dozen paddlers, who drove them through the water with great precision. It was fascinating to watch them.

He went on to say that there was no other group of people in the entire island, or for that matter the whole of the Pacific, who knew more about crocodiles. Not only were they an important source of protein, but also they were closely interwoven in their legends. They caught them alive, brought them back to their villages and kept them tied up under their houses, which were built high off the ground, and killed them for food. It seemed they had no use for the skins and just threw them away. I couldn't get there quick enough. Just before we turned in he said that we'd be away at first light, adding that 'it was uphill all the way', referring to the current that would be against us.

We plugged along all the next day, passing Marienberg Mission in the afternoon. Before the First World War, New Guinea was German Territory and at the conclusion of hostilities it had been ceded to Australia under a mandate. Many places, including this mission, had retained their German place names. The German Lutherans were still conspicuous but the Catholics seemed to predominate in most places and appeared to have the strongest followings. This was probably due to their flexibility – they seemed to have a more workable system of forgiveness and the priests certainly had more autonomy.

We came round a bend and Angoram came into sight. A great deal of shouting from natives along the bank heralded our arrival and when we tied up at the wharf, the population of Angoram had gathered to welcome us. A jeep arrived soon after, driven by a man of huge proportions who Shanghai said was Ralph Ormsby, the ADO. After greetings were exchanged, some perishables from his refrigerator were delivered, the ADO had roared off and we all walked up to the club.

Shanghai Brown was a legend in his own right, but here there were others who had claims to fame. Another ex-Coastwatcher, Sepik Robbie had been decorated with a well earned DSO. Ralph Ormsby, the ADO, apart from his considerable bulk (he'd been on a diet and was down to twenty-two stone I was told), was another character about whom there were tales aplenty. Ken McLean and Peter England ran a sawmill, Fred Eichorn was a trader, Andy Anderson was a Patrol Officer, and Bob Mankie was another labour recruiter. Sepik Robbie, whose name I eventually found out was Eric Robinson, although I never ever heard him referred to as such, was one of the three married men on the station, the other two being Ken McLean and Peter England. They brought a nice balance to the outpost.

The station occupied an eminence overlooking the river. It was a pretty setting with a sprinkling of African tulip trees that carried a profusion of bright scarlet flowers; undulating and grass covered, it was well cared for. The road from the wharf was formed of crushed coral, known as coronus, of which there was unlimited supplies. The rise on which the station sat was a solid mass left by the receding sea perhaps a million years ago. Because of the heavy tropical rains, ditches were dug each side of the road to carry the floodwaters away; these were known by the pidgin word, barats, and were very deep. There was a well formed road going up from the wharf, past the District offices and other buildings, and dwellings to the Club House and on to the ADO's house. Further back were a group of buildings occupied by the native police and behind them again was a barbed wire enclosure, which was the prison compound.

Down river from the wharf following the bank was Tobacco Road and here were a string of buildings and trade stores. Fred Eichorn had a house and one of the trade stores, as did Bob Mackie, also John Young, who I hadn't met, and a Chinese trader named Chu Leong.

Chu Leong was the oldest inhabitant of this remote outstation by many years. He was married to a Sepik River woman (although not perhaps churched), and they had a small daughter, Tai Foon. He first arrived on the river some years before the Second World War and with the tenacity that his race applied to everything they undertook, he prospered. Then, because of trading opportunities among the villages along the river, he built himself a boat. Not a very big boat, perhaps thirty feet in length, it was very well constructed and he was rightly proud of it.

War was declared in September 1939, which at first was a long, long way away. Then Japan joined the fray and swept through the Pacific; they bombed and occupied Rabaul which, you might say, was just over the horizon, and Chu Leong was informed that he would be evacuated to Australia. He was terrified; he had a trade store, a boat and a wife and small child, but a burly sergeant told him that he was going – his wife and child could go back to the mother's village and when it was all over he could come back and get his wife and daughter back. Some organisation called the War Damage Commission would recompense him for his losses. Chu Leong was not so confident, and it may have crossed his mind that Australia might not win the war – they weren't doing too well so far.

Anyway, the invaders weren't going to get his beloved boat. He got a labour line together and with ropes they dragged it out of the water to above the highest flood level. He then got the biggest crosscut saw that he could find and with the help of some muscular Sepik River men he worked all one day and half the night. When he finished he had his boat cut in half. The next day, with a group of missionaries, he was bundled into a plane and packed off to Australia.

It was not long before the Japanese occupied New Guinea in vast numbers; there were thousands on the Sepik and when the Allied forces had cut them off and isolated them, their supplies were exhausted and they ravaged the country like a plague of locusts.

When it was all over, Chu Leong was repatriated and he found to his surprise that everything that the sergeant had told him was true. The War Damage Commission recompensed him handsomely – they even paid him for cutting his boat in half! And all the villages that had been devastated were compensated. The Assistant District Officer loaded the Government launch, the *Osprey*, to the Plimsoll line with bags of silver and journeyed from village to village. He was met by the village policemen who, having heard the good news on the grapevine, presented him with imposing lists of pigs, chickens and coconut trees that had been lost, gardens destroyed and goodness knows what else. They were all generously recompensed. They had more money than they had ever seen before and nothing to spend it on.

Chu Leong wasted no time; he had to get back into business as soon as possible and help those villagers out. He had to stick his boat together again, but with all that money on the river it wasn't big enough – he decided to enlarge it. It took a lot longer to build than to saw in half, partly because he spliced an extra ten feet into it. No one would have guessed that it had been lying round in two pieces all those years.

As in all wars, there were many stories of great fortitude and heroism that were still fresh in people's memories. There were stories of the Coastwatchers, who went far beyond the call of duty; there were stories of human endeavour under tremendous strain and appalling conditions; tales of great sacrifice.

Harold Hindwood, tall, spare and active, told me how with ten other men he walked across New Guinea when the Japanese landed. He was at Salamaua with others when the last aeroplane flew out, and when Rabaul fell they knew that it was only a matter of days before the enemy reached the town that was the gateway to the goldfields. They were all experienced island men – there were two or three miners, some planters, a couple of labour recruiters, and some like Hindwood who were traders. Port Moresby and most of Papua was firmly in Allied hands and they planned to walk to the Sepik River, follow it up, cross the divide and pick up the headwaters of the Fly River and float, raft or canoe their way down that river to safety.

The island had been crossed earlier by the Karius–Champion patrol from the other side, coming up the Fly and down the Sepik. Although they would certainly have known about it, it is unlikely that they had read the report, otherwise they may have had second thoughts. Their confidence was no doubt fortified by the availability of supplies, equipment and money for paying carriers. When the town was abandoned, the stores were well stocked and because of weight considerations, coin was left behind; there were bags of it.

With a line of carriers they made their way across to the Sepik, which did not present any difficulties, the Japanese were busy consolidating at Finschhafen, and it was to be some weeks before they spread their forces further along the coast and inland. Harold told me that they reached the Sepik River at a point some miles upstream from the coast, maybe somewhere around Kambaramba. They paid their carriers off and negotiated with the local people for canoes.

Harold said that looking back, he never ceases to be amazed at their naivety and complete ignorance. They thought the crossing would take about six weeks, maybe eight at the outside. Experience, he said, was something you don't seem to get until after you need it.

There was no difficulty arranging for canoes and although the current was against them, the first three or four hundred miles were reasonable. After they passed the Government station at Ambunti, which was abandoned, the force of the river increased to such an extent that it became impossible to navigate and they were forced to walk. Fortunately the natives were friendly and they were able to obtain carriers. Week after week, month after month they battled on. They reached a formidable barrier of limestone peaks somewhere about the divide, which in their exhausted state took weeks to negotiate.

They found the headwaters of the Fly River, but because of the mountainous nature of the country and the turbulence of the river, it was many more weeks before it was possible to use it for portage. Once they were able to do this travelling again became bearable.

They made their camps on the bank of the river and Harold told me of an extraordinary and frightening experience. In the middle of the night on the riverbank close to the edge of the jungle, they were awakened by the most terrifying shrieks from one of their native paddlers screaming, 'Gai-Gai! Gai-Gai' – their word for snake. Everybody woke at once and they ran over to where the porters were camped. Writhing on the ground was one of the men, completely wrapped in a huge python, a species of boa constrictor. At first no one knew what to do until one man drew a revolver and fired at the snake. He didn't hit it which, under the circumstances, was fairly predictable, but he did hit the unfortunate porter, breaking his leg. The python made a lightning decision and streaked off into the jungle. A week or so later they reached Madiri Plantation and from there they were able to get a boat to Port Moresby. The journey had taken seven and a half months.

Having got rid of the last of the 'finish time', and with the boat hosed down and scrubbed out, we headed upstream. Shanghai seemed as anxious as I was to get to a village and show me, if not crocodile hunters in action, at least the spoils of the chase. He may have thought that I doubted his stories of the men who caught man-eating crocodiles with their bare hands, which I didn't because it had been confirmed by too many others.

We stopped at a village called Moim, which seemed to be a fairly big one judging by the number of canoes along the bank, fishing nets hanging up drying, and baskets that were a kind of fish trap. We went ashore and were soon surrounded by a large group of villagers, a village policeman shook Brownie's hand vigorously and talked rapidly in pidgin. I was able to catch a few words but couldn't follow the gist of it, although I knew that 'puk-puk' was the word for crocodile.

We walked between a row of houses, neat and tidy with colourful crotons planted in between. We hadn't gone very far before I saw it –

everything I had been told was true. Secured to one of the house stumps by a length of lawyer vine, which they called kunda, was a live crocodile fully eight feet long. One end of the vine was around its neck, the other fastened to the house stump. I expect that my eyes were popping out of my head, if not literally then certainly figuratively. It was a fascinating situation: we were surrounded by men and women, and the children played nonchalantly around a man-eating crocodile, although keeping well clear of its jaws.

In the meantime Shanghai was explaining to a group of villagers the purpose of our visit. All we wanted was the skins, which they had been throwing away; no we didn't want any of the meat, they could keep that, and I would pay them for the skins. They were obviously perplexed by this unaccountable generosity and, as Brownie explained to me later, questioned him closely as to why we wanted the skins – were we going to eat them? They were well aware that the white man was a bit peculiar in some of his tastes.

He tried to explain that the skins would be made into all sorts of things, shoes and bags, but the main thing was that I was going to pay them for their skins, and when this was made clear they were happy to get on with the business. The next question was how much would they get? It was then suggested that if they would like to kill one I would skin it and show them all about it; when it was killed and the skin taken off I could work it out. All of this involved an incredible amount of explanation and talking, which was by no means simple because they were all talking at once. Eventually the creature was despatched with a couple of axe blows to its head. I grabbed a couple of skinning knives from the boat and a bag of salt, and set about the skinning, showing them where the initial cuts were made and emphasising the importance of not cutting any holes in the skin. When it was finished I then demonstrated how the measuring was done: across the belly at the widest part, which came to twenty-two inches, for which I paid the owner of the croc twenty-two marks, a mark being the pidgin term for a shilling.

At this they became almost hysterical and quickly brought two more crocodiles, killed them and clamoured for them to be skinned. I had so many enthusiastic helpers that they were in one another's way and I had to restrain them. When they were finished, I then explained the importance of salting the skins to preserve them and showed them the correct way to roll up the finished skins.

In the meantime, the village policeman was telling Shanghai that while they could get plenty of crocodiles, they had no salt – it was very costly, and perhaps it wasn't such a wonderful deal after all. I thought perhaps Brownie had been purposely delaying until the last minute the dramatic effect of his trump card. He listened carefully to the village policeman agonising over the salt, then he held up his hand for silence. When all the talk and chattering had ceased, he solemnly announced that Master Tom would give them the salt for nothing. There was a stunned silence for a fraction of a second and then they all roared their approval. I was surrounded by pretty well the entire village, all trying to shake my hand, rub me and pat my back. The enthusiasm was incredible and quite embarrassing, too, but I must admit that with such overwhelming adulation I was starting to feel like the last of The Great White Hunters.

We went back to the *Mubo* escorted by the entire village and when I gave them four fifty-pound bags of salt, there were more roars of approval. The anchor was raised and we proceeded up river again – and I started to worry about salt supplies. This was going to be a bigger operation than I first thought. Shanghai told me that between Angoram and Ambunti there were probably about twenty villages; some were on the main river while others were on tributaries, and they were all crocodile hunters. He told me about Chambri Lakes, ten or fifteen miles up a navigable creek, which were famous for crocodiles.

The next village was Tambanum, which was strung along the riverbank for about a mile, and here again we went through the same performance as at Moim. They brought eight crocodiles out and this time the *Mubo* crew were a great help. I hadn't realised it, but they had watched the skinning at Moim closely; of course, it wasn't that complicated.

The Tambanum people said that there were plenty of big 'roundwaters', their term for lagoons and billabongs, which were not far away at the back. Brownie went through the same rigmarole when they got to the subject of salt. He loved the reaction when he told them that salt was free; I wasn't averse to it either. Again they roared their approval – and it was a very loud roar: there were a lot more of them; this was a very big village.

When we left Tambanum we were three days out of Angoram and although we passed a number of villages, we didn't stop. I was starting to get concerned about the salt supplies. I would have to start rationing it and also get a substantial shipment out as soon as possible. I had started this venture without any proper idea of how it was likely to develop, but now I could see that it was going to be a very big operation. Talking it over with Shanghai, I reckoned that it was better to go directly to the village where he intended getting a load of recruits. This was up a tributary of the Sepik at Chambri Lakes. It would take a couple of days for him to collect his recruits, maybe longer because he explained there was an awful lot of talking involved, as well as the bargaining with the village policeman for the twenty-five or so men.

We passed a number of villages, some quite big, and Brownie explained that there were other recruiters and as a rule they each had their favourite places and that they all had 'understandings'. He mentioned Les Ingle and Bob Mackie, both of whom recruited for plantations. I made a mental note of their names; they would no doubt be interested in a sideline. We passed a big village called Timbunke and then turned into a fairly big river, a tributary coming in from Chambri Lakes. It was narrow, but very deep and on each side were extensive swamps smothered with wildlife. We anchored close to a village called Kabriman and we were immediately surrounded by canoes. Two village policemen clambered up the side, greeted Brown like an old friend and asked for tobacco. Obviously prepared for this, he took a few sticks from one pocket and a sheet of newspaper from the other. Newsprint was preferred for rolling the black twist into a smoke. In between, of course, they chewed betel nut, a combination that, if it could be viewed during mastication, would undoubtedly reveal an interior in a startling and vivid technicolour that any film producer would give his right arm to possess.

The recruiting procedure didn't take long once the applicants were assembled, and it was interesting to watch Shanghai make his selection. He knocked back several – one had a bad sore on his leg, another a racking cough and two on account of their age, probably about fifteen or sixteen. In the end he had nineteen and said that he would have no trouble collecting another six or seven on the way back down river.

The village policemen received some commission in silver, I thought perhaps about £10, some tobacco, and lengths of material that would end up as lap-laps, or loincloths. We then got to the important matter of crocodiles, or puk-puk, not to be confused with pek-pek, the word for excreta. A frequently told tale is of the tourist relating to a spellbound audience how he saw a fifteen-foot pek-pek swimming down the river. I was doing my best to get the hang of pidgin and had been practising on the crew; I wasn't doing too bad, at any rate they were understanding me a lot better than I could them, mainly because they spoke at such rapid fire rate. There were only two live crocs in the village; they had killed and eaten a big one only yesterday. They said that there were plenty in the lake and there was another big stretch of water nearly as big as Chambri further over. After the skinning and salting was finished, Shanghai gave a long talk to probably thirty or forty people, about half of whom, I was pleased to learn, came from nearby villages – it all helped to spread my gospel.

The next day we left, promising to return soon, and in the evening anchored off Timbunke village. This was where Japanese had machine gunned the people and when we went ashore, they pointed out a number of bullet scarred trees; although it was a long time ago, the bullet marks were clearly visible. Not entirely to my surprise, they knew all about me and my activities; canoes continually plied the river and news of that nature would spread quickly. There were six live crocodiles that were quickly dealt with and I left them four bags of salt from my supplies, which were now getting perilously low.

We continued down river and were hailed at Tambanum by several natives who paddled out and said that they had some skins. We stopped and they brought three over in canoes. When I unrolled the skins to measure them, I saw that they had cut the tails short, thereby reducing the skins to second class; my buyers would react to that very promptly. They were putting in a short cut, as it were; also, skinning down the tail became progressively more awkward. I explained that they must take the entire skin off from one end to the other, at which they smiled tolerantly. We stopped at Moim and here again to my annoyance three had shortened tails. After giving it some thought, I decided that the best way to overcome this problem was to buy them by the foot lengthways. It was a nuisance having to change over; with primitive people it is difficult trying to explain things like this – that they think we are peculiar in many respects is often a help.

We cruised on down river and Shanghai told me that he was leaving the company very soon. He had been up and down the river recruiting for Bulolo for the last five years and, as men do the world over, he had developed an affection for it – 'Ol' Man River' he called it. He wanted to settle at Angoram. This crocodile skin business was interesting, could we come to a deal? I thought this was a very good idea: I certainly needed someone on the river and a man of Shanghai's experience would be invaluable. Right now I had just about as much as I could handle. This was going to be a big operation and I couldn't afford to let it foul up, which it could easily do if I didn't keep a grip of the developing situation. I came to an immediate decision and asked him when he thought he would be leaving the Bulolo company. He said any time. Charlie Groves, who was the company's native labour supervisor in Lae, was anxious to go to sea again; he had all the qualifications and tickets necessary. We soon had it worked out: I made him an offer and told him that I could help him with finance to buy skins. I flew back to Madang and arranged for a load of salt to go to Angoram on the next ship. I grabbed a seat on a plane to Port Moresby, where there were nearly 500 skins stacked up. I sent cables to buyers in London, New York and Singapore.

I sent a signal through the oil company to Roy Edwards – wherever he was, I was confident they would find him – asking him to take over my boat. I sent cables to Sydney for two outboard motors to go to Madang on the next plane. I arranged for Vince Sanders, who was just starting out in business, to act as my agent, and pack and ship my skins. I got two replies to my cables, one from New York and one from Singapore, and settled for Singapore. Apart from the fact that their offer was fractionally higher, they offered to establish a credit at my bank.

FIVE

MASSACRE MOST BLOODY

I FLEW back to Madang and took a day off – nearly. Brian Holloway, who was the Madang police inspector, came to the hotel looking for Tom Cole. When I was pointed out to him he came over, introduced himself and asked if I would mind shooting a crocodile that was in a lagoon 'just over the road'. The lawn at the back of his house ran down to the water's edge and he was concerned because his children and their friends often played dangerously close, probably paddled in it, too, I thought. He said that we could pick up some prisoners from the calaboose and borrow a dinghy somewhere. What did I think about that? I thought it was a good idea, but we would have to wait until dark and then we could go out and pick it up with my spotlight and that would be that. In the meantime we could fill in the time profitably, or maybe unprofitably, at the bar. As darkness fell, we went to the police barracks, picked up a police corporal and then went to the calaboose where we got four prisoners, who very happy to lift a dinghy from the harbour onto the back of the utility.

We drove to the lagoon and launched the dinghy; it was a beautiful, cool clear night, and I could hear the sound of music and voices from other houses that were fringing the lagoon. I switched on my spotlight and quickly picked up the red eyes of a crocodile glaring straight at me. We glided over towards it and I shot it between the eyes. It sank immediately, but the water was shallow and in a few moments we had it aboard. The dinghy was returned to the harbour and we went back to the hotel. The prisoners carried the crocodile in – it took up the entire length of the bar. Mrs Gilmore, who owned the hotel, complained of the smell, but no one took any notice and, anyway, it brought a few extra customers who stayed right up to closing time. Next day Brian Holloway got his prisoners to skin it; the meat saved them a day's issue of bully beef so everybody was happy, especially me. I had no difficulty finding an agent in Madang. Alan Strachan had been a purser before coming ashore and setting up as agent, and he was familiar with the ramifications of shipping.

It was now getting towards the end of 1953 and I had to get back to Angoram. The next day I was on a Gibbes Sepik Airways Norseman piloted by Bob Gibbes himself, a jovial character who had been one of Australia's most distinguished fighter pilots, decorated with a DSO, DFC and Bar. He had been shot down a few times – once walking back from behind the enemy lines and once badly burnt when his Spitfire was shot down in flames. He was on his way to Wewak and when I asked him if he would mind diverting to Angoram, he said that it was no trouble. I was pleased to find Shanghai Brown had already handed *Mubo* over to Charlie Groves and had settled in. He hadn't wasted any time, which was an indication of his enthusiasm for his new career. He said that two Archimedes outboard motors had arrived consigned to me, which was very fast work. We got the keys of the cargo shed from Sepik Robbie and went down and inspected them; they were powerful looking horizontal twins. There were plenty of good canoes around and we could soon get ourselves mobile. We were now on the verge of the wet season and once the river started to rise, it would be the end of hunting until next year. I wanted to do one trip up the river to consolidate what I had already started. We got the keys of the club, again from Robbie, and settled in to do some forward planning.

The following morning we did some bargaining with canoe owners and settled for a couple of forty-footers. One I noted had been cut from what must have been a magnificent cedar and I couldn't help thinking what a waste of beautiful timber. The next day the Burns Philp ship *Kulau*, skippered by Les Ingle, pulled into the wharf with five tons of salt for me. Burns Philp owned many plantations all over the islands, in fact, right through the Pacific. As well as carrying cargo, Ingle also recruited labour, and, as I anticipated, was very interested in skin buying. He was going up river and as it turned out we all went up together and towed the canoes. After talking it over, I suggested Shanghai and Les, on this trip at least, take every alternate village starting at Moim.

It was a remarkable trip – the word had spread that someone was buying the skins that previously they had thrown away and they all had live crocodiles tied up. The salt I had dropped off previously had all been used, and altogether I collected more than 150 skins; it was getting better and better. Les Ingle told me that he averaged about a trip a month, sometimes more if he got an unexpected order due to some sort of an emergency, as had happened recently when a fight broke out and living quarters had been burnt down; some were arrested and some were out of action with spear wounds. Sometimes they killed one another, but they rarely ran away because a portion of their pay was held until they had finished their time, and if they cleared out they would forfeit it. Not that this was their legal position, it was just that they never endeavoured to claim it. There was always a demand for labour and Les Ingle was anxious to own his own boat; this crocodile skin sideline would be of considerable help, he hoped. So did I – it was certainly beneficial to me if he had some additional inducement to collect crocodile skins.

We arrived at Tambanum and it was Shanghai's turn. There were twenty-seven live crocodiles and as Les had to be back in Madang in about a week, he wasn't keen on waiting until they were all killed and skinned, which would take some time. It was decided that Shanghai would stay and tidy up, and so we left him with the canoes while we went on to Timbunke. Here there were thirty salted skins and twelve live crocs; one of them was eleven feet long and they gave a graphic account of its capture. There were four men, three women and three children in a canoe paddling down river when they saw it up on the bank. They drifted quietly on downstream for about a hundred yards where they all went ashore. They sent the women off into the jungle, which was some distance away, to get some lengths of kunda (lawyer vine), while the men crept up as close as they could to watch it, but it soon became suspicious. All wild animals have a highly developed inbuilt sense of approaching danger and this croc became uneasy and started to move towards the river. They realised that it might be some time before the women returned, so they made an instant decision and rushed up and grabbed it by the tail. It must have been a titanic struggle, the crocodile trying to attack them and at the same time endeavouring to get back to the river. When the women arrived it had almost thrashed its way to the water's edge. They then had to fashion the lawyer vine into a loop and get it around its neck and when this was done they had to get another length around its body. Eventually they secured the beast and lashed it to a long pole. They hailed a passing canoe, which was much bigger than the one they were in, and triumphantly brought it back to their village. I recalled the crocodile I had brought back alive over on the Fly River and what a struggle that was – and it was half stunned with a bullet in the head.

Les Ingle started recruiting and quickly got what he called a 'full book', it was standing room only on the *Kulau*. Shanghai caught us up that evening and I decided to go back with Ingle with all the skins while I had him for transport. The wet season was building up, the level of the river was surely creeping up and it was starting to turn slightly muddy from runoff feeding in from upstream. I measured up all the skins and paid Les Ingle nearly £1000 and Shanghai just over £1000. I realised that I had better get back to Madang and arrange for packing and shipping. Shanghai wanted to make one last trip to Chambri Lakes and off he went.

Two days later we were at Angoram and while Les was busy getting his paperwork done and signing up his recruits, I asked Sepik Robbie to send a signal to Wewak asking Bob Gibbes to send a Norseman out to take me to Madang. Nothing happened that day so I resigned myself to another night at Angoram, which was no great hardship. The next day I hung around the office hoping for some word from Gibbes, but all I got was a deathly silence until late in the evening when Robbie informed me that there was no plane available. Les Ingle laughed and said I could get a lift to Madang with him. 'It won't cost you anything,' he said.

The following morning there was still no news and Robbie was puzzled, too. 'Something's happened,' he said, but he couldn't imagine what it might be. 'Gibbesy's got five bloody Norsemans and an Auster – they can't all be tied up.' Then the shattering news came through, very garbled at first – the Telefomin Patrol Post had been attacked and wiped out.

This was one of the most remote outstations in the whole country, at the headwaters of the Sepik, near the cloud-covered peaks of the Star Mountains. Robbie was in his radio office all day and gradually details of the massacre emerged. The station head was Patrol Officer Gerald Szarka, his junior was Cadet Patrol Officer Geoff Harris. With a detachment of six police and a line of carriers, they set off on a census of the Eliptimin Valley, which was a short day's walk from the Telefomin Patrol Post. The people who inhabit this mountainous region are among the most primitive in the world; few have been outside their mountain fastness and even fewer could speak pidgin, all communication with authority was through an interpreter. They believe that their origins go back to Afek, a legendary woman who gave birth to the people of those rain-drenched mountains.

Their customs go back thousands of years and their preservation was of overriding importance, particularly to the headmen, who were becoming uneasy at the new laws thrust upon them by these white men who had suddenly come among them; laws that undermined their authority, and which they could not understand. The law that they were not to kill anyone any more was the most inexplicable of all.

There had been a succession of bad years, too. The taro and yam crops had been disastrous, which, the headmen explained, was caused by these white interlopers. And the missionaries, too, they were bad men – they would all have to go, they must all be killed. The natives planned carefully and they waited; they knew that the white man's guns were very strong, they had seen them belch flame and make a terrifying noise.

The Eliptimin census patrol was to be a straightforward operation. The policeman of each village held a book containing the names of all the villagers and from time to time a census patrol came to the village and added to the names in the book all the children that had been born since the last official visit. In order to simplify the work, Szarka decided to split his patrol, for not only was it a routine job, but also it was an opportunity to give the young cadet experience that would increase his confidence. This was what the plotters had been patiently waiting for – this division, a weakening of the forces. They planned to steal the rifles and then kill the Patrol Officers and all the native policemen, who were not of this country; to these mountain men they were foreigners who ordered them around and wanted their women. The priest at the mission station, always talking about God and wanting them to change their ways, would be easy to kill. After that they would strew logs all over the airstrip so that the 'balus' (aeroplane) would be unable to land. They could go back to their old ways in peace, untroubled by the white man's laws that stopped them from killing their enemies.

This action had been planned for a long time and at last the opportunity presented itself. On the morning of that terrible day, the two young officers were busy preparing for the patrol, checking their supplies, calling for carriers. The time had come: two runners quietly left the station to inform the headmen of the impending patrol and of the decision to split the party.

That night, not very far away, at the village of Ankavip four headmen assembled to plot the massacre. That the patrol plans were well known was perfectly normal, there was no reason for secrecy. The policemen would be told where they would be going and the object of the patrol, as would the carriers, most of whom, being local men, would know of the treacherous plans to be put into action by their chiefs.

Gerald Szarka with three native policemen and a line of carriers set off in one direction while Geoff Harris, the young cadet, leaving at the same time, headed for the opposite end of the Eliptimin Valley with an almost identical retinue. As soon as the patrols had departed, word was sent to the headman of Okfekamin, telling him what he had to do. But by the time the message reached him, it had become garbled and so he walked across to where the plotters were still assembled, sending out runners in all directions. From them he received direct instructions – he was to kill Szarka at Misinamin, a further day's walk. When he reached Misinamin he found that the patrol had settled in, prior to starting their census work, and so he called a meeting to relate in detail the instructions he had received from those who were undoubtedly the No. 1 headmen.

Among the group who listened to the harangue were two of the Patrol Officer's carriers. As stated earlier, Szarka set out with three native policemen, but the day he arrived at Misinamin he sent one of his constables and an interpreter to the next village to advise of his arrival, and for them to gather and prepare for the census. Now he had two policemen, who were going about tasks such as arranging firewood supplies, tidying up the rest house and so on.

Szarka and one policeman were together when they were rushed by about ten or twelve men and it was so sudden that they had no chance whatever, they were quickly hacked to death. The axe used on Szarka was one of special significance; it was kept in a certain Dubu House and was known to the people as 'Arigaptin'. It had unusual hieroglyphic characters cut into one side that no one had been able to decipher; constant grinding over many years had worn the blade back almost to the handle.

The other policeman who was with Szarka was immediately surrounded by tribesmen intent on killing him, but managed to escape and here there is a strange story of tribal superstitions. The policeman ran along a road that had been built some time previously by a gang of prisoners from Telefomin to facilitate travelling among the villages; it would not have been a vehicular road, there were no vehicles, more like an improved track. Suddenly, the fleeing policeman came upon a woman returning from her garden. When they met, she gave him a piece of a bush known as 'tanket' and a broken arrow which, because of tribal significance, gave him immunity from attack. She stood firmly in the path of his assailants and as strange as it may seem, they turned back. No reason was ever suggested for this woman's action, which undoubtedly saved his life. I think that possibly there had been a previous association that went beyond ordinary friendship.

There was one more policeman in the Szarka party to be killed – the one who had gone ahead with an interpreter to advise the next village to prepare for a census. The interpreter who went with him had been in the employ of the Administration for some years, and was well thought of by all at the Telefomin Station. They ate together, slept under the same roof on patrol, and joked among themselves, but when he accompanied the policeman to the next village to tell them of the Kiap's coming, he knew that his companion was to be killed. Such was the depth of the treachery that he gave no hint or warning. They came the next day and killed the constable while the interpreter stood by.

Patrol Officer Szarka was dead, two of his policemen were dead – at the other end of this Valley of Death, Geoffrey Harris was at the village of Terapdavit. It was the morning of 6 November; Harris had risen and was almost ready to start his census work. He had found it all very simple and straightforward, the people had been cooperative, having been through it many times previously. There were a few young children running around, perhaps thinking that he would be away from this village by midday. The drama was about to explode.

One constable had wandered away from the barracks and was chatting to an old couple, two others were sitting on one side of the house, enjoying the early sun. Unseen, a man sneaked around the back of the constables' quarters and took two rifles away. It is surprising that the man who stole the rifles did not realise that there were three policemen – and therefore three rifles. One of the constables had laid his rifle on his bed and it was covered with a blanket. The signal was given to attack and Harris and the constable who had been in conversation with the old couple were immediately surrounded by men armed with axes.

Harris was struck about the head and the constable was seized by several men, who chopped savagely at him. But this man, whose name was Kombo, was very strong and although badly hurt, he managed to break away from his attackers. He wanted to get to the rifle that none of the tribesmen knew about. Kombo was hit several times with an axe and fell to the ground; he was slashed on the right shoulder as he was rising, but his powers of endurance were amazing – he flung off some of his attackers, who may have thought that to finish him off was now a simple matter. At the same time the other two constables were fighting a losing battle behind the barracks, they also were surrounded and all had received blows from axes and bush knives. At last Kombo reached his rifle, but because of his wounds he could only use his left hand. He got a cartridge into the breech and holding the butt against his stomach, he got a shot away at an assailant who was about to chop him down with an axe.

The sudden and unexpected appearance of the rifle must have shaken the attackers considerably – the report when it was fired and one of them being hit caused them to withdraw, but not before they managed to set fire to the thatched roof of the police quarters. The temporary withdrawal enabled the other two constables to join Kombo; they had all received some savage blows, but Kombo was now in a state of near collapse and in great pain – and their quarters were burning fiercely. They carried Kombo over to the Patrol Officer's Rest House. Harris was lying outside semi-conscious and bleeding badly. They carried him into the house, too, and placed him on his bed.

Geoff Harris, as was normal, had a personal boy whose duties were to make his bed, heat his shaving water and generally attend to his requirements, and he was not of these people. The boy was sent off with instructions to run to Telefomin to get help. He raced away like a hare, and it is unlikely that he was even seen.

The party now consisted of the dying Patrol Officer, the badly wounded Kombo, who was in great pain, and the two constables, who although they had sustained some injuries could still use the rifle. The attackers changed tactics and started using a type of arrow with three prongs that is used for bringing down birds. Between the prongs they jammed red-hot coals and fired them into the thatched roof of the Rest House; before long it caught fire and they were compelled to leave, carrying the Patrol Officer and Kombo. The afternoon wore on slowly; they were being attacked less frequently – most probably they were running out of arrows, which were not easily fashioned. The wounded men were now in an old house that was in an advanced state of disrepair and for that reason it had been abandoned. The young Patrol Officer called for water, but there was none. He knew that he was dying for he told the policemen to be sure to tell the Kiap to write to his parents. Shortly after he died. Then came a brief rally from the attackers, perhaps to find out if there was any ammunition left. One man, a little bolder than the rest, could have told them except that a bullet in the head effectively limited his conversational abilities.

The sun was getting low and there was another attack with a flurry of arrows to which they responded. Then, just before sundown, they heard a distant shot echoing through the ranges – it was a relief party from Telefomin. The party sadly made its way back to the station that night carrying the body of their Patrol Officer; Kombo also had to be carried, as his wounds were severe and he was in great pain. When they got back to the station the next morning, word had already gone to Wewak, which was the District Headquarters, and a Gibbes Sepik Airways plane arrived with medical supplies and reinforcements.

When the full story became known, the District Commissioner, Alan Timperley, sent in ADO George Wearne and Medical Assistant Rhys Healey and 100 native policemen. These primitive mountain people, who had never been beyond their tribal boundaries, began to feel uneasy – they never imagined that there were so many policemen or that they could appear in so short a time. It began to dawn on them that perhaps they had made a mistake. ADO Brian Corrigan arrived: he was to go out and recover the body of Gerald Szarka and his dead constables. Two more ADOs, Alec Zweck and Bill Crellin, arrived with more police. Those who were responsible for the murders were going to be brought to justice, and that was going to be a long haul.

Nevertheless, these people began to realise that Nemesis was closing in on them and they dispersed into the dark, impenetrable rainforest that they knew so well. But if the men thought they could escape the white man's laws, they underestimated the determination of the men who set out to capture those who had slain their comrades. After long months of weary slogging in bleak, wet and miserable conditions, following the wraith-like tribesmen over mountains, through jungles and across surging rivers, they rounded up 165 suspects and witnesses.

There was a lengthy trial held at Wewak before Mr Justice Gore. There was a lot of hurried changing of sides as a number of the accused made frantic attempts to appear as lilywhite supporters of the Patrol Officers, but the judge had no difficulty cutting through their transparent attempts to place the blame on their fellow conspirators. In the course of his summing up, Mr Justice Gore said of the three constables who were with Patrol Officer Harris, 'It was a story of heroism, resolution and loyalty which, in the cold marshalling of facts in a judgment, must appear sublime'.

In telling this story of the killing of the Patrol Officers, Szarka and Harris, and the two police constables, for the sake of continuity I took the drama through to its final conclusion, which was to take many months. It will be remembered that I was at Angoram endeavouring to get an aeroplane to transport me to Madang, but because of the events at Telefomin, none were available. Eventually I gratefully accepted a ride on a Catholic Mission Cessna, which deposited me at Madang. Everything was in hand; Alan Strachan proved to be a very efficient agent and between us we graded and packed five cases of skins for

The first aircraft (a Junker) to land at Mount Hagen, 1933 (National Library)

Mick Leahy, 1934 (National Library)

Roy Edwards, a crocodile hunter, sharpening his harpoon

A friendly crocodile!

'Taking up the white man's burden'

Eric Jolliffe, after a good night's hunting

Tom Cole and friend before a duck shoot

Dragging the kill ashore

Tom Cole with crocodile shot on the Fly River

Crocodile being carried to camp for skinning

Crocodile skinning

Results of an average night's shooting

The author supervising skinning

Measuring the skin

Examining the skins

Crocodile skin, Angoram, Sepik River

With one of the hunters

Hunter's canoe in Kikori Delta

An eighteen-foot crocodile skin

*Mount Lamington at moment of eruption — photo taken by Captain Jacobsen, a
Qantas captain (Department of Mineral Resources)*

Cecil Cowley's (the district commissioner) jeep immediately after the Mount Lamington eruption (Department of Mineral Resources)

Mount Lamington, after the main eruption (Department of Mineral Resources)

Left to right: Kathleen, Kathryn, Gabrielle and Tom Cole, 1959

Native carving, Sepik River area

Gabrielle and Kathryn Cole, 1960

View over the Chimbu Valley

A Goaribari headhunter

Scene on the Kikori River

Singapore which were, I calculated, worth close to £5000, which filled my heart with joy because there were still quite a lot more to come in from that prolific river before the season closed. Moresby was next stop, and everything was proceeding smoothly; then it was off to Sydney for a Happy Christmas.

The time passed pleasantly; 1953 disappeared and 1954 took over where it left off and in March I was once more back in Port Moresby. I was happy to find out that I was wanted in several places at once – two Danes had arrived in Madang from somewhere; they had their own boat and were anxious to go crocodile hunting.

Someone else over in New Britain was complaining that crocodiles were eating his cattle: 'Where's this Cole fellow?' Roy Edwards wanted me to come out to the Purari Delta and take *Seabird* off his hands. It was only a bloody nuisance, why don't I take it round to New Guinea? he complained. But the more I thought about it, the less attractive it sounded; with boats, canoes and outboard motors scattered all over New Guinea, I wasn't sure whether I was Arthur or Martha, although come to think of it, I was sure I wasn't Martha.

A cable arrived from Singapore advising that the buyers were able to increase the price of skins to twelve shillings an inch. I headed for the Snake Pit, which seemed an appropriate venue sufficiently well equipped to not only supply the support required for some forward planning, but also at the same time repair the wasted tissues. A couple of days later I took off in a Gibbes Sepik Airways Norseman for Madang; I was developing a happy rapport with this company. This time my pilot was Peter Manser and we were going via Lae, but got trapped in heavy cloud over the Markham Valley and had to make an emergency landing on an old wartime airstrip made of Marsden matting – perforated steel sheets that made a hell of a racket when the wheels touched down. We spent an uncomfortable night fighting off mosquitoes, but in the morning the weather had cleared and we got off the ground early, made a brief stop at Lae and reached Madang by midday.

I found the 'Danes' but there weren't two, there were three – and only one was Danish, Nils Madsen. The second man was a tall Swede named Petersen and the third was an Englishman who had been a professional hunter in Africa. John Hartley had run some kind of a big game safari in Rhodesia. He was an interesting man and told me that life was becoming very difficult in Africa, saying that the white man's rule was rapidly diminishing with, in most places, tragic results. He had a powerful Holland & Holland double-barrelled .450 calibre rifle and by the look of the cartridges, they would go into an elephant one end and come out the other.

We got down to business, Madsen and Hartley wanted to go croco-dile shooting while Petersen, a baker by trade, hoped to start a bakery in Madang. I suggested they go to the Ramu River, which had been on my 'croc list' for some time. The following day we loaded up with a ton of salt, fuel, stores for a fortnight and, to be on the safe side, a month's supply of rum. They had been drinking some peculiar kind of white spirit that smelt terrible, but after they tasted rum, they took to it like a duck to water, or something. We left Madang with the Plimsoll line slightly under water, but by the time we had got through a drum or so of fuel, it would probably surface, we thought. We cruised along the coast and anchored at Bogia the first day, where three young fel-lows asked us to give them a lift to Awar Plantation. It was not a very long walk, but they were burdened with a substantial amount of stores, having been on a shopping spree. Madsen said that he didn't mind and I was curious to see a hunk of machinery on the beach, which had achieved considerable fame and was the focal point of a story involv-ing the boss boy of Awar Plantation, who was known rather indeli-cately as 'The Man Who Fucked the Steamroller'.

Awar Plantation was at Hansa Bay where, during the war, there had been a large concentration of Japanese troops. The bay provided good shelter for shipping and its gently sloping beach was suitable for unloading machinery and equipment from landing barges. It had come under heavy attack from Allied bombing and a lot of ships were still there, with just their masts sticking up out of the water. Closer in were landing barges that had been blown to smithereens, others with gaping holes in them, and tanks that had been knocked sideways and were rusting away, half buried in the sand. There was also one steamroller. Actually it wasn't a steamroller, I think that it was a piece of road-making machinery, but once the story started there was no way it was going to be anything but a steamroller.

The boss boy was a Tolai from Rabaul, a people who are noted for their sporting prowess in every field. It seemed that on his day off, he went to the beach where the golden sand sloped gently down to the sea, where the rise and fall of the tide was gradually eroding the rusting hulks and barges – and steamrollers. After lazily swimming around in the warm tropic waters, he drifted towards the piece of machinery that, as I have explained, was probably a piece of road-making equipment; it doesn't matter, a spade doesn't have to be a spade all the time. He climbed onto the steamroller to sun himself and just where he sat, in a very convenient position, was a bolt hole, without a bolt. Then in an idle, carefree moment he slipped his member into the hole, perhaps trying it for size – who knows. Here was a man of different calibre, perhaps one might say of different mettle – not for him the soft embrace. And then, as one might expect, swelling took place – a logical sequence of events I suppose. Normally, one imagines, once nature had run its course, the swelling would subside, anyway I would have thought so, but then I've never had anything to do with steamrollers. In this case nothing of the sort happened and the poor fellow couldn't get it out. A lot of people may say, 'Here's a nice how do you do', but somehow it doesn't seem an appropriate expression to describe a situation where a man has got his cock stuck inextricably in a steamroller, the water lapping at his ankles and the tide rising.

Although overcome with shame, he called for help and was soon surrounded by a large group of people whose sympathy was no doubt exceeded only by their astonishment. Nobody knew what to do – no precedent I suppose. The manager of the plantation, Dave Paxton, arrived and took in the situation immediately – he didn't know what to do either, it looked as though by high tide he'd be without a boss boy. Someone suggested cutting it off, a suggestion that was strongly supported – with one notable exception. The tide was inexorably creeping up; it was now halfway up his legs. The manager came to the conclusion that he wouldn't drown as the water would come halfway up his body – it was a neap tide, he'd be all right for a week anyway.

The nearest doctor was in Madang, more than 100 miles away, and the only post office and means of communication was at Bogia, some twenty miles distant, which was the headquarters of ADO Jack Worcester. His wife Ray operated the post office and radio.

Dave Paxton could see only one course open to him: he would have to get to Bogia and get a message through to Madang requesting medical assistance. After one last look at the unfortunate boss boy to assure himself that he was in no immediate danger of drowning, he got into his truck and drove to Bogia where he did his best to explain to a surprised Mrs Worcester the predicament at Awar.

Ray Worcester, being the wife of a District Services officer, was used to unusual situations. Dave Paxton, with some difficulty, outlined the problem, but it was a while before he was able to manage the finer details. When the situation finally became clear to the bemused ADO's wife, she called Madang, where her counterpart, Mrs Eileen Leyer, was the radio operator.

Mrs Leyer worked in a corrugated iron shed alongside the Madang Post Office, an uncomfortable building that had one door and three shutters, which were kept propped open during office hours in an endeavour to combat the unrelenting tropical heat. Any kind of privacy was impossible.

When Eileen Leyer first received the startling radio message from Ray Worcester, who endeavoured to express it as delicately as possible, she could not believe what she was hearing and asked her to repeat it. On the other hand, Eileen Leyer, who possessed a very keen sense of humour, may have heard the message quite clearly, but was savouring the delicious humour of the situation. Ray Worcester came back, 'I repeat, Dave Paxton's boss boy is trapped on a steamroller. His penis is caught and the tide is rising they need immediate medical attention'.

At that moment Hec Longmore, the Madang stevedore, was passing Mrs Leyer's office just as she was asking Bogia to repeat the message. He didn't need very acute hearing to realise that an unusual situation had developed at Awar Plantation.

As Hector said later, although his imagination was not quite up to grasping the seriousness of the situation, he did realise that it was an unusual occurrence. He wasted no time getting over to the Madang Club, which was not very far away, informing all those at the bar of the drama at Awar. He didn't get the story quite right – he had the poor unfortunate fellow in the last stages of drowning with his penis caught up in some machinery, but it was sufficient for the barman to close the bar and follow everyone over to Mrs Leyer's office.

By this time Eileen Leyer had been in touch with the hospital requesting that the local medical officer, Dr Ozols, be flown to Awar immediately. Unfortunately, the good doctor was in the operating theatre and could not get away, and a medical orderly asked that the patient be flown to Madang. In the background Dave Paxton was heard to say to Ray Worcester, 'Tell them to send an aeroplane that can lift a steamroller'. The best Eileen Leyer could do was to assure Ray Worcester that Bob Gibbes would fly Dr Ozols in the following day.

The manager went back to the patient who, naturally, was in great pain and told some of the plantation workers to gather enough material to build a house over him; the tide was up to his waist and probably wouldn't get much higher. The unfortunate fellow endured a most uncomfortable night, although the pain had subsided, his pride and joy had become completely numb – though still upstanding. Some of his friends stayed with him through the long, dark hours and in the morning everybody was anxiously scanning the sky for the aeroplane.

Eventually they heard the steady drone of the engine and when it landed at the plantation airstrip, the manager met them and drove the doctor down to the beach in the plantation truck. He had a quick look at the patient, gave him an injection – some kind of anaesthetic I suppose – and then picked out a burly plantation lad and told him to put his arms around the patient's chest and pull, 'Quick fella', he said. The man must have been more than a little apprehensive because he said to the doctor, 'By 'n by cock bilong 'im broke'. 'Pull him,' the doctor shouted, 'it's not my bloody cock!' It came away all right, but was very badly torn and, as the story goes, about three feet long. I suspect the story has lost nothing in the telling.

From Awar Plantation to the Ramu was a short run – we left at midday and turned into the river just before sundown, dropping anchor off Marangis village just inside the mouth. When it got dark I switched a light on and swung it around, there was quite a few crocodiles but mostly small. We lowered a dinghy into the water and in a very short time I had shot three.

There seemed to be swarms of small ones about a foot long, all about the same size and playing around in the shallow water, no doubt from one hatching. The next morning, while the three crocs were being skinned, a couple of canoes came over from the village. They brought some bananas and yams and asked if they could have the crocodile meat. I asked them if they caught crocodiles, thinking that they might hunt them like the Sepiks did, but surprising they said they didn't savvy. The mouth of the Ramu was only about twenty or thirty miles from the Sepik and because of its proximity I thought they might have hunted them, too.

We recruited a couple of Marangis lads and headed upstream. It didn't take long to find out that it was a very awkward river to navigate and by midday we were well and truly stuck on a sandbank. We rolled a few drums of fuel overboard to lighten the little boat and after a lot of churning, we got off. The drums were lifted back on board with the boom and we proceeded on our way with a great deal more caution. To get stuck at this time of the year when the river was falling could be quite serious. Our idea was to go as far as Annenberg, a mission that was maybe about 200 miles by river; it twisted and turned a lot, like any other river, and it could be more. The Marangis lads didn't have any idea. The first day we passed only one village, and as I had noticed at Marangis, there were very few canoes; they seemed a completely different type of people. If we'd been travelling the Sepik, over a similar distance we would have passed several villages and they would have a much more virile appearance with far more canoes.

Every night we did some shooting and built up a fair tally. On the third day Annenberg came into sight. The priest in charge was Father Cahill, a most delightful character who made us welcome and asked us over to the mission for dinner that night, where we enjoyed a pleasant and entertaining evening. The next morning he took us for a long walk, the only form of locomotion, he explained; we probably walked about ten miles, and for a man of the cloth he was extremely active. There was a series of lakes where, he assured us, there were plenty of crocodiles. I knew that there wouldn't be any doubt about that. He was quite enthusiastic, but said there was no chance of the natives being induced to hunt like the Sepiks did, which he knew about, but he said that the meat would be a welcome addition to their diet – and by the look of them anything would be a help.

Madsen and Hartley were keen, but realised that they didn't have sufficient supplies to last for more than a few weeks and by then the river would be too low for them to get out and back; whatever they were going to do would have to be immediately. I asked Father Cahill where his supplies came from; I hadn't seen any sign of a boat although there was a jetty of sorts. He said that the river was too unreliable and that everything had to be flown in. A mission plane called once a week with supplies and mail: 'Should be here tomorrow,' he said, 'depending on which way he came; it services four of our stations.' I was able to get a seat, as there was no particular reason why I should go back on the *Angler*; they might get stuck somewhere down river, which was the last thing I wanted.

The father said getting a lift on the plane would not be a problem; by the time he reached Annenberg he had dropped off half his cargo. I thought that it would be a good escape route for me: I had visions of being stuck on a sandbank until the wet season broke. The plane was due in two days. Madsen and Hartley didn't mind me leaving; there was nothing I could do now – they had shot most of the crocodiles on our way up the river and knew what it was all about. They packed up and left the next day and the day after that the mission Cessna arrived. The pilot was a young God botherer who had been with the mission for about four years and flying for two. He had done his training, he told me, at Bankstown Flying School and had held a licence for two years. I remembered about the old pilots and bold pilots saying and hoped that he aimed to be an old pilot – his landings weren't too bad.

We reached Madang in the early afternoon and I had hardly settled in when Brian Holloway, the police inspector, turned up at the hotel wanting to go crocodile shooting; he really had the bug. There was a forty-foot Government launch at the wharf, he said, and he could have it for the weekend. 'It's all ready to go: what about getting away this afternoon? I'd like to go to the Golgol River, it's not far,' he said. I couldn't easily get out of it, not that I wanted to, but I would have preferred to settle for the next morning. We went down to the wharf in the police utility with a couple of policemen and two prisoners and went aboard. It was well stocked with stores and supplies, and there were two comfortable bunks, an icebox full of beer, and a cupboard with a more than ample supply of spirits, to which he had thoughtfully added a couple of bottles of my favourite tipple – if it wasn't enough I could make do with whisky, gin or vodka. I checked my side of the expedition – my .275 rifle and ammo, a powerful spotlight and battery.

It was an hour's run to the mouth of the river, which had a bar across it. Surf was breaking on the bar so the launch had to stand off while we loaded all our gear and other necessities into a dinghy. It was touch and go getting through the surf and bouncing over the sandy bar, but once we got through the breakers we were in deep, calm water. Just inside the river mouth we found a thatched hut that was probably a temporary shelter for native fishermen. It looked as though it hadn't been used for some time, the ashes of a fire were weeks old, but whoever had been there last must have been successful – there were bones and scales lying around that had come from very large fish. We tidied the site and made it our headquarters; the prisoners made a fire and we boiled a billy, made some coffee that, after being suitably fortified, gave us strength.

It was a beautiful night: tall trees along the bank were mostly smothered in creepers, and closer to the water grew clumps of sago palm; there were also quite a few of the palm that produces betel nut, which would have been planted by villagers. It got dark quickly, and soon we slid the dinghy into the water. Brian and I got in, followed by the policemen and prisoners; they did not have proper oars, but had paddles with which they were more familiar and were more suitable for navigating narrow creeks and getting in close to the bank.

Brian hadn't shot before, but he'd seen me shooting in the lagoon in town. I suggested that I take the first shot and he took over the spotlight. We hadn't gone very far when I picked one up and soon disposed of it with a clean shot to the head. Brian then took over the shooting seat and I grabbed the spotlight; half a mile further on, another one obligingly showed up. Brian did a good job – he was about a foot or more longer than the one I had shot. After dragging him up on the bank to be picked up on the way home, I was thinking that we wouldn't get many more in the dinghy. It was now my turn and, apart from a few tiddlers a foot or so long, we went quite a long way before sighting anything – I was beginning to think that we had run out of crocodiles.

I had the lamp, idly swinging it around, when suddenly I saw it – and drew a quick breath. I estimated that it was something like a quarter of a mile away, but I knew it was a big one – the reflected eyes were blood red. I passed the light around and let the crew have a look and they redoubled their paddling efforts. I handed the lamp to Brian and slipped a cartridge into the breach of my rifle and sat back, comfortably relaxed. As we got closer, I was sure that it was going to be the twenty-footer that had almost become an obsession with me. I whispered to Brian, 'It must be twenty bloody feet'.

We glided up closer and closer, it was twenty feet I was sure, I was elated. I put the rifle to my shoulder, I estimated that we were fifteen feet away; the croc was under some leaning mangroves, and there were no obstructions. I had a clear view of his head and half his body out of the water; the great, broad, serrated back looked to be three feet across. He was facing me and appeared to be exhibiting some curiosity at the dazzling lamp. It was something he had never seen before, but I knew that his curiosity would soon develop into alarm.

I pressed the trigger – the bullet went straight into his head between the eyes, and he didn't even shudder. The water was shallow and one of the policemen told the prisoners to jump in and grab the croc as it was starting to drift away. They got it by the tail, but it was enormous and they couldn't hold on; it must have weighed a ton. Holloway told the policemen to get in and help them, and after a struggle they dragged it into shallow water and we got out of the boat to have a better look – I was anxious to establish its length; had I made my twenty foot ambition?

I asked Brian how long the dinghy was, as we could gauge the length. He thought it was about ten or twelve feet: 'But I've got a tape measure on the launch' – I might have guessed. We now had one croc in the boat, which was taking up a lot of room, and the one up on a bank downstream. There was no way to get this monster in the boat – even without the other two and we hadn't finished shooting yet, although I was beginning to think that perhaps we should call it a day – or a night.

I said to Brian, 'We'd better tie this fellow up, we'll have to come back early tomorrow morning and get him'. There was no way we could have dragged him up on to the bank and I didn't want to risk him drifting away. When it was properly secured with the rope that was used for towing the dinghy, a good hitch around his tail and the other end tied to a mangrove, I gave him a friendly pat on the head and we started back. We picked up the first one we had shot and we had a very full boat, but as we were going downstream we travelled comfortably. We were close to our camp, as I could hear the surf booming over the bar. As we were about to turn into the little creek where the native hut was, I idly swung the light around, keeping a lookout for logs and obstructions, and caught a fleeting glimpse of a crocodile on the edge of the surf. I steadied the paddlers and turned them towards the surf to get a better look and there sure enough was a big crocodile at the edge of the bar, rising and falling with the breaking waves. I said to Holloway, 'We'll go back to the camp and unload these two and come back and get this fellow'. We turned into the creek and our crew unloaded the crocs while Brian and I fortified ourselves with a couple of stiff ones.

When we got back to the bar, the crocodile was still there, but had moved into deeper water. 'We'll have to walk,' I said. We beached the dinghy and one of the policemen was left to mind it, while a prisoner carried the heavy battery to which the spotlight was attached by a long cable. The crocodile was about fifty yards away, bobbing up and down in the surf as we walked towards it. The water was knee deep and the waves were surging back and forth, but the sand was firm underfoot.

Holloway walking beside me kept the light steady and I was hoping that the creature would keep still long enough for me to get a shot away, a couple of seconds would do – I only needed one shot. I would only get one, if I didn't kill it there would be no second chance. As we approached, the spotlight suddenly started to flash round all over the place and Holloway turned to the prisoner who was carrying the battery and gave him a whispered tongue lashing for not keeping up – the cable had tightened and had caused the light to waver around. Brian whispered to me, 'I think this bloke's got the wind up'. I nodded; he was probably from some place where there were no crocodiles, had never seen one in his life before and was terrified. To see one for the first time under these conditions, in the middle of the night, would have to be a frightening experience.

We were getting closer, so I put the rifle to my shoulder and went forward a step at a time – if only the bloody thing would keep still. I stopped – this was close enough – and then was trying to decide whether to take it on the rise or on the fall of the waves. It turned and looked towards us. I decided to take it on the top of the next wave, there was no depth of water. I sighted and pressed the trigger, the report booming across the water. I didn't miss it, but I cursed as I realised that I hadn't killed it – it half leapt out of the water, its jaws opening terrifyingly wide as it rolled and thrashed around. The prisoner carrying the battery gave a frightened yell, dropped the battery, turned and ran. The light went out; I said to Holloway, 'Quick, grab that bloody battery' – it would be totally finished once salt water got in. He realised it, too, quickly recovered it, clipped the leads back on and the light came on, much to our relief. No damage had been done. He called to a policeman to carry it, 'And don't bloody well throw it away'. He swung the light around and picked up the crocodile, which had partially recovered and was swimming around in deep water. We walked towards it, but soon the water was up to our waists and shelving away sharply – all we could do was stand and watch it, and hope that it would turn and come towards us. But it went further and further away and eventually disappeared over on the other side. I knew we wouldn't get it now, although a part of its head had been blown away and it would probably die.

We returned to the camp, but the prisoner who had run away was nowhere to be seen – everybody was quite philosophical about it. One of the policemen said, 'Me think 'im 'e run away finish'. Brian thought he'd probably turn up. There was no point in me worrying about it; 'Plenty more where he came from, I suppose' was my contribution, to which Holloway agreed. The next morning we were up bright and early; the two crocodiles that we had in hand were in the water, surrounded by a few stakes to stop them drifting away. The idea was to keep them cool, or putrefaction would set in, the scales would lift and the skins would be useless.

We had to go up river to bring the big fellow back, which would take the best part of an hour. I was anxious to find out his size, thinking of my twenty foot ambition. I wasn't quite sure whether we'd be able to lift him into the boat, we were a man short; we'd have to tie him alongside. The sun was just coming up when we got there and he looked tremendous. We had absolutely no hope of lifting him into the dinghy and had we been able to do so, there would have been no room for anyone else. We lashed him alongside, which made it awkward for the paddlers, but we were going downstream and were soon back at camp.

While we were untying the crocodile, the prisoner who had run away the night before appeared, apologetically explaining that he was, 'Big fella fright too much' and then, 'Me 'ungry'. One of the policemen gave him a tin of meat and some biscuits and all was forgiven. Holloway had previously arranged for the launch, which had been sheltering behind a nearby island, to come over in the morning in case we needed anything and she was now swinging at anchor just over the bar. He sent a policeman to get the tape measure, 'meta' as it was called in pidgin. I had come to the conclusion that it wasn't going to make twenty feet – and so it turned out, it tipped the scales at eighteen feet three inches, and although I was disappointed, it was a monster just the same. That night we went out and shot five and the next night four, which just about wrapped it up, and early the following morning we returned to Madang.

Madsen and Hartley had been and gone, and were now on their way to the Ramu River. Alan Strachan drove me out to the airport and once again I was on my way to Angoram. The Sepik was in top gear, Shanghai was doing well, in fact, he was doing so well that he decided to bring his wife and daughter from Hong Kong; would I fix it up for him when I next went to Sydney? I wasn't too sure how I was going to accomplish this. I asked where in Hong Kong they lived, but he didn't know. I said, 'But you must have an address?' 'Yes, it's care of Sime Darby'. I was a bit dubious about it, but put it out of my mind as I wouldn't be going to Sydney for a couple of months. That didn't worry him. 'There's no great hurry,' he said. There were a lot of skins stacked up in a shed down by the wharf that kept me busy for the next few days and I put it out of my mind.

Two months later I was on my way to Sydney. Before I left, Shanghai reminded me about his wife and daughter, but having been away from my family for eight months, his rather casual request for his wife and daughter had taken a low priority; in fact, it was just about at the bottom of my shopping list. Then one day I received a large envelope with details of skins that he had shipped to Madang and a request for some money. At the end was a postscript: 'Have you been able to make contact with Emily?' I thought of my good friends Nelson & Robertson, island agents who had extensive interests reaching far and wide. I rang and asked for Ray Laws who, after we had exchanged pleasantries, and yes, they knew Sime Darby, said he would make some enquiries and let me know. It was a fortnight before I heard from him again. He rang to say that he had arranged to have Mrs Brown and her daughter, Della, flown to Port Moresby the following week, where arrangements were in hand for accommodation, and the ongoing flights.

Not unexpectedly, 1955 was soon upon us, and after a brief recuperation period I got myself back into gear. I had been giving a lot of thought to some land – which I had heard about through a very reliable grapevine – that shortly would be made available for agricultural purposes. It was in the Wahgi Valley in the Western Highlands, about 100 miles to the west of Goroka. In Goroka there were a few plantations, all of which were growing coffee; it was regarded as the most suitable crop for that area, the climate was ideal and the market was strong.

What little had been produced had realised £1000 a ton, a fantastic price. I wasn't getting entirely carried away, but I was giving it a lot of thought. There was nothing particularly attractive about the lifestyle of a professional crocodile hunter. Although it had a lot of entertainment value in a pub or a party, the real nitty gritty was that it was a dull, hard and, at times, miserable life, particularly at night when it was wet and cold. The real attraction lay in the rewards, which were substantial, but at the same time I was not building anything up – I was destroying.

There was an end to the road along there somewhere and I wasn't sure how far it was – it mightn't be too far away. I talked it over with my wife, sounding her out; she was not keen about the idea of leaving our comfortable home and going up to New Guinea, a place that was almost entirely inhabited with man-eating crocodiles and cannibals. It had no appeal at all, and I realised that some of the stories I had related when entertaining were starting to rebound. I let the subject drop; I pushed it to the back of my mind, but not too far.

The time passed pleasantly and at the end of March we drove to Rose Bay, where a new company, Oceanic Airways, had started a flying boat service from Sydney to Port Moresby. I had travelled in flying boats before and found them very comfortable; a further attraction was that the journey would be broken at Townsville where we would stop overnight – much better than flying all night and landing with a hangover. At the Rose Bay terminal, a great, cumbersome-looking Sunderland was gently rocking at its moorings.

My wife had been noticeably pensive for some time, which I put down to my departure. She asked me if I would be back by September or October. I said that I thought it was unlikely. I was wondering what was on her mind, and she then said, 'Well, try and manage it if you can – our family will be doubled about that time'.

That really shook me. 'You mean...?'

'Yes, that's what I mean.' She was smiling now, enjoying my astonishment.

I was last to board the flying boat; in fact, I nearly missed the boat and it took 500 miles and the frequent ministrations of the hostess to get me back to normal.

Next day we landed at Port Moresby and taxied up to a mooring beside a Catalina, an inter-island flying boat. Vince Sanders was there to meet me. I was concerned to learn that production was falling off, particularly in the Fly River. I thought of the land that was coming up in the Highlands and asked him if he knew anything about it. He didn't subscribe to the Government Gazette, which listed such items, but promised to keep an eye out for it. He told me that an inquiry had come from New Britain and I recalled that a planter there had complained that his cattle were being eaten by crocodiles. I might look into that. I asked Vince to try and sell *Seabird* and I flew back to Madang. After a stint on the Sepik, Madsen and Hartley were back from the Ramu with more than 300 skins and did not want go back there. After settling up, they came to some satisfactory arrangements between themselves – Hartley took the boat and sailed off into the sunset, or maybe it was the sunrise; Madsen took my canoes and went up to Ambunti.

I liked Madsen, he was a very efficient bloke and when I suggested he take my canoes he jumped at it. Shanghai Brown seemed to be on a downhill run, rarely sober. Things weren't all sweetness and light on the matrimonial front. He told me that he'd just received Nelson & Robertson's account for his wife's fares and et ceteras, which came to more than £400 – maybe he hadn't got his money's worth. Apart from the addition of Shanghai's wife, nothing had changed at Angoram. I always stayed with Ken and Kath McLean, whose hospitality and kindness I was again grateful to accept. That they would not hear of me making any contribution to their household probably had a tendency to prolong my stay.

SIX

A LIVE VOLCANO OR TWO

BEFORE THE Second World War, Rabaul had been the capital and executive headquarters of New Guinea which, prior to the Great War of 1914-18 had been under German domination. It was ceded to Australia as a mandate by the League of Nations and included New Britain, New Ireland, Bougainville and other islands, of which Manus was the largest and most important, having been a naval base. The New Guinea group of islands, up to the outbreak of war, had been administered separately, from Rabaul, but after the war New Guinea was combined with Papua under one Administrator in Port Moresby. It then became known as the Territory of Papua and New Guinea, and later still, simply Papua New Guinea.

I landed at Rabaul on an airstrip at the foot of a volcano which gave forth steam and smoke and an occasional rumble. It had erupted in 1937, causing an evacuation of the town. The only casualty was a sailor who fell overboard in the harbour, but there was some doubt that it was as a result of the eruption – it was before the days of breath-testing, of course. Rabaul was a tropical town with a lot of character. The main street, heavily shaded with mango trees and appropriately known as Mango Avenue, was pretty well the business centre, which was dominated by Chinese traders. Here again Burns Philp was the principal European business house, closely followed by Colyer Watson. There were two hotels, the Ascot and Cosmopolitan, and I had previously made a booking at the former. I caught up with Ian MacDougall, the man whose cattle were being taken by crocodiles, when he turned up at the hotel in the evening. He said there were lots of crocodiles in the creeks and lagoons down his way, but they were awkward to get into – they all had sandbars. There was an island not far from Bialla, his plantation, where there was an extinct volcano, and the crater was now a big lake that was full of crocs. I was curious to know more about it, but he couldn't tell me much. 'We'll have a look if you like, but the natives are scared of it,' he said. His boat, a forty-foot workboat, was up on the slips and would not be back in the water for a couple of days. He also said that a Chinese trader with whom he did business wanted to see me. I was naturally curious to know what that was about, but he couldn't tell me much, 'Something to do with croc gall bladders'.

'What would they want them for?'

'I've got no idea,' he said, 'but, you know, they're funny buggers.' I thought that he was right there, and we arranged to go down and see him in the afternoon.

Wing Wah Loong's store was an enormous shed, choc-a-block with every conceivable thing, provided you could find it. Here was a most incredible jumble and it had the very distinct smell of a Chinese trading store. We found him in his office, an old man flicking away at an abacus, a sort of Chinese cash register. I guessed that he could work anything out to about three decimal points. I have always found the Chinese very good people, friendly and very honest in their dealings. After greetings were exchanged, he produced three bottles of beer from a refrigerator. Ian told him that I was the crocodile man and we were here to talk about crocodile gall bladders. His eyes sparkled when he mentioned them: 'How much?' he asked. I had no idea and shook my head: 'How much you like buy 'im?' I asked. He thought for a moment, 'Me like buy 'im one pound one biladder'.

Although it could hardly be described as an appropriate simile, I thought that a quid for one 'biladder' was fruit for the sideboard. He then explained that they must be dried out thoroughly in the sun and when I suggested that I would pack them in salt said, 'All li, velly good'. He then produced some more beer to seal the deal. I was curious

about what use they would be put to and asked him, to which he chuck-
led and said, 'Velly strong melisin (medicine), good fella bilong push-
push'. We all laughed – I'd always thought that 'push-push' was an
appropriately descriptive word for sexual intercourse. He explained
that it was ground into a powder. I wondered how many doses they
would get from one gall bladder. I'd heard the expression 'as bitter as
gall'. If Aphrodite was hovering around anywhere she would have
been in a state of shock. 'You like tly him?' he asked me. 'No thanks,
I want something that works the other way.'

We left Rabaul a couple of days later: the weather was fine and we
cruised along, dodging islands and reefs. It was a long day's journey
to the plantation. The house was a few hundred yards back from the
beach and unloading was soon accomplished, an island a few miles
offshore affording protection. Ian was keen to start shooting immediately; he had good canoes and outboards that he used for loading and
unloading his boat. We left after sundown and followed the coast until
we came to a river that had a sandbar across the mouth. We rode the
surf over it quite comfortably and entered a wide stream. We found
three crocodiles within three miles, but were then held up by fallen
timber and logs plaited up from bank to bank.

We turned back, crossed the bar again and went on until we came
to another, almost identical river. I asked Ian to do the shooting and he
settled himself comfortably into a canvas chair. We came round a bend
– the spotlight was a very powerful new one, and I soon had a big croc
in its beam. I showed Ian, and the size quite startled him. He whistled
and suggested I shoot it; he wasn't feeling too confident at first. I could
see that it had been feeding on something, which I thought was one of
his cows, but as we came closer it was clear that it was something else,
something I couldn't identify. We gradually closed on it and suddenly
I realised that it was feeding on another huge crocodile. It turned towards us, its eyes shining malevolently.

The creek was running very strongly and we had some timber to get
around – I wasn't going to get an easy shot. The craft swung broadside,

but I dare not speak out loud or the croc would dive. We were almost up to it when I fired, but it wasn't a killing shot. It thrashed around, creating a minor whirlpool and giving us a heavy shower into the bargain. The crew picked up their paddles and backed the canoe away – they were all a bit scared. I cursed and got a quick shot away, which probably missed, as it didn't slow him down. I was hoping that he'd weaken and maybe suddenly die, which wasn't very positive thinking – he had no intention of dying, not unless I gave him some help. He jumped out of the water and up on the bank and just as I had him lined up, he jumped back again. Then he started to roll over and over and got under a leaning mangrove; he came out the other side, looked around and I blew the top of his head off – that stopped him.

MacDougall heaved a sigh of relief; so did I but I let it sneak out quietly. 'Christ, that frightened shit out of me,' he said. 'Yes, well I can tell you I wasn't enjoying it, but there was no way your paddlers were going to let him join us on the canoes. They were all ready to break a few water speed records.' We got a rope around him and pulled him alongside. We left him where he was and went over to check out his interrupted lunch – we were all curious to have a look. We paddled up to where the other croc was floating, bloated and stinking, and one of our paddlers said, 'Two fella makim big fella fight'. They'd had a big fight, that was for sure; he was horribly torn about. When he had died, the victor began to eat him, starting on his tail just behind the hind legs. Had we not come along and disrupted his plans, he could have had a couple of weeks uninterrupted gormandising. The law of the jungle – the survival of the fittest – was running its full course.

When the big fellow was lifted aboard, it was the limit of the canoe's capacity and when we rode through the surf and over the sandbar, there wasn't much freeboard to spare. There was a slight offshore breeze and the sea was calm as we cruised back. I questioned Ian on the crater lake that was supposedly full of crocodiles. It was Lolobau Island, straight opposite Bialla, five or six miles away, and the crater that was several hundred feet high could be clearly seen from the plantation. MacDougall appeared to be sceptical about there being crocodiles in the waters of the crater, and I had considerable doubt, too.

I asked him if he knew of anyone who had actually seen them, but he shook his head. He then questioned his boss boy, who was adamant that they were there, but when Ian asked him, 'Eye bilong you lookim true?' he said, 'No, plenty man lookim'. Then, ''im 'e no puk-puk true, 'im 'e masalai'.

'All this devil-devil stuff, that's what they've always told me, but you know, they've got masalai behind every tree if you listen to them,' Ian said. It was getting interesting, I wanted to have a look at a crocodile that was really an evil spirit, and suggested we take a walk up into the lake. Charlie Blake was the owner of the plantation that covered the southern half of the island, and it was managed by Bert Jacobsen. Charlie lived in Rabaul and sometimes came out in his boat *Three Brothers*, which picked up copra and cocoa and kept them supplied with stores. Ian said: 'My boat has to go into Rabaul tomorrow with a load of copra, but if the sea isn't rough we could go across in the canoes. I'd like to find out whether it's true or 'gammon' (the pidgin word for 'bullshit'); I've heard the story of it being full of masalai ever since I've been here. Besides, I haven't seen the Jacobsens for a while; we'll pay them a surprise visit, his wife's a good cook.'

In the morning Ian was busy loading his boat with copra while I attended to skinning and salting. By the time everything was tidied up and the boat had left, the wind had got up, which effectively put a stop to our proposed trip to Lolobau with canoes. The wind ran to a pattern and by afternoon the sea was down, but there was only one thing for us to do, so we pushed the canoes out and went off for another night's shooting.

We went back into the creek where we shot the big fellow. I reasoned that the stinking dead one would have attracted some others that would have been frightened away by the big fellow; he would have been very much the boss round there. Sure enough, there were a couple of six- or seven-footers, one of which I shot, but the report of the rifle was enough to scare the other one away. Ian took the shooting seat and we went further upstream where he shot two more. We turned back, shot another close to the beach and then turned for home.

The wind kept to its set pattern and the next day was the same. In the afternoon a cry went up: 'Kiap 'e come!' We looked along the beach and saw a line of carriers approaching with two white men walking in the lead. As they got closer, Ian recognised them: 'It's Dave Goodger and Ken Pike.' He told me Goodger was a Patrol Officer from Talasea and Pike was an Administration medical officer.

There were about forty carriers, so I guessed that they had been on a fairly long patrol and when they walked up to the homestead, I saw that they both had heavy growths of beard and looked a bit done in. After introductions, Ian asked them what they wanted most – a drink or a shower, to which they both said, 'Yes'. He got a couple of bottles of cold beer from his refrigerator and called to his cook to pump up plenty of water.

Ian asked: 'Where have you fellows been?'

'Out in the Namatanai country, chasing Kanakas up hill and down dale,' Dave Goodger answered, then, glancing towards the beach, 'I've got some prisoners and witnesses coming along behind who are travelling a bit slow, some old fellows and a couple of women.' After they had cleaned up, we settled down on the verandah and the PO told us a bit about his patrol. 'It's the same old thing – pouri-pouri; they killed a young fellow, they wanted his guts to make some devil's brew, that's why I took Ken along,' indicating the young doctor.

Ken Pike laughed: 'I wasn't much help, unfortunately we don't do a witch doctor's course at St Lucia. Since I've been here, I've often thought it would be a good idea.' Shortly after, the prisoners walked in escorted by two policemen. They were walking in a line, secured by a light chain from one to the other. Half a dozen others, who would have been witnesses, were not chained, and there were two women with small children.

We talked about the crocodiles that were supposed to be in the crater, but, like everyone else, they had heard the story – knew somebody who knew somebody.

I asked Dave Goodger when they were going back to Talasea, the station that was his headquarters. He said that the main reason why they had come to Bialla was to get on Ian's radio to call up Talasea and request a ship to take their prisoners and witnesses to the station. 'They're just about buggered,' he said, 'those two women with the kids are all in, and there's an old fellow that's not too good, either.'

There was no shooting that night, and the next morning Dave and Ken were huddled over the blower calling Talasea. It didn't take long to get through. The ADO, Royce Webb, said that he would send the *Matoka* and that it would probably get there the next day. MacDougall then suggested that the boat drop us off at Lolobau Island, which I thought was a good idea.

I asked: 'How are we going to get back?' He said that there wouldn't be any problems there: 'My boat will be back before we're likely to have shot the lake out – if there's anything to shoot, of course.'

That night we all went out shooting, but it wasn't very successful – maybe if we'd only taken one bottle of rum we would have done better. However, it was a success from the entertainment angle. Ian shot the first and, as it turned out, the last – they all wanted to taste crocodile meat, something that I was almost ashamed to admit I hadn't experienced either.

The one we had was about eight feet long and as the Patrol Officer and the doctor were so insistent, a couple of boys skinned it while a fire was lit. We cut the tail into four pieces and waited for the fire to burn down until we had a bed of glowing, red-hot coals. Ken Goodger announced that it was midnight as he extracted the cork from the second bottle of rum.

Everybody was throwing their portion onto the coals and just as I was about to toss mine on, I made the mistake of smelling it. I can't describe what it smelt like except that I have never smelt anything so revolting in my life, not anything I was about to eat anyway. I turned away as my stomach heaved. I did my best, but there was no hope – everything came up. My companions thought it was a wonderful joke, but I was too busy to give expression to what I thought of them as they laughed their fool heads off.

Ken Pike, who, in his medical capacity one would think would have at least made some sympathetic noises, if anything laughed louder than the others, said that I'd been drinking too much rum. I knew, of course, that it had nothing to do with the rum – if I hadn't had the rum I would have probably been a lot worse. When the meat was cooked, it was noticeable that my companions' enthusiasm for their epicurean dish did not send them into transports of delight, no rhapsodies on the delicacy of flavour; in fact, no one finished their portion. They blamed me for putting them off, but I don't think that was strictly accurate. Their hunting enthusiasm was at a low ebb, too, so we headed back downstream. When we got back to Bialla it was three o'clock.

The next day Ian called Lolobau up and had a long talk with Bert Jacobsen, who was very keen for us to come over and have a look in the crater. Ian asked him if he knew whether there were really any crocodiles there, but he said that he didn't know, but was confident that there were. I heard him say: 'I'm sure that there are crocodiles there; the story has been going on for too long and is too consistent. But you might have a job getting any natives to go in with you.' I said to Mac-Dougall, 'Let's have a look anyway. I'd like to establish once and for all whether it's true or not', to which he agreed.

The *Matoka* arrived and anchored just beyond the surf. The prisoners and witnesses were ferried across and then we went aboard with our gear and a few bags of salt. It was a short run across to the island and Bert Jacobsen was at the wharf to meet us. We drove up to his house where I met his wife, who was equally excited about the expedition. Bert said that it was about two miles from the house to the foot of the crater, and there was a road that petered out about halfway. Bert said he was sure that we would find crocs there.

'I've often thought about going up and having a look, but it's never been very important to me – I wasn't interested whether there were puk-puks in the crater or not.'

The next morning we piled into Bert's truck, picked up his boss boy and followed a winding track between rows of coconuts and the beach that soon turned inland and petered out. We walked to the foot of the crater, but it was a fairly steep climb to the top. We stood on the edge and looked down into the lake, about fifty feet below. Tall trees grew all around the rim, shading the water. The crater was enormous, far bigger than I expected, oval in shape, about a mile long and at least half a mile wide. Not a breeze ruffled the surface, which looked like a huge sheet of oil. I said to Bert, 'I can understand the natives not wanting to come here, it's an evil-looking place'.

Birds called raucously from the trees and I caught a glimpse of a pair of birds of paradise, their brilliant plumage flashing as it caught the sunlight. The boss boy didn't seem to be exhibiting any signs of fear, contrary to what I expected. I mentioned this and Bert said that he came from the Sepik, and, as a 'foreigner', wasn't so concerned about the local variety of evil spirits: 'But don't be fooled, he would know all about the masalai stories.' Nevertheless, he was taking a great interest and suddenly pointed to a disturbance on the water surface. 'Puk-Puk!' he whispered excitedly. We all stared at where he was pointing, but all I could see was a slight ripple. Then it surfaced – there was no doubt about it this time. The croc's head was clearly visible as it swam towards some overhanging branches and then disappeared.

I was elated, 'Well, that settles it once and for all. I suppose there are some more in there'.

Bert said, 'I would think that there are quite a few. I've been hearing about them ever since I've been here'.

All I could think of was getting in there, but it was going to be quite an exercise. Canoes would have to be carried up over the rim, and persuading paddlers to accompany us was going to be the biggest hurdle. We sat on a fallen log and talked it over.

Ian said, 'We won't get any of the local people to come with us, that's for sure'. Jacobsen nodded and spoke rapidly to his boss boy in pidgin. I could see he wasn't all that keen, but gradually came round; perhaps the thought of a feed of croc meat encouraged him. Bert's labour line had about 100 men and he said there were about thirty Sepiks among them. I said we'd need four paddlers, which he was sure would be okay: 'As long as this fellow's on side, you'll be all right.'

We went back down the mountainside, slipping and sliding our way to the bottom and drove back to the house. Bert was most enthusiastic and couldn't do enough to help. He drove us down to the beach, where a dozen or so canoes were pulled up under trees. I picked out a couple about twenty feet long, which I reckoned four boys could carry comfortably – where the ground was level anyway. The job was simplified when they told us of a spur that ran out into the crater and gave an easier approach.

With bush knives they hacked a fairly good track that enabled the truck to get to the foot of the crater. Bert let us have his boss boy, which was a very generous gesture, and he had talked three of his fellow Sepiks into accompanying us, but it was difficult to detect any enthusiasm, which they would have normally displayed when we were going anywhere else – 'Bloody masalai,' I thought.

After unloading the canoes, Ian went back with the truck for some salt (the crocodiles would have to be skinned in the crater), rifles, harpoons and spotlight and a box with enough food for a week. Bert left us and went back to his interrupted work while we settled in and prepared for the coming night's action.

The canoes were soon lashed together with vines and ropes; it wasn't very elaborate, but we didn't expect to be there more than a couple of nights. When the job was finished, the craft was launched and tied up, and we lit a fire, boiled a billy and had a meal.

As darkness approached, our crew was obviously apprehensive, talking in whispers. Unless one has made a study of anthropology specialising in certain areas, it is impossible to know and understand the superstitions and beliefs of primitive people. I was among Melanesians who were, one could say, between three cultures – that of the missionary teaching, the trader and businessman, and their own. It is significant that they copied us in so many ways and, as they say, imitation is the sincerest form of flattery. But it is fairly true to say that they are greatly influenced by their own culture.

There is no doubt they believed that the crocodiles in the crater were masalai because the local people had told them so, but also they probably regarded them as belonging to the Lolobau people, for although I couldn't have got the local people to come with me, the Sepiks were prepared to give it a go. I was the puk-puk man who knew all about them. I suppose everybody's masalai was different, too. Ian and I talked and joked with them in an endeavour to settle them down, and as darkness closed in I buckled on my cartridge belt and said, 'Let's go'.

I sensed their reluctance as they picked up their paddles and as we glided over the water, I turned on the spotlight, which seemed to give them confidence, the rhythm of the paddles increased noticeably. As we approached the far side of the lake, I waved to turn the canoes to where I was sure I had caught a fleeting glimpse of a reflection that could be a crocodile. I was not sure, as frogs' eyes also reflected a light, although they were much lighter; one soon learnt to distinguish the difference, as crocodiles were distinctly red.

Then suddenly there it was, the unmistakable, evil-looking eye of a crocodile. The crew didn't display any enthusiasm for getting close to my quarry, and I dared not urge them on with any spoken word, it would only alarm it; I had to kill it with my first shot and break the spell. We crept up closer, agonisingly slowly, Ian holding a spotlight steady on its head. I put my rifle to my shoulder and although we were further away than I would have liked, I pressed the trigger. The report echoed across the lake and blood spurted from the skull of an eight-footer – it wasn't a masalai after all; there it was, completely lifeless. It didn't change into some awful shape and devour us all.

Now there was an entirely different atmosphere, the change was remarkable; suddenly they were chattering and laughing among themselves, a great relief to me after the almost sullen attitude that they had displayed previously. I knew we had a crew who would be taking a lively interest in the operation.

The boss boy was the harpoon man and, being a Sepik was traditionally an expert, but I knew there would be difficulties recovering the crocs after we'd shot them. The ideal situation is gradually shelving banks, but being a crater, a lot of the shoreline was steep, falling away into deep water. My diary records: 'This lake is about a mile long and half a mile wide; it has steep sides and a lot of overhanging foliage – not the best for shooting or recovering.'

My crew now was full of enthusiasm and we hadn't gone very far when I sighted another – I knew that we were going to do well. It was recovered, but not without difficulty. I told Ian to have a shot and took over the spotlight. The next one was an easy shot, but it sank so quickly the harpoon man had no chance; where we were the water could have been 100 feet deep. It would surface eventually, but by then putrefaction would have set in, making the skins worthless.

We moved on; the shoreline was quite irregular and we came round a point and turned into a small bay with a shelving, gravelly beach and there lying twenty yards or so from the water was a big crocodile lying side on – a perfect shot. MacDougall drew a deep breath and whispered, 'Christ, what a beauty'. Then, 'Tom, you take him. I'd never live it down it I missed him'.

The target was very small at this distance, and if it wasn't hit in the head it would get away. We glided in and the canoes grounded. I think everyone was holding their breath as I took aim; I know I was. I hit him just behind the eye – he never moved. We all waded ashore, as the water was only knee-deep. It was lying with its tail curved round, so Ian straightened it out and paced its length, saying that it was a bit over twelve feet; it had an enormous girth.

We now had two on board and I was thinking that this croc posed a problem. My idea was to take them over at the other side where our base camp was, skin them and carry them to where they could be picked up by the plantation truck. The only way to get this fellow across the lake would be to either tow him or lash him alongside, but first we had to get him down to the water and lying there the croc looked monstrously heavy.

There were six of us. Ian MacDougall was a big man and I was no lightweight, our four canoe men were quite strong, although not up to us in weight. I told each of them to take a leg while MacDougall and I picked up its tail. Perhaps the six of us could drag it down to the water, but it took about ten seconds to find out that we had no hope. I said to Ian that we'd call it a night. We would have to be up early in the morning to get the skinning done before it got hot; this fellow would have to be skinned where he lay and the skin brought back to the camp.

Early the next morning we all went across to the other side and it didn't take long for the six of us to take the skin off; it was rolled up sideways and the four Sepiks carried it on their shoulders down to the canoes. The croc skin looked like a huge snake and it was by no means easy to carry – it was very heavy, even without its owner. We had the other two finished and carried out of the crater to where the road ended; they were salted down and covered with bushes to be picked up with the truck later.

We walked back to the plantation – there was nothing to do for the rest of the day, but we might have another strenuous night ahead of us. I thought that one more night would probably clean out the area. The truck came and collected the skins and a load of crocodile meat.

That evening it rained so heavily we were kept inside, which was no great hardship. I was glad that it started before we were out, it would have been cold and miserable. The following night was clear and we headed back to the crater again; as the sun settled behind the trees, our crew's impatience was in sharp contrast to their reluctance the previous night. I waited until dark before giving the signal to start. This would be our last night's shooting, and should clean it out. I said to Ian that if we saw any crocs where the water appeared to be very deep, we wouldn't bother with them; not only was it almost impossible to recover them, but also it was a waste of time and ammunition.

I took the spotlight, we went round the opposite way this time and before long we had two. Cruising quietly along we came to where the lake tapered off, cliffs rising sheer. The shoreline developed into a series of sharp rocks rising from the water, and pockets with small sandy beaches. We came around the headland near the little bay where we had shot the big fellow on the beach. I intended going straight past, but to my astonishment, over towards the shore I saw an amazing sight.

The crocodile that I had shot a couple of nights ago, and which six of us had been unable to lift, had been dragged down to the water and a portion of its tail eaten away. Close by with its head clearly showing was another monster. Had I not seen it I would not have believed it. I knew of their tremendous strength in the water – they could drag a big bullock in and drown it – but to have pulled this crocodile that six of us couldn't move, down to the water's edge, was amazing. The fact that we had skinned it made not a lot of difference. I swung the canoes around as Ian glanced along the beam and said something. The feeding croc turned towards us, no doubt having heard the sounds of our paddles splashing, curious at the water movement that we were causing. It would have immediately thought of an intruder – another crocodile was approaching, which not only would be encroaching on its territory, but also perhaps challenging its right to its recently discovered supply of food.

We were two or three hundred yards away when it started to swim slowly towards us. I thought that it could be dangerous and handed the light to Ian saying, 'I'll take it'. We were closing on one another at about the same speed, and Ian kept the light steadily on its head as it swam towards us, creating a miniature bow wave.

I slipped a cartridge into the breech of my rifle as I guided the paddlers. Standing up in the bow of the right-hand canoe, I would see that it was enormous, and tensed up I waited until it was alongside. My rifle was pointing down, following it as it swam steadily towards us. When it came level, my rifle was no more than a hand's breadth from its head.

I pressed the trigger, it rolled over as the report of my rifle reverberated around the lake and sunk in about three feet of water. The release from the build-up of tension affected everyone. The crew, laughing and talking excitedly, jumped overboard and feeling around in the water brought it to the surface. Its great broad head must have been a foot across, and rows of gleaming white savage-looking teeth showed as they pulled its jaw open. In the light of the shooting lamp, its evil look was intensified. They dragged it closer inshore to the shallow water where it rested on the bottom, the serrations along its back and tail intensified this look of enormous strength.

The night was young, so I decided to leave it for a while – there would be perhaps a couple or so left and it would definitely be our last night here. We only got one more and that wrapped it up. We left the big fellow where he was until the next morning. I doubted whether there was anything big enough to eat him. He turned out to be fifteen feet, which is an awful lot of crocodile. The skinning and salting was soon completed, and MacDougall's boat came over in the evening.

I was well satisfied with the adventure, for we had proved there were crocodiles in the crater. I believed that they had walked overland from the sea – there was no other logical explanation. It was probably a breeding area. I knew that in the rivers they went upstream well beyond the tidal limits to make their nests, but there was a great lot I didn't know about them.

We returned to Bialla. I was concerned with what was happening in the great big outside world. Ian immediately got on the blower and came back to the house with a sheaf of telegrams for me. The most important being from Sanders advising that seven blocks of land in the Western Highlands were advertised. I made a lightning decision – I would become a planter. There was an accumulation of mail that had come from Rabaul, the most important being from Kath reporting on the progress of the approaching addition to our family.

There was mail from the Sepik River, a letter from Madsen saying that he had more than 500 skins in hand. Shanghai Brown, he said, was on a downhill run. Alan Strachan wrote saying that the Singapore market had dropped slightly. Well, I thought, there was a fair bit of leeway. I realised that I'd been here long enough and I'd better get back into what was known as the real world – a pity, but needs must when the devil drives; everything still revolved around filthy lucre.

Ian MacDougall said that he would take me to Talasea the next day. There was an airstrip at a place called Hoskins, but the planes were a bit haphazard, with no definite schedule. There was a District Office at Talasea, and the ADO, Royce Webb, would know all about the aircraft movements.

The next day we left early, calling at Lew Searle's plantation for lunch, which was about halfway, arriving at Talasea just after sundown. Ian, who knew his way around, took me straight to the club, an institution that no self-respecting outstation would be without. The local population was just starting to string in. The ADO, Royce Webb, was a commanding personality, more than six feet tall, he had the kind of blond, Nordic good looks that could be guaranteed to keep him in permanent trouble with the opposite sex. It was apparent, too, that he was respected on the station; he had a personality to match.

Ken Pike and Bert Goodger had recently passed through Bialla, and so they all knew of me and were eager to hear of our venture into the Lolobau crater. Until now everyone had heard the stories, but no one knew whether to believe them or not as most people found it difficult to believe that crocodiles had climbed into it. We were able to give them a very good account of our two-night adventure and didn't have to exaggerate to make it interesting.

I asked the ADO about the chances of getting a plane to Rabaul, but he said that the airstrip was closed, although Bert Goodger would be inspecting it tomorrow and because of the weather they had been experiencing lately he was sure that he would be able to open it to traffic. Even so, it was obvious that I was going to be here for a few days. Ken Pike, who had been following the conversation, said, 'I've got a spare bed, you can stay with me'. I was very grateful for this. One thing about this country: there was no way a man would ever be left out on a limb.

Talasea was not only surrounded by craters of varying sizes, but also was literally sitting on one. Not far away was an area of boiling volcanic springs. Some bubbled merrily away, while others shot into the air periodically; they boomed and cascaded boiling water, which the natives often used for cooking. There were stretches of grey, dried mud that were of a dangerous thickness – tempting to walk on but covering a seething cauldron that broke through in places and bubbled grey mud, almost obscene in appearance. The whole area boomed and rumbled, and occasional tremors shook the earth.

I idled away a couple of days while Royce Webb sought a plane. He was soon able to inform me that there would be one available. 'There's a DC3 coming in tomorrow; how's that for service?' There was no strain staying at Talasea, it was all very pleasant but the path of duty is the road to something or other.

We went to Hoskins by boat – the airstrip was a short walk from the jetty. It was an old wartime strip and seemed in good shape. There were no buildings of any description so we selected a couple of oil drums to sit on while we waited for the plane. When it arrived, I made my farewells and climbed in. The first officer locked the door and I looked around for something to sit on. I found a bale of something that was fairly comfortable. It was a short flight and I was in Rabaul by midday.

Two days later I was winging my way across the Solomon Sea, heading for Wewak. From there it was a short hop to Angoram, courtesy of a Sepik Airways Norseman, and I was back where I started.

In the Angoram club I gave a rundown on my travels since I had last seen them, a bare month ago. Just relating it made me dizzy before I finished. Then Madsen dropped a bombshell: he had bought a lugger and wanted to go trochus fishing, would I come into partnership with him? I started to get dizzy all over again.

He'd bought the boat, which I'd seen a couple of times, from the Catholic Mission for £1000. It was a lugger type similar to the pearling luggers working out of Darwin. Its mission name was *Gabriel*, which he'd changed to *Heron*. I had seen it occasionally on the river, but had never taken much notice; the last time it was being towed from somewhere up the river. It was powered by a diesel engine that gave a lot of trouble, which was why they'd sold it so cheaply. They reckoned that before long they were certain to lose it on a reef or something.

Madsen said there wasn't much wrong with the engine – it needed new injectors and a set of rings, and it was a Ruston, which I knew was top of the line in diesels. Next morning we went down to the jetty where it was tied up. It looked a well found boat to my inexperienced eye. The engine, which he had polished up, was aft – this made for extra efficiency because of a shorter tail shaft and allowed more hold space.

'Tell me all about the trochus fishing?' I said.

'Well, the market is very strong, the pearl shell beds are getting fished out, there's lashings of trochus out on the shallow reefs that's easily got at. As you probably know, they can't make a button from plastic that will stand boiling.' I knew that from experience – whenever I bought a shirt I made sure that the buttons weren't plastic.

He went on: 'When we came up from Australia in the *Angler*, we had a good look over the reefs around Samarai, I don't think it's ever been fished, it's lousy with shell. I wanted to stop and fish, but the others didn't and I was outvoted. Right now, the market is at about £150 a ton, and there're miles of reefs loaded with trochus all through that chain of islands. If I can't pick up a ton a day I'll eat my hat.'

I thought his indigestion wasn't likely to suffer from this exercise – I was sure that he never owned a hat. He explained the gathering process, which was done by divers using goggles, a skill that all coastal islanders had mastered.

The shell was cone-shaped and fairly large, containing a rubbery, small creature that was inedible and was extracted by boiling in forty-four gallon drums. A lot of it, particularly the older shell, was often heavily encrusted with lime that had to be cleaned off. He made it sound so easy and very attractive. I knew of the chains of islands off

Samarai, which tailed off into several groups. The Louisiade Archipelago, the D'Entrecasteaux Islands, the Trobriand Islands and a mass of reefs in between.

He suggested I take a quarter share for £250 plus as much again for working capital. I hesitated for a moment, as I had enough on my plate already. He went on, 'Burns Philp will buy as much as they can get their hands on, and once I've delivered the first load I can get an advance.'

'Then all you want from me to start is £500?'

'Yes, that's all.'

It sounded an excellent proposition and I suddenly had visions of joining him for a couple of carefree weeks for a spot of lotus-eating among the Isles of Love – if I ever got the time, of course, as I was reminded that I planned to become a coffee planter, too.

Madsen intended to leave for the Trobriands sometime after Christmas. In the meantime he would make sure that the crocodile skins were being packed and shipped out. Shanghai Brown had acquired a new lease of life and a young native girl. Cedric the Saxon was doing quite well with crocodile skins.

The land for sale in the Wahgi Valley was giving me plenty to think about. If I took it on, I would be diving headlong into something that I knew nothing about, so I better have a look at it. I asked Sepik Robbie to whistle up an aeroplane and the next day I was on my way to Madang. There was no difficulty arranging a radio-telephone conversation with the Minj District Office. My talk with the ADO was most rewarding. There was, he said, a Government charter leaving Madang for Minj in a couple of days: 'See the District Commissioner, I'm sure he'll be able to arrange a seat.' The DC was Les Williams and as the Minj ADO predicted, there were no problems about a seat on the plane.

There were already a sprinkling of planters recently established in the valley, most of whom I knew. I was confident that I would be able to get some valuable advice and help from men who were familiar with the area. Norman Plant was there, so was Bill Matthew and Alan

Ferguson, partners in a big block. Bob Gibbes, too, was one of the first and was experimenting with tea, coffee and a few other things.

Two days later I was out at the aerodrome watching the last of the cargo being loaded. I made myself comfortable on some bags of rice and we were soon airborne. We flew in from an altitude of 8000 feet and as the valley came into view, it presented a striking contrast to the jagged and formidable peaks of the Bismarck Ranges, which formed the northern wall of the valley. We broke through some light cloud and a beautiful vista of a green, undulating country unfolded. The Wahgi River, which rose high up in the distant whale-backed Mount Hagen, wound its leisurely way to the Papuan Gulf.

The Highlands cover a large area of very rugged country interspersed with lush valleys, which are heavily populated with the greatest concentration of warrior tribes in the whole of New Guinea. The Leahy brothers, Mick and Dan, were the first white men to venture into what was then completely unknown country. Of aggressive, red-blooded Irish stock, theirs was an heroic epic of exploration, the stuff of which legends are made.

From 1930 to 1934 they led several expeditions penetrating through from Kainantu at the eastern end to beyond Mount Hagen, more than 200 miles to the west. They encountered people who had never ventured beyond their tribal boundaries, had never seen white men before, and their incredulity when they first met was embarrassing. The natives believed that the whites were their ancestors returned from some distant world, which was reinforced by the sight of the food that they carried (which came from tins), the mirrors, and the clothes they wore. To them such things could only have come from some nether region. They cried inconsolably and when they approached the whites, they touched them to see if they were real. The natives prostrated themselves on the ground, crying out in fear.

The carriers, although the same colour as themselves, were also believed to be returned spirits. That they wore loincloths of brightly coloured material, carried bedding and ate this strange food from tins was probably regarded as evidence of this.

The firearms they carried created a combination of terror and wonder. Mick illustrated their fearsome power by shooting a pig, which he bought to supplement their rations. This, of course, was the first, fine, careless rapture. It was not long before they were assailed by doubts as to the strangers' spiritual origin. Every move they made was closely watched, even their excreta was collected and carefully wrapped in banana leaves.

Perhaps this is where the first doubts crept in. Is there such a thing as ethereal shit? Mick and Dan would have been in no doubt that the adulation they received at first would change. Mick, a born leader, never allowed their vigilance to relax. He was well blooded before he ventured into the Highlands, surviving, but only just, a dawn attack on his prospecting camp. His brother, Pat, who was with him in his earlier ventures, took several arrows and Mick was clubbed about the head. They were only a small party, but fought a savage, rearguard action in which six tribesmen were shot. He was tough and disciplined, with all the qualities of which Empire builders are made. There were many occasions when lesser men would not have survived.

The Leahys, while making valuable contributions towards the meagre geographical knowledge, were mainly concerned with prospecting on behalf of the Bulolo Gold Dredging Company. By 1933 they had penetrated through Bena Valley to the Asaro River. Before them lay the formidable barriers of the Chimbu Ranges. To the north, rising to 15,000 feet, was Mt Wilhelm. Further to the west was the Wahgi Valley, located between the Bismarcks and the Kuber Range.

Somewhere out there to the west was Michael Leahy's pot of gold – and 1933 was to see the biggest expedition mounted by the Leahy brothers. They made Bena-Bena their base camp and an airstrip was built. All their supplies were flown in from Salamaua.

By now, the Administration was very impressed with his ability to open up what was classified as 'uncontrolled territory'. Furthermore, not only was he highly respected as an explorer and prospector, but also he was working for the Bulolo Gold Dredging Company, a powerful international conglomerate that governments treated with respect.

Leahy told the Administration that his next expedition would be of great significance. Mick believed that he was on the verge of great discoveries. The Administration decided to have a hand in it, too, and Jim Taylor, an experienced Patrol Officer, was instructed to accompany them. At the end of March they were ready and early one morning Mick Leahy and Jim Taylor strode out of their camp at the head of ninety carriers. Dan Leahy and a company geologist brought up the rear. The white men were armed and Leahy had also armed six trusted Waria tribesmen, who had been with him for some time and were trained in the use of firearms. Taylor had four native police with him.

To reach the Chimbu country they climbed to 8000 feet, where the nights were bitterly cold with icy winds sweeping through the gorges, all making the carriers' task an unenviable one. They soon came to the heaviest populated area of New Guinea and again the people treated them with a mixture of awe and astonishment. Whenever the natives could find them, they collected their faeces, and if an opportunity presented itself, they would pluck hairs from their legs and wrap them in leaves. Their efforts to prospect were continually hampered by the crowds that followed them wherever they went. These people were perplexed by the white man's careful examination of the creek beds, and when they broke samples from reefs with their knapping hammers, keeping some, discarding others, the natives brought stones to them, indicating by signs that they were far more suitable as axes.

Apart from a few isolated streams with minuscule traces of gold, the Chimbu country was a disappointment and the Leahys prepared to leave. Their planned departure shocked the mountain people, who did everything they could to persuade them to stay, offering their choicest young women as an inducement. Followed by thousands of wailing people, the long line of carriers headed by Mick Leahy and Jim Taylor walked from the rugged confines of the Chimbu Ranges. As the column marched from one tribal area to another, the dialects gradually changed and by the time they had passed through several clans, the language changed completely. Communication was at all times a problem. Tribal boundaries were fiercely maintained and one group would take over from the last. Decked out in magnificent bird of paradise plumes, chanting in unison, they presented a spectacular and unforgettable escort.

The mountains gradually gave way to valleys intersected by crystal clear streams, and the walking became less arduous. Then from a ridge they suddenly saw beautiful rolling downs-like country unfolding before them – the Wahgi Valley.

Although they were continually surrounded by curious and fearful highlanders, no hostility had been shown, as many believed they were returned ancestors. But it was necessary to curb their curiosity and enthusiasm and so they ran a rope around the perimeter of their camp wherever they stopped. None were allowed inside the area unless invited. If this had not been done they would have been quickly overrun and pilfering would have been inevitable.

They walked on through country that was essentially farming land as the intense activity testified. Neat little checkerboard gardens covered hundreds of acres: taro, sweet potato and sugarcane were in abundance. Mick Leahy was anxious to establish a base from where he could prospect and it was already arranged that he was to be supplied by air, which, of course, required an airstrip. The arrival of the first aeroplane had been determined at the time of their departure and as this time approached, the preparation of a landing ground was an immediate task. They made camp at Kelawere, close to the present-day town of Mt Hagen, the mountain after which it is named rising a few miles to the west. It was also a good base from where they could extend their prospecting activities.

The party was becoming proficient at making themselves understood by sign language and with their carriers giving them a lead, they soon had several thousand warriors removing bushes and levelling the country with sharp sticks and other crude implements. It was with some difficulty that the workers were restrained from digging it up – to them there was only one reason to prepare land and that was to plant crops. These newcomers were strange people indeed – after going to all the trouble of clearing an area of very good ground, they then wanted it rammed and stamped so hard that nothing could possibly grow!

Eventually it was ready and the white men anxiously awaited the arrival of the aeroplane, while these Stone Age people hung around in a state of mystification, one would assume. The plane would be flying into unknown territory after negotiating the fearsome Bismarck Ranges. They were concerned at having the landing ground clear because at all times there were a number of tribesmen wandering over it and because they had experienced the reaction and impact of an aircraft arriving on a couple of previous occasions.

The arrival of the white man in the Highlands, with their astonishing possessions and weaponry, was undoubtedly a cataclysmic event in the lives of these people, who immediately elevated him to legendary status. But all this would be reduced to insignificance when an aeroplane arrived and a white man stepped out of it. The only event in the white man's world that would bear any kind of comparison would be the Second Coming of Christ.

I believe that in the entire history of exploration there has never been anything to compare with it. There are similarities up to a point in the annals of African exploration, with white men arriving with their guns and strange equipment, but the aeroplane came much more gradually, probably in picture form in the first instance.

It was one of the carriers that heard it first, a distant humming. Then, as it gradually increased in volume, everyone heard it – a steady drone to the east. Then someone saw it floating lazily, losing altitude after its strenuous climb over the Bismarcks. There was a rush to set fire to the debris lining the landing ground to provide signals for the pilot. It gradually turned towards them, the pilot had seen the smoke. It was no more than ten miles away now, gradually descending. By now the pilot would have been able to clearly discern the encampment, the group of tents and the rapidly accumulating mass of natives.

Mick and Dan got all the carriers together who knew what had to be done and, with Jim Taylor and Hector Kingsbury, the geologist, they endeavoured to clear the landing area of the now terrified natives. As the aeroplane made its first approach at just over tree-top level, they flung themselves to the ground in terror. The pilot, having experienced it before, kept making low runs until eventually the airstrip was clear and he was able to land.

There were probably thousands of natives all around the Leahy's camp and the airstrip, with huge numbers of them lying on the ground moaning and crying fearfully. Then this strange bird, the engine roaring and smoking, came to a halt and a white man climbed out of it. Dressed similarly to the men on the ground, it proved beyond doubt that these strangers came from the sky.

This was the first aeroplane to arrive and it was followed by others, and although their curiosity and enthusiasm never diminished, they became used to it. Mick persuaded a young highlander to go on a flight to the coast. His name was Kopia Rebia and when he left, his parents and relatives were terrified they would never see him again. His own terror can only be imagined. Mick made sure that he was well taken care of. It was of the greatest importance as a public relations exercise. He saw the sea and many other wonders, including horses. He was taken to a trade store and told to help himself. He returned with a bottle of sea water, hairs from a horse's tail and numerous other treasures.

Mick and Dan continued to prospect, their travels taking them as far as the Dutch border. Jim Taylor accompanied them and sometimes Hector Kingsbury. These men knew from their earlier experiences that the euphoria all these things generated would not last. They were four white men in a country where the ratio was probably something like half a million to one. At any one time they were surrounded by up to a thousand of the most primitive tribesmen in the world, whose own laws were dominated by 'might is right', and it is remarkable as well as a tribute to their own personality and commonsense that they had travelled thus far unscathed.

Mick Leahy was leading an expedition with three white men and 100 carriers from a distant part of the country, who were 'foreigners' to these people. On their own, they would have been chopped to pieces overnight. As we know, they were at first regarded as returned ancestors, or some kind of spirits. This could not last for ever. The visits to the coast did a lot to dispel it.

One of the earliest incidents occurred when the carrier line was strung out heading for Mt Hagen. It was 18 April 1933 and they were being followed by several hundred belligerent tribesmen who were demonstrably hostile. In their book on the Leahys, *First Contact*, authors Bob Connolly and Robin Anderson quote Ndika Nihints, who relates:

'The Yamka and the Kuklika (two clans) and all the people around us were making a lot of noise, shouting and calling out war cries. They were saying that they wanted to take everything from the white men. Some people snatched things from the carriers, like tins and trade goods. Then Kiap Taylor broke this thing he was carrying (loading it) and before we knew anything we heard it crack. Then everything happened at once, everyone was pissing and shitting themselves in terror. Mother! Father! I was horrified.

'I wanted to run away. The muskets got the people – their stomachs come out – their heads came off! Three men were killed and one was wounded. The dead ones were a Yamka Manamp man, a Kawelka Goimpa man and a Ndika Klimbil. I said, 'Oh, Mother', but that didn't help. I breathed deeply and that didn't help. I was desperate. Why did I come here? We thought it was lightning eating the people up.'

One can imagine this old man, who was a youth at the time, relating the dramatic events, endeavouring to explain it with his limited English. Seeing people's heads blown off, bullets going in one side and coming out the other, leaving a gaping hole – a chilling experience for people whose most fearsome weapons were sharp sticks and pieces of stone wedged into a piece of wood – their spears and axes.

There was another clash some time later, far more serious and but for the vigilance of Mick Leahy, the expedition would undoubtedly have been wiped out. The prospectors had stopped in a beautiful valley, which the people had told them was Doi. They set up camp and, as usual, ran a light rope around the area, running from trees to pegs to trees, inside which they rigged their tents. Although there were always crowds of curious onlookers peering at them, watching every move, that simple, single rope encircling their camp was always respected. Inside it, they and their carriers could relax and rest.

Mick Leahy, never still for a moment, walked away from the camp, going a few hundred yards to an eminence nearby, where he took some photographs of the camp. Returning, he shouldered his way through the crowds of curious onlookers that were packed right around the boundary rope. Back in his tent, Mick's attention was suddenly drawn to a man with a spear who started haranguing his people. Waving the spear belligerently, what he was saying did not have to be translated. It was all too obvious – he was urging them to attack the camp. For this man, whose name was Pinketa, to have urged his people to murder the prospecting party was a reckless and foolhardy act, for although none of the Doi people had seen a firearm discharged, they most certainly by then would have heard of the white man's guns, if only in a garbled form. But in their world of spears and axes, until they had actually seen the devastating effect – a man's head disintegrating under the impact of a soft-nosed bullet, or passing through two or three people, and leaving a hole the size of a coconut – they would not have much idea of the frightful destructive power of the rifles.

Mick Leahy shot Pinketa as he raised his spear to drive it into the carrier, who was the closest man to him. His brother Dan fired at the oncoming mob at the same time. Jim Taylor fired and so too did Jim Taylor's police, and those men of Mick Leahy's who were trusted with firearms. Ten or twelve people were killed instantly, perhaps more; a number were wounded and the rest retreated. It would be impossible to estimate the final number of casualties, but certainly some of those wounded would not have survived. When the long line of carriers walked from Doi soon after, they were watched by the fearful villagers, none of whom carried a spear.

Some criticism has been levelled at Leahy and his companions that was largely unwarranted. As leader, Mick always did his best to maintain good relations with the people through whose country he passed. It was most important for many reasons, not the least of which was their lives. He knew only too well that he was among people to whom killing was not only a way of life, but also something that carried a good deal of prestige. Maybe it is difficult for people who have never been in such an isolated position to visualise what it is even remotely like. Those who are furthest from a problem are often the most moral.

The two brothers prospected far and wide in every direction with determination. They travelled through country that, because of its rugged nature, yielded little in the way of sustenance and the inhabitants were reluctant to offer any supplies. The belief that they were spirits from another world persisted. There were attacks and, inevitably, there were shootings.

They found gold at a place called Kuta, which raised their hopes. It had every appearance of a major deposit. Unfortunately, further examination failed to disclose anything of a sufficiently substantial nature to interest a company the size of Bulolo. It must be remembered that the international market price of gold was about £4 an ounce, a far cry from today's $400, and so because of the magnitude of their operations, any find would have to be big enough to support one or more dredges. These were the Depression years, too. Mick Leahy's greatest success had been in extracting finance from southern businessmen, but after a while that lode petered out, too.

The company backing him at the time of the Kuta discovery, because of the expense involved, decided that it was not big enough for them and the two brothers took it over. Even then it was not enough for two, and Mick Leahy sold his interest to Dan, who continued to work it and at the same time started a farm.

When war broke out in 1939, the impact was not felt in New Guinea until the Japanese entered the war in late 1941. Mick and Dan Leahy were commissioned at once, as their knowledge of the people and the country was invaluable, particularly in searching for airmen who had parachuted into the unknown and terrifying wilderness. They served with distinction and Mick Leahy was decorated – by the Americans.

After the war Dan continued to work the gold and his new farm. Mick made a home at Zenag, not far from the goldmining town of Wau. Another brother, Jim, went into business and farming at Goroka. At the time of writing in early 1990, Dan is the only survivor and is still living at Kuta. They were all my friends.

Many, many years later, I was sitting with Jim Taylor on the verandah of a bush house he had at Banz. By then he had married a local girl, Yerema, to whom he had a daughter, Meg, who was studying law at a Sydney university. He was a fascinating and erudite man, and I was never tired of hearing him talk of his early years in the Highlands, and his exploring trips with Mick Leahy, for whom he had a great regard. Jim was a very humane man, and always went to a considerable amount of trouble to understand the native people on his travels. I do not know of anyone who had a better rapport with them.

As the shadows lengthened and the sun slowly disappeared behind the Bismarcks, he quoted a few lines from a poem by, I think, Ella Wheeler Wilcox. I have always remembered them:

> *Wherever the white man's pathway leads,*
> *Far, far, has that pathway gone,*
> *The earth is littered with broken creeds*
> *And always the dark man's tent recedes*
> *And the white man pushes on.*
> *For this is the law, be it good or ill,*
> *The weak must yield to the stronger will.*

SEVEN

BANZ COFFEE GROWER

LANDING AT Minj the first time and knowing, as I did, the history of the opening up of the Wahgi, I found it difficult to believe that it was little more than twenty years since the first white man set eyes on this valley, since Mick Leahy led the first expedition into what was completely unknown country – a little more than twenty years since the first aeroplane landed. And, of course, it must also have been unique in the annals of exploration that these primitive people saw a plane before they saw a motor car, or for that matter a wheel.

I looked around me: the ADO was busy supervising twenty or so near-naked workers who were cheerfully unloading the aeroplane and carrying everything across to a group of buildings – the district headquarters, and nothing very elaborate, mostly built of bush timber and thatched roofs. The station hadn't been established long. When the unloading was finished the ADO, Bob McIlwain, asked me to lunch, 'While we work something out', he said. We went to his house, the only building with an iron roof, which, as I knew, was to catch rainwater that then ran into a couple of 1000-gallon tanks. I met his wife, a very pleasant animated lady; the table I noted was already laid for an extra person.

After lunch we went over to his office and for the next hour or so poured over a map examining several blocks of land that had been allocated and advertised. Bob took it for granted that I intended settling in the valley and by the time he had given me a rundown on the district and the two or three settlers that were already established, I had pretty well convinced myself. Of the people in the valley, those I didn't know I had heard of: Bob Gibbes, of airways fame, had a big property; Norm Plant was here, too, having come from the Lands Department to try his hand at coffee planting; Peter Maxtone-Graham, a former Administration officer from the Department of Agriculture; Bill Matthew; Alan Ferguson and Colin Toole. In the afternoon Bill Matthew and Alan Ferguson roared up, each piloting a three-wheel contraption fitted with a tray. They had come to collect cargo that had come on my plane. They were a jovial pair of characters who had been in the valley for about a year. Their plantation, Kinjibi, was well advanced. I had met both of them previously in my travels and I unhesitatingly accepted their offer to come and stay with them while looking around.

I bid farewell to the McIlwains and, with some misgivings, fitted myself onto a kind of tray on Bill's motor tricycle between some cargo. Leaving Minj must have sounded like the start of a grand prix, except it seemed a lot more dangerous. We tore over what was described as a road, scattering natives right, left and centre. We came to the Wahgi River, which was spanned by a crazy-looking suspension bridge that, to my surprise, we negotiated safely. We called at an embryo plantation for the purpose of, as Bill said, 'steadying our nerves'. Norman Plant and his attractive wife were just starting up. After refreshing ourselves there we went on a few more miles and came to Colin Toole's property, another newcomer. The one thing that impressed me was everyone's tremendous enthusiasm, it was convincing and infectious. Bill and Alan, who were old RAAF mates, lived with their wives in bush buildings, thatched with walls of woven bamboo.

It was getting cold as night closed in, but they soon had a roaring log fire going which, considering the nature of the building material, seemed a bit risky. After dinner they filled me in on a few facts and figures: labour was plentiful and they were happy workers. Apart from the local tracks such as the one over which we had just travelled, there were no outlets to the coast. Everything had to be flown in and out, and air freight was one shilling or, in local terms, one mark a pound. From the day a planter put his first coffee seedlings in the ground, it was five years before he could expect to see any return.

Bill and Alan were exceptionally resourceful men: they had built a waterwheel and, with a generator they had scrounged from an ex-army dump, they had an inexhaustible supply of electric light. With several rolls of wire from the same source, at a price Alan said no one would quibble at, they ran a telephone line from Kinjibi to Col Toole's place, on to Norm Plant's and from there to the Banz airstrip. The telephones were ex-army field phones, activated by strenuous cranking of the handle. They were also making very good beer, an activity that caught the gimlet eye of the Madang Collector of Customs. There had been the matter of certain items on a consignment note – malt, hops and crown seals – made out to Bill Matthew and Alan Ferguson. Here was essential brewing and bottling ingredients with illegal overtones – moonshine in the mountains!

Bill Dishon was the very competent District Commissioner stationed at Mount Hagen and when he called at Kinjibi Plantation and explained his mission, he was very apologetic. Bill and Alan had every reason to be concerned because not only was their beer's specific gravity – the measure of its strength – considerably above the legal limit, but also it was powerful enough to explode a bottle. As I can personally attest, this happened frequently.

They opened a bottle for the District Commissioner to sample, watched anxiously as he poured a glass, and intently peered at the bubbles rising to form a good healthy head; watched him taking a mouthful and swill it around in the approved professional manner, rolling it over his tongue, savouring its flavour. He turned to the two anxious brewers and delivered his verdict: 'Not as good as mine.'

The next few days I inspected various blocks that would be the subject of a Land Court to be held in Minj. The court would decide on the merits of the various applicants, which boiled down to 'whoever had the best story and was well backed financially'. There were a lot of pros and cons and although I realised that a pro was better than a con, or vice versa, I disregarded them. I eventually settled for 250 acres about five miles from the Banz airstrip. I filled in an application form, posted it off and made plans to return to the Sepik River area, where most of my income was generated. I also remembered that I had a partner in the Coral Sea dicing with death among man-eating sharks, filling our boat with trochus shell. Finance, I said bravely, was no problem.

We went to Banz airstrip and I hitched a ride on a Catholic Mission DC3 charter. Just before I boarded the plane, Bill Matthew said, 'You don't have to be mad to be a coffee planter, but it's a tremendous help'. I felt sure I could qualify.

I flew back to Angoram and as the aeroplane made its approach, I spotted a familiar boat tied up at the wharf, very much like the *Heron*. We landed and I went straight to the District Office to collect my mail. I asked Sepik Robbie about the boat at the wharf. 'It's the *Heron*,' he said, 'from what Madsen told me I think it's been a bit disappointing; you'll probably find him at the club.'

With some foreboding, I made my way to the club and found him sitting disconsolately at the bar with a woman and two ringtailed possums. The sad story didn't take long to tell. It seemed that pretty well the day he started his diving operations someone discovered how to make a plastic button that would stand up to boiling. Looking back, I suppose it didn't take much thinking about really, it would have been a very short step for the plastic people to come up with the answer. He said that the reefs were loaded with shell and when he had ten bags ready he sailed into Samarai and took them to Burns Philp's store, where the manager gave him the bad news.

He introduced me to the woman as Mary somebody, I didn't catch her surname, and she seemed to be quite infatuated with the two possums, which she referred to as karpuls, the pidgin term. Shortly after, she left us saying that she was going to get dinner ready, telling Madsen to bring me for the evening meal. When she had gone, I asked him where he had won that collection. He told me that she was the wife of a Trobriand Island planter and that he'd sort of got her accidently when he was anchored off one of the islands. She had been sailing a lakatoi, at which she was very proficient, and presumably was curious to know who the trochus fisherman was and came alongside. He invited her aboard, after which she became a regular visitor. He didn't go into any details about what happened after that except to say that she was a good cook. 'After a while you get used to them,' he said.

We talked for a while and I told him that I had applied for a block of land in the Western Highlands, but didn't intend letting the crocodile skin business go for at least another year. He said that he would be happy to again go skin buying for me, which I was pleased to hear.

I went through my mail and after sorting out the wheat from the chaff, I opened a letter from Lee Robinson. Lee was a film-maker and had formed a company with the actor Chips Rafferty. I had known both for some time among a fairly wide circle of Journalists' Club friends. They were coming to New Guinea to make a film, some of which would be shot in the Highlands and some on the Sepik River. The letter went on to explain that there would be about twenty in his party and he hoped that we could meet up as he was depending on me for some advice on all kinds of things like natives and native canoes, and he might want a couple of snakes – quiet ones. The name of the film was *Walk into Paradise*, and they would be making a start in Goroka some time in early June 1955. I showed the letter to Madsen and suggested that he might be able to help them. I could see that I wasn't going to be on the river that much from now on. He said, 'I don't mind helping them out with canoes and natives, but I'm buggered if I'm going to start snake charming'.

The next few days we were busy packing skins and as September 1955 faded away and October arrived, I had to arrange for an aeroplane to pick me up and get me to the Land Court. The wet season was approaching and some savage storms were building up, consequently radio transmission was bad and after a couple of days I was starting to get the jitters. On Wednesday 5 October I shared a charter with Colin Buscombe, a recruiter. The next day I was in Madang and on Friday

I flew into Goroka (a roundabout route but I was gradually getting closer; the weather was getting worse – and not gradually either). All Goroka flights were grounded and radio communication wasn't much better. Then there was the rapidly approaching addition to my family – I didn't want to get my priorities wrong, but anyway there were no problems in Sydney associated with cyclonic weather.

By midday the weather had started to clear. I had a private Tiger Moth standing by, the best that was available. It was owned by one of Bob Gibbes's pilots, Adrian Nisbet, who looked at the sky every few minutes somewhat grimly; the racing clouds were dark and formidable. As I well knew, we would be heading through the distinctly inhospitable Chimbu country, the terrain of which was practically straight up and down. At midday two blue holes appeared in lowering cloud cover, but not for long. Adrian said, 'Come on, let's get out of here while we've got a chance'.

I climbed into the open cockpit, buckled the seat belt as someone swung the prop, which quickly caught and fired, and we trundled down the runway and were soon airborne. It was hazy for a start, but it gradually cleared as we weaved our way from one hole to another. Once we got through the Chimbu Ranges, we saw the sun and were in the clear, and soon the Wahgi Valley was in front of us. We landed at Minj, where I was informed that the Land Court had been postponed until Monday. I was almost annoyed – all that exercise in apoplexy that I had been going through was wasted.

I went to Kinjibi with Bill Matthew and Alan Ferguson for the weekend and it didn't stop raining. By Monday the suspension bridge over the Wahgi River had washed away and the only way to get to the Land Court was to fly, if we could get an aeroplane. Alan got on to his Air Radio transmitter and after a lot of talking and pleading, extracted a promise from Bob Gibbes to send a Norseman over from Goroka. Adrian Nisbet was once again the pilot, and he was also an applicant for a block of land, which was good insurance. We piled into the plane – it was only three or four minutes' flying and I looked down on the surging Wahgi River and saw the suspension bridge dangling in the water. We landed and made our way to the Land Court, which was already in progress in the District Office. There was only Adrian and myself to be heard. Adrian was first and then I breasted 'the bar' and presented my credentials to the court, which consisted of the Director of Lands, the ADO and one other fellow I didn't know. I said my piece, not very confidently, and left immediately. Adrian was already in the plane with the engine ticking over, I climbed in and we took off for Goroka. Now it was a matter for the Land Court to assess the various applicants on their merits. All I had to do now was to sweat it out; I imagined that it would take at least a week, perhaps longer.

I spent a few days in Madang supervising the shipping of eight cases of crocodile skins to Sydney; the tannery had been sending out an SOS. From there I headed for Wewak and back once more to Angoram. Sepik Robbie said that Madang was asking where I was – they had some telegrams for me. They all came on the afternoon radio schedule at four o'clock. I found that I had a daughter born on the ninth, the Land Board recommended that I be granted a block of land in the Wahgi Valley, and, lastly, a telegram from Singapore advised that the crocodile skin market had taken a slight rise – my cup was overflowing.

I went back to the club and threw a handful of notes on the bar, inviting all and sundry to drink the health of my new daughter, an offer that was taken up with enthusiasm the depth of which I underestimated, it being necessary to replenish the offer a few times – how many times I am unable to say.

We put the *Heron* up for sale and in the meantime it would earn its keep carrying salt up the river and skins back. I flew back to New Britain, where I shipped a few cases of skins to Singapore and from there I flew to Moresby where I caught up with Lee Robinson and Chips Rafferty, who were doing a preliminary survey. They planned to start filming after the wet and plied me with questions about the Sepik River, but when it got to snakes I wasn't much help. I suggested a crocodile, but Lee said that Michelle, their leading lady, was scared of crocodiles – what she thought about snakes they didn't say. I can't remember quite how that particular scene went, but as far as I can recall there was to be a very tense moment where she was to be bitten by a snake, which they wanted to be as authentic as possible. Couldn't some of my lads get them a nice, quiet snake? I said that I'd see what I could do and asked whereabouts she was going to be bitten, but they hadn't worked that out. I then asked what the leading lady thought about all this, recalling her crocodile allergy. 'She doesn't know about that part yet,' Lee said, 'Chips dreamt it up and I thought that well handled, it would make an exciting scene.' I reckoned it might, too – especially when Michelle found out about it.

I didn't get back to Sydney until the end of January 1956 and I concentrated on getting to know the not-so-new arrival, Gabrielle, who treated me with a mixture of curiosity and disdain; very young children have a great capacity for disdain. I started to study books, some on agricultural machinery and others on how to grow coffee, most of the latter being unhelpful.

My friends, with few exceptions, thought that I was out of my mind, especially when I described the completely inaccessible Shangri La that could only be reached by aeroplane. I never attempted to argue with anyone about the state of my mind, after all, I'd known I was crazy a lot longer than them. Even when I was reasonably normal I don't think anyone would have noticed much difference.

We went to the mountains for ten days, where I hired some good horses and took Kathryn for her first ride. Then it was back to Sydney where, according to my diary, I was busy tidying up a few loose ends. Today I find some of the entries a little mystifying. It appears that Alan Anderson and I planned to buy the Angoram sawmill, but beyond that brief statement, nothing seems to have happened. I bought a Geiger counter for someone, today I can't imagine why, maybe he was radioactive. An artificial horizon had to be picked up at Bankstown for someone else, obviously an airman.

I had shopping to do for myself, too, and spent some time looking for a tractor that would fit into an aeroplane like a Douglas freighter. Going from crocodile hunting to coffee planting was a flying leap in the dark, but I was starting to look forward to the new challenge. I also was looking forward to getting my family together, but that wouldn't be for a year or so as there was so much to do.

There was one very heartening feature: the group of planters already established in the Wahgi Valley were staunch, sensible and helpful. The first week in April I reluctantly dragged myself away and flew back to Port Moresby. Vince Sanders greeted me with good news, or what sounded like good news. He had sold my boat to an adventurous, young crocodile hunter from whom I received neither the money nor any skins; he just disappeared – maybe he ended up in a Goaribari cooking pot, I hoped so anyway.

After a couple of days I headed for the Highlands to look over my latest acquisition, my 150 acres that ran down on to the Wahgi River, bounded on one side by the Anye Creek and on the other by another creek called Sigri. I decided that Sigri would do for a name and so Sigri Plantation came into being. Getting the place started didn't seem to present any difficulties: there was a village nearby that was a logical source of labour. Norman Plant, who had a property adjoining, had signified his willingness to manage it initially. After a talk we came to a satisfactory arrangement. The first thing was to get a labour line together. I thought about fifty, it didn't need too many for a start.

We sent a runner across to the village for the headman to come over for discussions, but as I had already found out a long time ago, nothing happens in a hurry and it wasn't until the next day that the village policeman appeared, flanked by a couple of tribesmen carrying deadly looking spears. He gravely explained that while they would be happy to start work, they couldn't begin right away because there was a fight coming up, which would start the next day. As soon as the fight was over he would bring a line of workers to Sigri.

I asked what it was about and it seemed that two women who had been working in an isolated garden had been captured and taken back to a village in the mountains. The two tribes involved were traditional enemies and from what I could make out, there was something of an ongoing war that broke out periodically. They thought they would be ready to come to work in two or three days. I gave the village policeman, whose name was Mek, some tobacco and away they went, presumably to sharpen their spears and arrows for the coming conflict. Fights such as these were very much a part of their lifestyle. If they got serious sometimes the Kiap would step in and read the riot act, but usually it was all over by the time he found out.

I went back to Kinjibi Plantation to get myself clued up on coffee planting. Norman would give me a ring over the field telephone as soon as the skirmish was over. A couple of days later I called up to find out how the hostilities were proceeding and was told one of Mek's warriors had been wounded. Norman doubted he would survive, which turned out to be true. Another spanner in the works. There was a compulsory sing-sing accompanied by funeral rites and maybe another 'payback' fight. It could go on for some time. As it turned out, they were glad to postpone any further hostilities for the time being. There was always another day for a fight.

Eventually the smoke of battle had died away and we were able to muster and sign on fifty workers. Their names were entered in a book that was used for calling the roll in the morning. This took time, as some of the names were quite complicated, or seemed so to us, many of them being of several syllables with a pronounced guttural sound. A boss boy was appointed, and a spade and a sarif (a long steel blade for grass cutting) was issued to each worker. In the Highlands the workers were known as 'cargo boys'. I never found out how or why they were referred to thus. The expression was not used on the coastal plantations.

Work started at seven o'clock in the morning and finished at five o'clock. They were summoned by a bell in the morning; it sounded again at midday for an hour's break and at knock-off time. The first task was to get a seedbed going. I had obtained a half hundred weight of seed for this purpose from one of the Government experimental agricultural stations.

I was starting to realise what kind of mammoth job I had taken on when this job was finished – from the time of planting the seed to the first picking of coffee beans was, at the earliest, five years. I would have liked going into a state of suspended animation for the next few years. I stayed another week, but Norman Plant seemed to have the situation well in hand and I decided I'd be better off generating some income. I flew back to the Sepik. Crocodile skins were my life's blood and would continue to be for some time.

There was a stack of mail at the post office, among which was a brief missive from the Superintendent of Police at Wewak, John Grainger, saying that one of his native police had been taken by a shark, and would I please come over and catch it. I was surprised that he asked me – I didn't know anything about sharks – but I was quite happy to have a look, it was something different. The following day I was on my way to Wewak. It was only a half hour flight and the superintendent was at the airport to meet me. On the drive into town, which was five miles away, he told me about the attack. There were two policemen spear-fishing off Moem Point, and the shark circled them once before attacking. From the description the survivor gave, it must have come in very fast and had taken his partner's head off in one savage bite. Grainger was surprised at how white the body was when they fished him from the water. I could easily believe it, the salt water would have drawn every drop of blood from the body.

The Government launch had gone out almost immediately and re-covered the body and the head, too, which I thought surprising. The superintendent wasn't by any means surprised. 'He was one of my best policemen, but I always made sure I was well to the windward of him whenever I was talking to him – his breath was something terrible. As soon as that shark got his head in his mouth, he would have spat it out and not wasted any time either.'

I had brought some cable with me and a few hooks. They obtained a dead dog from somewhere and we went out in the police launch to where the man had been taken. I spliced a trace onto a couple of hooks and fastened each one to an empty four-gallon drum, which in turn were anchored to the reef. After that was completed, we went up to the hotel to strengthen ourselves for the coming ordeal. One of the policemen would keep us informed. The next day one of them appeared at the hotel: we had caught a grey nurse, but the policeman who brought the news was most emphatic that it wasn't the right one. However, the superintendent was happy with the catch and said it would keep the prisoners in food for a couple of days. It certainly wasn't big enough to bite a man's head off. We were all in agreement that the man-eater was still enjoying life out on the reef somewhere, hoping for another spearfisherman to turn up. After killing the grey nurse, a jubilant sergeant took it away to the police barracks cook house. Another day went by and just before sundown a police truck raced up to the hotel, its horn blowing furiously, with half a dozen policemen in the back sitting on a fourteen-foot grey nurse. This time there was no doubt that we had captured the man-eater.

In the meantime, I was becoming interested in a murder trial that had been in progress for the last couple of days. It was remarkable for several reasons: the number of prisoners, the number of people killed, and the manner of the killing, which could more accurately be described as a massacre. Forty Iwam tribesmen from the May River, a tributary of the Sepik, were being tried for the murder of twenty-nine people from the upper reaches of the Yellow River. The Iwam people were a fairly large and warlike group whose villages were clustered along the May River, and, as was common among the people of the middle and upper reaches of the Sepik, they were enthusiastic cannibals. The region came under the jurisdiction of the Telefomin patrol post. The country was difficult of access and the people of such a ferocious nature, coupled with their enthusiasm for human flesh, that their neighbours were in a permanent state of mortal terror.

Some time earlier, an Iwam man had died under a hail of arrows. He was the eldest son of one of the tribal elders, a man of considerable standing, his prestige having been gained in battle, as a number of decorated skulls in the men's Dubu House testified. The death of his eldest son had shocked and saddened him. It was a personal affront by a distinctly inferior people. He called a meeting, telling the assembled tribesmen that the death must be avenged – at the same time reminding them that a successful raid would not only repair a serious vitamin deficiency, but also make a valuable contribution to the men's Dubu House, where the spoils of the chase in the shape of aesthetically and tastefully decorated heads testified to their artistic abilities.

Recalling the Telefomin murders mentioned earlier, it had been some time since the killing of Harris and Szarka, and the Iwam may have been under the impression that due to the isolation of their villages and the difficult rain-drenched terrain, as well as the infrequency of Government patrols, they could kill a few neighbouring tribesmen without any interference. They had always done it – it was a way of life.

Nahi, whose son Kwaso had been killed, was an accomplished orator and it did not take long for him to work his fellow tribesmen into a state of frenzy. Since the Harris and Szarka murders, there had been a falling away in internecine warfare. Having secured the backing of most of the warriors, a plan of action was worked out. The fact that they had lost only one tribesman had no bearing whatever on their plan for reprisal. Whether they were men, women or children was of no consequence whatever; in their raids no one was spared, except perhaps a comely girl who happened to take someone's fancy.

The Iwam tribal leaders, after several days of deliberation, planned a massacre of unparalleled, cold-blooded treachery. They first had to gain the confidence of the people they intended to slaughter and so several unarmed men, a couple of old women and children to dispel suspicion, set off in two canoes to make friendly overtures. After some initial scouting they came across some women making sago. They called to them, declaring friendship, saying that the Kiap had told them that the fighting must stop and that they wanted to meet with the Yellow River leaders. They would go through the ritual of breaking spears, and bows and arrows and exchanging gifts.

Having been killed and eaten at fairly regular intervals for untold generations, they would undoubtedly have been happy with the approach. Furthermore, when the Iwams said that the Kiap had been lecturing them on the evils of fighting and telling them that they were to give it up, it was perfectly true; he told them the same thing on every patrol. No one took much notice; they nodded their heads respectfully while they impatiently dug the ground with their toes, wishing he would go away and mind his own business. There were so many things Kiaps didn't understand. Anyway, this time perhaps it was true – if the Iwams wanted peace he must have been very impressive.

A meeting was arranged at a place on the Sepik River. The headmen and village policemen were to have their ceremonial spear, and bow and arrow breaking ceremony in a week's time when the moon was full. The Iwam people in five canoes reached the rendezvous first, which was part of their devious plan. By so doing they could choose the most advantageous position and have their weapons strategically placed and covered. In order to dispel suspicion further, they also brought two or three old women and a couple of lads.

When the intended victims arrived, they were greeted with a great demonstration of goodwill. Gifts were exchanged and they sat down together, declaring friendship and peace for ever and a day. Then the ceremonial weapon breaking and burning began with great rejoicing. When the Iwams were satisfied that their victims had smashed and burnt the last spear, the last bow and arrow, they tensely waited for the fatal words that were to signal the start of an horrific massacre.

At this point a group of women crossed the river for some purpose, perhaps to collect some kind of fruit, when one of the Iwams stood up and said, 'Nakuno, I want to eat sago'. Taken completely unawares, surrounded, unarmed and outnumbered, the frenzied killing began, and apart from the terrified women watching from the other bank, none escaped. Men, women and children were mercilessly slaughtered with spear, tomahawk and arrows. When the carnage was over, twenty-nine lay dead. The bodies were cut up, the heads removed and taking as much flesh as they could carry, they returned to their village. Although twenty-nine were killed only twenty heads were taken – in the frenzy of killing some were so badly smashed that they were unsuitable for decoration. They took their gruesome spoils to the village of Wanimoi, the biggest of the group.

Because of my own affairs, I was unable to follow the trial for more than a few hours over a couple of days, the translation of evidence being a laborious business. However, it was well covered by local journalists and reporters from several southern newspapers. The evidence was overwhelming and the prosecution was ably assisted by one of the Iwams, who enthusiastically turned Queen's evidence. This was by no means uncommon and the one who turned on his fellows would return happily to his tribe where none would bear him ill will. The forty prisoners were condemned to death, but as was normal the sentences were commuted to a term of imprisonment. Before the curtain rang down on this grisly episode, the judge instructed that the twenty skulls, which were exhibits at the trial, be returned to the Yellow River people. It is interesting to note that although these people were known to be practising cannibals and that canoe-loads of human flesh were taken back to Wanimoi, unquestionably for the purpose of a feast, it was not brought up at the trial – for there was no law against cannibalism in Papua New Guinea.

Some were cruel and ruthless people who killed with equal savagery and indifference. An example of the latter was related in Judge Gore's splendid book, *Justice versus Sorcery*, in which he told of a case that came before him. In a fit of ungovernable rage, a man speared his wife to death over a minor domestic matter. She came from a village some distance away and when the news reached the ears of her relatives, two brothers set off to avenge the killing. It was a two-day walk and they spent the first night at a village, where they were well known and made welcome. When they explained their mission, one of their hosts, as a matter of goodwill, offered to accompany them and assist in the 'payback'. This generous offer was gratefully accepted and on the following morning the three set off together.

It was some distance to their destination, and the heat of the tropical sun became so great that they began to lose their enthusiasm for their crusade. They came to a stream where a man was sitting on a log, singing quietly to himself and making arrows. Remaining hidden they had a brief conference and quickly came to the conclusion that he would do. They crept up on the unsuspecting maker of arrows and shot him dead. Regarding their mission as having been accomplished, they returned to their respective villages.

In the fullness of time, the relatives of the unfortunate arrowmaker learned who the killers were, which was not very difficult. The friend who so unselfishly gave his assistance saw no reason why he should keep his sporting activity to himself, and the two brothers of the dead woman they set out to avenge were anxious to claim their share of notoriety. The very worst they could expect, or so they thought, was a further extension of the 'payback' system, a lifestyle they grew up with. However, in this case, the fellow tribesmen of the unfortunate arrowmaker went to the Kiap who, without a great deal of difficulty, rounded them up and brought them back to his station. At the trial, the three killers eloquently and confidently explained to Mr Justice Gore why they had killed the unfortunate arrowmaker, emphasising that it was their way of life or, as the interpreter translated it into pidgin English, 'fashion bilong me fella'. The judge was equally eloquent and far more confident in his summing up. He sentenced them to death, which was commuted to a term of imprisonment.

I got back to the Sepik the same day as Les Ingle arrived from up river in the *Sealark* with a load of recruits and 300 crocodile skins. He was anxious to get away the same day and asked me to come with him, which I thought was a good idea; he was good company and flying was very boring. We left that evening, cruised down the river and anchored at the mouth where one of the crew caught some fine fish. At four o'clock in the morning I heard the anchor being raised and the engine throbbing into life. I joined Les in the wheelhouse for a mug of coffee as we turned into the open sea. The weather was good and we tied up at Madang some time after sundown.

I spent a week in Madang grading and packing 1200 skins, mostly for Singapore, and suddenly November popped up. I decided that I'd like to have a look at Sigri Plantation and in a moment of alcoholic exuberance bought a BSA motorbike, which I was sure would be of some use to Norman Plant for transport from his place to Sigri. After a couple of trial rides around Madang, I put it on an aeroplane, accompanied it to Banz and startled Norman and terrified the cargo boys when I roared up to his house. As it turned out, he couldn't ride one, but I found it good fun to tear about on.

Sigri was undulating country covered with a broad-bladed grass known locally as kunai. It was used for thatching, but it all had to be cut and burnt off before the ground could be prepared for planting. The labour line now consisted of seventy workers and quite a lot of progress had been made, but the seedbed that had been established some time ago was very disappointing, and was making a gallant attempt to compete with the healthiest weed I'd ever seen.

On Norman's property, Amuliba, a comfortable house had been erected of native material, thatched roof and woven bamboo walls. Because of the cold nights, he had constructed a huge fireplace of cement and stone that, because of the nature of the building material, struck me as presenting an alarming fire hazard. His wife Suzanne was a beautiful young woman who was coping remarkably well with the primitive conditions, two children and another on the way. She was the daughter of a doctor who had served with some distinction in the First World War, as was evidenced by a personal letter from King George V in his own handwriting that was framed and took pride of place among various family photographs and other memorabilia.

After a few days I started to get bored – there was nothing I could do to speed things up and I probably was more a hindrance than a help. I went back to Madang and called at the only bank, housed in an ex-army Quonset hut that crackled in the intense heat. I arranged with the perspiring manager to keep Plant supplied with funds, if not liberally at least regularly. It was November when I flew back to Sydney. It was becoming increasingly important to be with my young family at Christmas, also to reassure them that it would not be too long before they would be able to join me in a new home on the plantation – something they were looking forward to with great anticipation.

I returned in April and Moresby was my first stop, but there wasn't a great deal to claim my attention. I drove up to the foothills of the Owen Stanley Ranges outside Moresby and spent the weekend with Colin and Joan Sefton at Koitaki Plantation, which Colin managed.

The Royal Yacht *Britannia* was in Moresby harbour and on Sunday Prince Philip came to lunch at the Seftons. There were two or three other luncheon guests and we were all presented. When the prince and I shook hands, I was surprised to find that he was not as tall as I had thought, or as he appeared to be in his photographs, but he was very natural and jolly, and quickly put everyone at ease.

Then it was back to earth and Port Moresby on Monday to find a plane heading for Madang. I boarded a Norseman full of plantation workers returning to their village; they smelt like several years of accumulated sweat. There was no difficulty in following Rudyard Kipling's injunction: 'Walk with kings yet not lose the common touch'.

In Madang I bought an ex-army jeep for £400 and a trailer for £200. It just fitted into a Douglas freighter. I went out to the aerodrome to arrange for a flight to Banz, but was told to come back tomorrow. I don't know exactly how it happened, but next day I found myself on a Mandated Airlines DC3 under charter to labour recruiter Colin Buscombe. Having flown over that route a few times, it seemed to me that we weren't on track for Banz. I walked up to the cockpit and asked the pilot where he was going. 'Goroka,' he said, 'why, where did you think we were going?' When I told him Banz he roared laughing, and said, 'Well, it's only a hundred-mile drive, if there haven't been any landslides, you should do it in a day'.

I found Buscombe in the bar of the only hotel and told him that I'd brought a jeep and trailer up on his charter, and that I thought the plane was going to Banz. He thought it was a great joke, too, and when I asked him how much he wanted for the flight, he airily waved a hand and said, 'Forget about it, buy me a few drinks and we'll call it square'.

Two days later, with some trepidation, I jumped in my jeep and set off for Banz. It was 100 miles of the most death-defying driving I'd ever undertaken. It wasn't too bad for the first twenty miles or so, but then the road started to climb towards Daulo Pass, which was more than 7000 feet in swirling mists and drizzling rain. In some places the road edged along the side of a mountain, which fell away in sheer drops of 1000 feet and more. The many creeks were crossed on rickety bridges of bush timber that swung perilously over surging torrents. It was terrifyingly beautiful.

Going through Chimbu district, I passed numerous villages. This was the most heavily populated area in the whole of the islands and the hillsides were covered with well kept gardens, mostly sweet potato, which seemed to be their staple diet. There was very little flat land and most cultivated areas were terraced to prevent them washing away. Many of them were almost vertical, so steep was the terrain. I passed Chuave, a Government station, and then through Kundiawa, which was not only a Government station but also an established outpost with a couple of trade stores, two Mission stations and an airstrip squashed in between the mountains. After leaving Kundiawa, the country started to level off slightly, enough for another airstrip for small, single-engine planes at Kerowagi, also a Government station. At last I came to Banz – it was the hardest 100 miles I had ever driven.

My crocodile business was now starting to tail off and Sigri was starting to take shape, beginning to look like a plantation. The labour

A smoked man from the Kukuku Tribe — the body is smoked and painted with red ochre, then placed on a ledge cave on a mountain top

Bringing a dead warrior home (National Library)

Prow of traditional Sepik canoe

Footbridge constructed entirely of vines
with bamboo walkway —
Western Highlands (National Library)

Robert Menzies' visit to Banz, 1962

A native policeman (left), a tribesman dressed for the sing-sing to welcome Sir Robert Menzies, and the author

Part of the sing-sing to welcome Sir Robert Menzies

Unloading the first Range Rover in Papua New Guinea

Gabrielle, Tom and Kathleen Cole on the Konigle Bridge on the road to Goroka

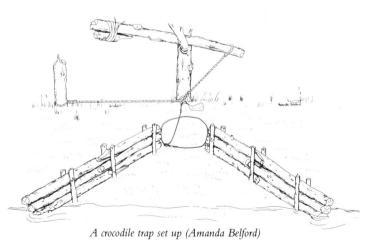

A crocodile trap set up (Amanda Belford)

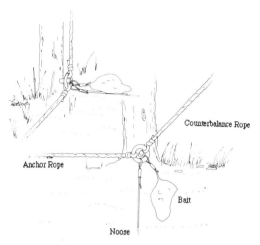

Crocodile trap in detail (Amanda Belford)

Crocodile taking the bait (Amanda Belford)

The maneater of Marshall Lagoon

Young coffee plants — on the author's plantation when it was first established

A crossing made easier by local assistance — near the plantation

Kathryn (left) and Gabrielle near the plantation, 1960

line was up to 100 men, and twenty acres of seedlings had been planted out. I had a large shed built of native material, which was serving, for the time being, as a residence for me and although the nights were cold, I resisted the temptation to install a fireplace. I had marked out a site for a house, but the thought of flying in enough material for even a very modest abode was more than daunting.

There were now quite a few settlers in the valley. Colin Toole, one of the earlier planters, was on the Kimil River, a few miles from my place. His wife had been one of Bob Gibbes's pilots, flying out of Wewak. Colin had managed the Wewak branch of Gibbes Sepik Airways. Pat Graham, as she was then, had once experienced an unnerving trip when returning to Wewak and heavy cloud obscured the Torricelli Ranges – the gap through which she had to fly to reach Wewak. There were no airstrips within range of her dwindling fuel supply, and she had to make a forced landing that would have been a frightening experience for the most experienced pilot. Pat chose a creek bed and executed a brilliant landing without damaging her aeroplane.

This was by no means the end of her worries; although she had no doubt that a search would be initiated at first light the next morning, Pat knew that she was in an area where the natives would only be regarded as partly controlled and were known to have cannibalistic tendencies. The sun set and darkness quickly enveloped the surrounding jungle. Pat locked herself in the cabin of the aeroplane and, as she told me, spent the night in a state of mortal terror in conditions that could only be compared to a pressure cooker.

At dawn the next day, half a dozen aeroplanes roared into life at Wewak. The aircraft with Pat standing beside it waving furiously was quickly discovered. Even then her troubles were by no means over and it was days later when Patrol Officer Laurie Nolen walked in with a line of carriers, who fashioned a kind of sedan chair from bush material to carry her out. It was several days more before she reached Wewak. The aeroplane was dismantled and also carried out, which was no mean achievement.

At that time she and Colin were engaged to be married and shortly after the knot was tied and they came to the Highlands and took up 300 acres of land, which they called Kalanga, the native name for that area. I had known both of them from my earliest crocodile hunting days and a close friendship had developed over the years. Now they were only a few miles from Sigri, and we saw quite a lot of each other. The Banz airstrip was a favoured meeting place when the weekly aeroplane arrived from Madang and most of us gathered to collect mail and the various necessities of life.

We were all leading a fairly primitive life in houses and shacks built of bush timber, thatched roofs and woven walls. Even the Government Patrol Officers were similarly housed. They appeared to be running on a very tight budget and as the Wahgi Valley was the most recent area opened up for settlement, it was a bit low on priorities.

There was a new sawmill up in the foothills of the Bismarcks run by a well known character, Bluey McNamara, a very tough bushman who could demolish a bottle of rum in a competent and workmanlike manner. There was an insatiable demand for his produce, particularly bridge decking, which would certainly have been his most profitable line. Enquiries about enough timber for a house had resulted in a quotation somewhere in the gold-plated class.

However, a small ray of sunshine seeped through when I heard that Bluey wasn't overwhelmingly happy in his mountain fastness. It was a long time between drinks when the nearest pub was something over 100 miles away. It was rumoured that Bluey would be more than happy to transfer his affections to somewhere where the proximity of hotels could be measured in yards instead of miles. Buying a sawmill was a bit beyond my resources. The following week at the Banz airstrip I put it to Colin, 'How would you feel about buying Bluey McNamara's sawmill?' I think it shook him a bit, 'Buy Bluey's sawmill? I don't know, do you think he would sell?'.

'Well,' I said cautiously, 'I have heard a rumour, maybe he would, if he would what about you and I buying it?'

'I'd have to give it a lot of thought, do you know what it's worth?'

'No idea at all and it depends how badly he wants to sell, he's got some good Government bridge decking contracts, but I don't know how much timber there is; for all we know it could be cut out.'

'Well, I'd certainly be interested, we could sound him out,' he said.

A few days later, armed with a couple of bottles of Bluey's favourite tipple, we headed for the sawmill. We went up there in Colin's jeep, a four-wheel drive, but it was a vile road and we got bogged several times. It was only five miles, but it took us an hour and a half. After some preliminary skirmishing and the first bottle of rum had bit the dust, Bluey said he'd think about it. By four o'clock the sun was getting low and the second bottle was finished. Bluey said he'd sleep on it, and was half asleep at that stage anyway. We decided to go – it was no kind of a road to travel in the dark. Col's jeep had only one headlight and we were in no shape to dig it out if we got stuck. We knew where the bad spots were and managed to avoid getting bogged.

A few days later we went back to the sawmill. We agreed that if he couldn't give us a decision, we'd drop the idea and perhaps start one of our own. I couldn't help thinking that we were going at it a bit blind, particularly in view of our knowledge of sawmills, which was five eighths of bugger-all. His equipment was pretty basic, at least I thought so. He had a big tractor for moving the logs; it also powered the circular saws. It seemed he pulled logs in the morning and cut timber in the afternoon. The mill was in the middle of a stand of timber, the bulk of which, as far as I could judge, was mostly good stuff.

Bluey greeted us effusively. We had some more grog, of course, and got down to business right away. Col said, 'What's the score Bluey? Do you want to sell or not?'.

He obviously sensed our mood. 'Yes, I'll sell for £3000 cash.'

Col and I looked at each other. All he had was a Fordson tractor, which if not clapped out certainly looked like it. There were some circular saws, belting snigging chains and various odds and ends. We opened a bottle of tiger juice and started arguing. After two or three hours we got him down to £2500, with £1000 deposit and the balance over six months. We exchanged letters, Bluey offering us the mill, walk in walk out for £2500, Colin and I agreeing to buy, the finer details to be fixed up in Madang the following week. We didn't waste any more time. We left him a couple of bottles of liquid dynamite and departed. We arrived at Kalanga just on dark. Pat didn't have to ask me to dinner twice – I gratefully accepted, and ended up staying overnight.

The next day was Tuesday 28 May 1957. The entry in my diary reads: 'Returned to Sigri this morning. There has been a fight while I was away. One of my cargo boys has been badly speared in the stomach and another in the arm. 150 natives have been arrested.' When the roll was called the next morning, I had nineteen workers left. It would take some time to get the labour line back to full strength. It was another occasion when it would have suited me fine to go into a state of suspended animation for a few weeks.

A few days later, the three of us, Colin, Bluey and I, hopped on to a DC3 freighter and flew down to Madang. It was normally about a half hour flight, but could take up to half a day depending on the weather. Today cloud hung over the Bismarcks and the pilot turned east until he found a break in the clouds, which brought us close to the towering peak of Mt Wilhelm, streaked with snow. From there we rapidly lost altitude, and the sea, dotted with islands, came into view. Shortly after, we landed on the crushed coral airstrip.

There was only one hotel, owned and run by a dear old character 'Ma' Gilmour. Ma, as she was known to everyone, had been through the mill, from mining fields to plantations to hotels, and there wasn't much about New Guinea that she and Jack, her husband, didn't know. The hotel overlooked the harbour and had well kept lawns running down to the water's edge.

We knew that if we wanted to get our timber mill business over and done with we'd have to keep a tight rein on McNamara. Once he got stuck into the booze, it wouldn't be long before he wouldn't be able to sign his name. There was one lawyer in the town and it didn't take long to arrange a meeting; I don't think he was overwhelmed with business. It all turned out to be very simple and straightforward. Bluey's anxiety to get his hands on our money was sufficient inducement to keep him on the straight and narrow.

When it was all tidied up, we chartered a DC3 and filled it up with four tons of corrugated roofing iron, cases of nails, guttering, assorted piping and miscellaneous material. Lew Connerty, a carpenter, was to come up in a week's time. There was every chance that my family would be able to join me for Christmas.

It was 1 June 1957 when a tragedy claimed everyone's attention. Jack Gray had a small charter airline, Territory Airlines. He was well known and popular. His fleet consisted of three or four aeroplanes, one of which was a Tiger Moth. I had flown with him in the little aeroplane more than once. On this occasion he had taken off from Goroka heading for Madang: with him was Jim Smith, who had a coffee plantation in which Jack Gray had an interest. He never arrived in Madang. A few days later the wreckage of the aircraft was found in Arona Gap. Both men had been killed. It was established that on that day the gap was clouded in. It was a classic example of the injunction, 'No see, no go'. Jack Gray was a bold pilot and, as we frequently heard, there were old pilots and bold pilots – but there were no old bold pilots.

While it could not be said that there were more fatal aircraft disasters in New Guinea than any other country, we certainly had our share, far more than Australia, or so it seemed. This was probably due to the fact that everybody just about knew everyone else, and I am sure there were not many countries in the world where it was almost the only form of travel. At that time there would have been very few pilots that I did not know personally; when one was killed we all felt it very much.

Apart from the odd skirmishes I soon found out that 100 or so on the labour line did not necessarily mean an equal number of workers – malaria was a rampant and savage decimator. I would buy the malaria suppressor Paludrine by the bucketful, and fortunately it was readily available from the Department of Health. A normal fall-out from this mosquito-born affliction was about eight per cent, the most common indicator being severe headache and high temperature. Mosquito nets were issued to every worker, but this savage insect was almost equally active in the daytime, especially in the shaded areas among the coffee. I was subject to frequent bouts so I knew exactly how they felt. It was a most unpleasant and depressing affliction that no one escaped.

Colin Toole and I were now beginning to find out what it was like to own a sawmill. The Bismarck foothills had long been a native battle-ground and felling trees for a sawmill was merely an interlude while fresh supplies of arrows were fashioned, spears sharpened and bark shields strengthened. War was always simmering in the background.

Colin took on the management, as he lived much closer to the mill. We had a miller named Bill Jones who took over the sawbench, but soon discovered that if we were going to fulfil our bridge decking orders and get enough timber for our houses, we'd need more equipment. At the top of the shopping list was another tractor, so we ordered one. Then, one morning, Colin arrived at Sigri as I was halfway through calling the roll. When I had finished and apportioned the work for the day, he asked me could I come over and run the labour line at the mill because he had to take Bill Jones to the hospital. He said that it wasn't serious, he'd been speared in the leg, a flesh wound but there was a bit of spear still in the leg. I was curious to know how Bill had managed to get himself wounded, but there wasn't much forthcoming; it seemed it was a domestic affair and Bill was anxious to avoid any publicity. I didn't pursue it further.

The day I spent at the sawmill overseeing the felling of majestic trees to feed our mill was one that I will always remember. It was long before any movement had developed to save the destruction of forests, although when one crashed to the ground I couldn't help feeling sorry to see such grandeur destroyed. After a chainsaw had cut through it, I attempted to count the rings to establish the age. I knew that each ring represented a year's growth, but it was not as simple as I thought. I believe some were more than 100 years old and in the prime of life.

Our boss boy, a powerful fellow with the sturdy legs of a mountain dweller, told me when I questioned him that there would be another fight, but was vague about when it was likely to take place. I noticed that while they worked, most of them would frequently cut saplings, which I had no doubt were for spear and arrow material. I thought the next battle would be when they had accumulated sufficient weapons.

We were building up a good supply of timber suitable for our houses and I had found a carpenter who was due any day. Lew Connerty had been working for the Administration, but had left the shelter of Government pay to start up on his own. Right now, he had been out of work for a week. He promised to have my house finished by Christmas.

Planting was proceeding apace. From the nurseries the young seedlings were taken to the newly prepared ground for planting out. In the early stages, the dark green foliage of the young plants had to be protected from the harsh rays of the sun, which was harmful to the delicate young seedlings in the early stages of their transfer. They were covered with an umbrella of dried grass, supported on a frame of sticks. As they strengthened, they would push their way through the flimsy covering, which would gradually disintegrate. To protect them further, a more permanent from of shade was planted, one of the Albizia group, which would spread a tracery of shade until the coffee plants reached a more mature stage. Some of the bushes of the earliest plantings, as is normal with nature, were exhibiting a precociousness and were endeavouring to flaunt their maturity with a display of flowers, a delicate, white, fragile blossom that gave off a delightful, haunting scent.

Because of the paucity of coffee-growing information available, I had taken every opportunity that presented itself to familiarise myself with the young industry. The earliest plantings were in the Goroka district and some of the plantations were in production. I found that the planters there were generous with their advice and I was always welcome to visit them. I grasped every opportunity to increase my meagre knowledge of the various aspects of the industry.

When the flowering had run its course, the berries appeared, dark green at first, gradually changing colour as they developed to yellow, orange, and finally a bright red when, because of their similarity, they were known as cherries. It always seemed that the final ripening process took place overnight – one day the crop would be an orange colour and the next the entire plantation would have turned bright red. Then would start the frenzy of picking.

The cherries would be picked and carried to a central point from where they would be carted by truck or tractor to the factory. Here they were put through a machine called a pulper, which expressed two kidney-shaped beans from the soft covering that enveloped them. The pulping machine diverted the pulp one way and the beans into a large concrete tank. When expressed from the cherry, the beans were covered with a mucilage, a slimy coating, which had to be removed. This was quite simple: they were left for two or three days during which a natural fermentation took place. The next step was washing, which involved pouring thousands of gallons of water into the fermenting vat, washing the slime away. It was then put out to dry.

The drying could either be achieved by exposing the beans to the sun or using a mechanical dryer. When dried, the stage was known as parchment, so-called because of a parchment-like skin covering the beans. This had to be removed and this was done in a machine called a huller. The resulting bean was a grey-green colour known as a green bean. The beans were then graded according to size and bagged.

It was obvious that before a planter could enjoy any benefits from his labours, he would require lots of patience and a kindly and well disposed bank manager.

In August 1957, I received a bundle of remarkable correspondence which, judging by the redirection notices, had been taking its time to catch up with me. Originally the letters were addressed to Sydney, and my wife, not being sure of my whereabouts, had redirected them to my

Port Moresby PO box. They had made a brief call at Madang and Wewak, finally arriving at Sigri in a very tired and battered state.

Earlier in the year the Sydney *Daily Telegraph* had run a 'New Guinea Supplement' and my crocodile hunting activities had enjoyed a couple of full pages. The interview for the article, which took place in the appropriately named Sportsman's Bar of the Hotel Australia, was spread over half a day of steady drinking, which would have stimulated my recollections to no small extent. In a comfortable bar and being plied with drinks at regular intervals, there would have been no reason to be unduly modest. In turn, the reporter had given it the kind of treatment that was usually dished out to any unusual occupation – never allowing the facts to spoil a good story.

The parcel that had been following me around the country for so long consisted of two letters: a covering letter from the Australian Crocodile and Big Game Hunters' Club, the other was two foolscap pages fully covered on both sides in a spindly hand that made it difficult to decipher. It was addressed to the club and ended with a request to forward it to me.

The Australian Crocodile and 'Big Game Hunters' Club

Secretary's Address:

7 Lysterville Ave.,
MALVERN, Vic,

Mr. T. Cole,
28 Cooper Street,
STRATHFIELD,
N.S.W.

22nd. April 1957.

Dear Sir,

      We have received the enclosed letter from Mr. Charles
Ogilvie with his request that we pass it on to you.

      Mr. Ogilvie appears to be a man of no mean ability!

Yours faithfully,

A.R. Bentley, Hon. Sec.

The letter forwarded by the club from Mr Ogilvie read thus:

Box 7
Beverly Hills P.O.
Sydney N.S.W.
April 6th 1957

To the Crocodile Hunter's Association
7 Lysterville Avenue
Malvern Vic.

Dear Sirs,

*I hope you will not object to me writing to you and asking you
things when I am not a member of your association.*

*I am from Scotland and am one of the most experienced shotgun
and rifle shots that you might meet in most places at any rate.*

*I have had years of fast snap shots with rifle and shotgun and a
great deal of shooting out of rowing boats in salt and in fresh water*

by day and by night; at night, because of the specialised technique of aiming I have developed, I can shoot a rifle to kill a target the size of a rabbit at fifty yards in quarter moonlight and less at times without a light at all.

I have also shot some thousands of rabbits up to seventy yards range with a torch at night, I don't see the target in the sights because you haven't enough light, but when not using a torch I can kill it provided it is in short grass.

I am, or was a few years ago, a first class deer stalker and shot. I am also above average with automatic pistols and various types of machine guns. I am a proficient net fisherman by any standards you like to set.

I was an aircraft pilot during the war and am a first class seaman and expert oarsman.

By trade I am a carpenter and build any type of flat bottomed boats and design and draw them from personal knowledge. I am not a boat builder although I have built a number (7) of boats.

A few years ago I was firing five to seven thousand rounds a year between shotgun and rifle. Then I could usually split a bullet in half on the blade of a kitchen chopper stuck in the ground at seventy yards range from the standing position. I am sure I could not do it now but I would be shifting the side of it more or less.

I used to shoot an average of fifty to sixty running rabbits weekly either walking them up in the long grass or ferreting them. The best I ever did was 107 rabbits picked up from dawn to dusk in one day. I have killed as many ducks and geese as any living man has ever done. I love boats, nature in the raw, stalking animals, danger and wildness.

I am fed up with the dull ignorant people one has to meet in daily life in business but Sydney has been quite good to me, I have above average employment. Most certainly I cannot complain.

I have wondered if I could make more money at shooting croco-diles than carpentry. Do you know anyone I could shoot for to learn *about it and see if I liked it before taking it on on my own perhaps? I would imagine it would be foolish to be on your own because the local knowledge takes years to get.*

I was always able to outshoot all comers to the estuaries, I shot wildfowl because of a great store of local knowledge, I had to for I earned my living for some years solely by the sale of wildfowl that I shot. I never allowed anyone to shoot alongside me as other professionals did and get paid for it, I wanted the big bags of fowl for myself and I got them too, enough to run my house and live on.

I am forty-four and 5' 10' and strong and active build.

Now that you have read all this I am going to ask you to send this letter to someone I read about in the Sydney Daily Telegraph, New Guinea Supplement.

He is by far the biggest professional crocodile shooter and exporter in New Guinea. His name is Tom Cole and he used to shoot buffalo in the Northern Territory for ten years before the last war.

If Mr Tom Cole on receipt of this letter forwarded by your goodselves to him, would care to put up some sort of proposition to me re shooting for him then I might be glad to hear from him.

He might be able to let me have some idea of how much per week I might average at this work under his direction. If he did want me and his proposition was fair enough it is unlikely that I would want to learn from him and then go off and do it myself. Usually that type of business is foolish practice engendered by unthinking human greed, and it would not pay off if a man was working under fair conditions, for someone who knew all the areas for years.

Re languages, I can only speak French.

I now thank you for your kind attention and await your reply. Needless to say, I don't desire to have to write out all this over again and hence the request to forward it on please.

Yours faithfully,
Charlies Ogilvie.

I did not reply to Mr Ogilvie's letter, however, as a matter of courtesy, I wrote to the club which was kind enough to forward it:

> *Sigri Plantation*
> *Banz, New Guinea*
> *September 3rd, 1957*

The Hon. Secretary
Australian Crocodile and Big Game Hunters Club
Lysterville Avenue
Malvern, Vic.

Dear Sir,

I have for acknowledgement your communication dated April 22nd, enclosing a letter from a Mr Charles Ogilvie.

I have read Mr Ogilvie's letter closely and although he seems to have omitted any reference to walking on water, as you say, he is a man of no mean ability. However, it is with regret that I cannot help him in the direction he desires as my interests now are principally centred around planting coffee in the Western Highlands of New Guinea.

Nevertheless I do feel that he would have a tremendous future as a source of supply of bovine fertilizer, which would have the advantage of being far less dangerous and much more spectacular.

There would certainly be a very wide scope in this valley for a man with his exceptional output.

Thanking you for such interesting correspondence.
Yours faithfully,
T. E. Cole.

EIGHT

SIGRI FAMILY

THE VALLEY was filling up with settlers. Bob Gibbes had been a vocal advocate extolling everything except the cost of air freight, which was logical seeing that his company would be flying in a substantial amount of our requirements. Consequently, quite a number of Gibbes Sepik Airways employees, ex-employees, friends and associates were among the successful applicants for land in the valley. Mostly ex-air force types, they ranged from Group Captains to Wing Commanders, all the way down the line, as ex-servicemen were given priority at the Land Court.

There was one thing we all had in common – our knowledge of the coffee industry was five eighths of bugger-all. We were pioneers and, as is the way of pioneers, the way ahead was abounding in frustrations, trials and tribulations that, if we could have looked into the future, would have been terrifying. But there was no turning back and over those years friendships were forged that hold to this day.

All our supplies were flown in from the coast, mainly via Madang, which was a half-hour flight provided the weather was good. Gibbes's Sepik Airways fleet mainly consisted of Norsemans, a high-wing monoplane that would lift 2400 pounds from sea level. The Douglas freighter (DC3) would lift about 5200 pounds, but at this stage few of us would have this amount of cargo, although we would often combine to make up a load.

Weather was an all important factor and was always studied with a great deal of anxiety. From Madang it was a steady climb to an altitude

of 8000 to 10,000 feet to get over the Bismarcks and even after negotiating this formidable range, a ground mist frequently obscured the
airstrip. It was a nail-biting experience to listen to your charter circling
overhead at £10 a minute, waiting for a breeze to blow the mist away.
We quickly learned to time our charters for later in the day, when the
mist had dispersed.

The houses Colin Toole and I were building were nearing comple-
tion and, in addition to our requirements, there was continual demand
for bridge decking for the Administration, as the original flimsy bridges one after the other were swept away in floods. I note in my diary
of 9 June 1957 that the District Commissioner, Ian Skinner, was pressing us for delivery of a large order. Two weeks later I was helping out
by driving the tractor pulling a load out when I got horribly bogged. I
don't recall the incident very clearly, but anyway I got well and truly
stuck. The next day's entry reads: 'Col went to the mill to retrieve the
tractor. Got it out with 100 boys.' A few days later: 'Bought a sawbench and tractor.' On 30 July I briefly recorded: 'Qantas charter came
in late with sawbench and tractor.'

The roads were always in a vile state. On 9 August I noted: 'Drove
Ian Parsons to Nunga (his plantation), turned the jeep over on my way
back. Walked to Col Toole's and stayed the night.' And the next day:
'Retrieved the jeep this morning. No great harm done, half the acid ran
out of the battery but fortunately had more. Pig got into the coffee but
the boys captured it and tied it up.' Pigs can do a tremendous amount
of harm rooting up the ground, especially around young coffee plants.
Then on 3 August: 'Boss boy told that the pig got away and went back
into the coffee. When they caught it again, it bit one of the labour line
and they killed it, so that was one way out of it.'

The sawmill road was a permanent worry: 20 August: 'Sent fifty
boys to work on the sawmill road. Got the jeep in order again.' On 30
August: 'Sent the whole labour line to work on the sawmill road.' This
would have consisted of filling holes and bad patches with stone, and
draining work. But as soon as one place was fixed, another would pack

up somewhere else. I was beginning to think that buying a sawmill wasn't such a good idea after all. Malaria was ever-present and no one escaped. Like everyone else, I took my turn. Paludrine was, at the time, the suppressor and it wasn't until some years later that improved drugs became available.

By November my house was sufficiently advanced to make definite plans to bring my family up. We were renting a very nice flat in the suburb of Strathfield at what today seems a remarkably low rental, I am sure from memory that it was £3/10 a week. In early December I flew to Sydney and had no difficulty arranging for a friend to take over the lease of the flat and the furniture. It wasn't a proposition to freight our furniture into the Highlands. In Madang there was plenty of quite good cane furniture from Hong Kong available, which had the advantage of being lightweight, a very important consideration. My carpenter had done a good job making up tables and beds. I booked the family on the *Sinkiang* and flew back to what was going to be my permanent home for some time to come.

Bill Matthew and Alan Ferguson were the life and soul of the Wahgi Valley. Their plantation was the most advanced. Alan had been in the permanent air force before the war and had risen to Group Captain. Bill Matthew had been a Squadron Leader. Both were married.

The telephone line that ran from their plantation, Kinjibi, to Banz had been their idea. They had gone to a lot of trouble scrounging wire and ex-army field telephones that worked perfectly. It was a party line and everyone had their own call sign – Kinjibi's was one long ring, mine was four short. They also obtained a radio telephone licence so we could send and receive telegrams, which was invaluable. They laid down a tennis court and built a small clubhouse, and it became a focal point for most of the settlers up that end of the valley.

The *Sinkiang* was due at the end of December and as the house would not be quite finished, Pat and Colin Toole immediately offered me accommodation. A few days after Christmas I flew to Madang, there was the extra furniture to be purchased and when I had finished that job I knew that I wasn't going to have any trouble filling a Douglas freighter.

The ship berthed on New Year's Day 1958. I settled my family in at the hotel, where Mrs Gilmour immediately took Kath and the children under her wing, for which I was very grateful, while I sought out Barry Kelly, the manager of Mandated Airlines, and booked a DC3.

Three days later we climbed into the loaded aeroplane, wedging ourselves between the cargo. The children were thoroughly enjoying it all – there were new adventures every day. We cleared the Bismarcks in perfect weather and Tom Deegan, our pilot, made a perfect landing at Banz, where I was pleased to see most of my friends there to meet us. The flying time was forty-five minutes and I was fortunate in being able to arrange a back load of coffee from Kinjibi. The charter cost £160, the coffee enabling me to recoup £60.

It was a couple of weeks before I transported my family from the Tooles to the house at Sigri and it was now getting towards the end of January. January and February were the wettest months of the year and ploughing through the black soil was a permanent way of life. With Colin's assistance, I was able to move my family in one day. There was none of this carrying anyone over the threshold in what is sometimes called 'the time honoured fashion'; it was more like stumbling over sawn-off timber ends and sawdust. With the help of a few boys, we soon had the place in order. I had a good cook and he had a relative who was a kind of 'wood and water joey', who had been trained somewhere to make beds and keep the place reasonably clean. One thing that I was thankful for: there was a definite lull in the tribal fighting.

The sawmill was a continual worry and by now we had both had a bellyful of trying to keep the road in order and were giving serious thought to selling – if we could find a buyer. But before we could take any steps in that direction, we would have to get a fresh timber lease. We had been going further and further afield to get good logs and it was no simple matter getting them to the sawbench – and the country seemed to be getting steeper; as it was, it wasn't a saleable proposition. The forest country started at the foothill, and there was no shortage of timber, but finding something reasonably accessible wasn't at all simple.

We eventually settled for a good stand of timber at Kwianna, about fifteen miles from our mill. We notified the Administration, who were quite happy to cooperate, as they badly needed bridge decking. David Hook, a Patrol Officer stationed at Minj on the other side of the valley, started the ball rolling and he was joined later by an officer from the Forestry Department who had to give his okay, after which the negotiations started. There were about forty or fifty tribal owners in that particular area and I suppose it would be impossible to get that many people anywhere in the world to all agree on something, let alone forty or fifty primitive tribesmen, most of whom had no idea what it was all about. But David Hook was a very experienced Patrol Officer and he had lots and lots of patience. Jim Cavanagh was the Forestry Officer and had also been through it all many times before.

A transaction like this was a gala occasion and at the appointed time and place, the forty or fifty tribesmen with their women and children were gathered in all their feathers and finery, the men armed to the teeth with spears, bows and arrows – they all loved drama. Colin and I decided that we would go along for a look as a matter of interest and when we arrived, David and Jim were seated on a log surrounded by something like 200 people, all talking at once. Finally, and with a good deal of patience, David was able to get about ten 'Big Men' together and it was explained to them that the Administration did not want to buy their land, only the timber. Some were very much in favour of selling the timber because, as one pointed out, they would be getting their land cleared and they could use it for gardens, which was the only thing they used it for anyway.

The negotiations were conducted in pidgin and this was somewhat laborious; after a while, when they seemed to be coming around, we left. It took another week to finalise and although we were not yet legally entitled to cut timber, Dave Hook suggested we could start forming the access road. There was a track of sorts and two creeks to bridge so Colin and I took fifty cargo boys each and took it in sections of about a mile at a time.

It was pretty rough but we found we could get in and out reasonably well if it didn't rain too hard. Collecting a labour line for this work involved a lot of talking, too. There were 'Big Men' involved who were given a kind of verbal contract to supply labour with kau-hau (sweet potato), but of course there were the inevitable spanners in the works from time to time. Sometimes the labour line would be made up with a few meris (women), most of whom worked as well as the men.

A few days after we had started the road in to the new sawmill site, Colin and I were together at the furthest point that we had penetrated, comfortably pleased with ourselves, as everything was going smoothly. Suddenly, in the distance, I caught the undulating chant of a number of people. We listened intently for a while as it drew closer, then called to one of the road workers close by: 'All 'e come bilong what name?' (What are these people coming for?) I had no doubt that they would all be fairly well informed as to what was afoot. 'All Kulaga 'e come.'

The Kulaga were the people whose country we were just about to enter. I'd already realised that was who it would be.

'All 'e come bilong what name?' (What are they coming for?)

'All 'e come bilong this fella rote.' (It is to do with this road.)

It is often a convoluted business getting to the bottom of even the simplest matters. I turned to Colin, 'A hundred to one they're after more pay', but he didn't take me on, instead he said, 'Another job for Dave Hook'.

The Administration was paying for the road, mainly because of urgent bridge decking requirements. The only thing that we had to worry about was the Kulaga people suddenly backing out of the whole deal. I turned again to the man I was interrogating.

'Na you hearim talk-talk true, 'im 'e got cross bilong rote?' (Now have you heard the true story: are they annoyed about the road?)

'Na got, me 'earim all 'e like pay more.' (No, I have heard that they want more pay.)

Soon they came into sight, about fifty natives decorated in all their feathered finery, their chant rising and falling, and every one holding either deadly looking spears or bows and arrows. Anyone not familiar with their love of drama could easily be terrified at their approach. They came to a halt a few yards from us, the singing reaching a crescendo and then with a stamping of their feet it suddenly stopped. It was real theatre. They then walked toward us and extended their hands, all part of the act. We were soon surrounded; a large number of women and children who had been trailing along behind made the crowd up to about 100 people.

Although at this point they were enjoying themselves hugely, it was a situation that could easily turn into a nasty incident should an inexperienced person not enter into the spirit of it all, perhaps displaying unwarranted bravado by doing or saying something foolish. They were extremely volatile people and it took little to set a spark to a barrel of gunpowder.

When all the handshaking was done, one burly fellow, smelling of half-rancid pigs grease, said very gravely, 'Me fella come bilong talk-talk'. (We have come for a talk.)

'Bilong what name?' (What about?) Colin asked.

'Me fella like pay more belong this fella rote – pay 'e no enough.'

Colin said: 'Na you fella hearim, this fella pay bilong rote, me two fella no markim, 'im 'e something bilong Kiap, s'pose you like 'im pay more you must talk 'im Kiap, 'e no something bilong me fella.' (Now you fellows listen: the pay for the road is not determined by us, it is the Kiap's job so if you want more pay you will have to talk to him, it's nothing to do with us.)

They had planted several spears where the last bit of roadwork had finished, a clear warning that it was not to proceed any further. I looked at Col and said, 'I suppose we'll have to take some of these fellows over to Minj', which was Dave Hook's headquarters. We called the two boss boys and told them that work was suspended, for the time being anyway. After some discussion, four warriors were selected. One of them had a village policeman's badge strung round his neck, and being the Administration representative we were happy to see him go along. A couple of days later it was all settled. I don't have any record of how much extra the ADO paid them, but I wouldn't think it was much more than £10 or £15.

In the meantime, our benchsaw man, Bill Jones, had not been entirely idle. By applying himself industriously to the job of demolishing a case of rum, he had got himself into an advanced state of the DTs. From memory, I think he was fighting off hordes of cannibals. As a precautionary measure, we hid an old single-barrel shotgun he had, and a couple of days later took him to Mt Hagen Hospital. We were fortunate in being able to replace him soon after with a very good half-caste named Andrew.

Eventually everything fell into place. The road was reasonably navigable and buildings gradually appeared – a house for our sawmiller, then a large building to house the sawbenches and equipment. We built it big enough to have everything under one roof. They were all built of bush timber and thatched. The mill on the Kimil River was dismantled and transferred to Kwianna. There was a backlog of orders, mainly bridge decking. We let it be known the sawmill was for sale.

There was an immediate reaction. A Seventh Day Adventist pastor was the first to throw his hat into the ring, followed by an Administration carpenter from Minj, and finally an itinerant buyer of native coffee, one Alan Booth, who had a prospective partner, Frank Pemble-Smith, who was managing a coffee plantation for Sir Edward Hallstrom. They were all plagued with an identical problem – none of them had much money. The carpenter was the first to fall by the wayside, closely followed by the pastor. He was putting too much faith in the Lord, who is notoriously unreliable in matters secular. We listened respectfully to a moving and anguished sermon on a subject with which we were no doubt even more familiar than he. We explained simply and briefly that while we were allowing for a certain amount of flexibility, it was unlikely that we'd strike a deal, but would keep his offer in mind. We then came to Alan Booth and Frank Pemble-Smith with some anxiety – they were the last card in our limited pack. After a lot of haggling, we let it go for £4000, on extended terms. Neither Colin nor I attempted to work out what our respective homes cost, but I strongly suspect that they were very, very expensive. We went back to our plantations and settled down to uninterrupted coffee planting, for a while anyway.

I ran a water race off the creek and installed a hydraulic ram, which is a wonderful invention. Such a ram is powered by the volume of water that runs through it, which is utilised to propel a portion of the water through an outlet pipe to quite surprising heights. Water is its sole motive power and it clanks merrily away day and night, needing no fuel or lubrication. Although it was nowhere near sufficient to supply the mill, it kept a 1000-gallon overhead tank full, more than enough to supply our domestic needs. I couldn't bear to see the overflow going to waste so I had a swimming pool built, which was soon filled by the excess water, much to the delight of our children. Later on, most of the children in the valley learnt to swim there.

By this time, an increasing number of children in the valley were reaching school age. Kathryn was taking correspondence lessons on the verandah. Jock McGregor, a trader who lived at Minj, was married to a former school teacher. We put a proposition to the Administration: if we built a school would the Administration furnish it and pay a school teacher? They agreed, and we all contributed time and labour and in no time the Banz school was officially opened. Another addition to the social life of the district was the Banz Club. The Highlands Farmers' and Settlers' Association had been formed in Goroka in the very early years. We became the Western Highlands branch. We built a clubhouse at Banz, again with voluntary labour. This not only became the social centre, but also was also the farmers and settlers meeting place. On Sunday, Doug McGraw held services there, although this was strictly on condition that he finished his God Bothering by 11 a.m. It was probably the only place of worship that had a liquor licence.

A month or so after the sawmill deal was concluded, I thought it would be a good idea to buy a few head of cattle. There seemed to be an awful lot of grass going to waste and although we were getting fresh milk from one of the mission stations, it would be better to have it on tap, as it were, with fresh meat later as well. I scouted around and bought a couple of cows here, another one there from different mission stations that were starting to pop up like mushrooms all over the place, as is the fashion with missionaries. I fenced off ten acres of ground and to improve the native pastures I planted a few species of grasses, mainly kikuyu and molasses. The females, like all females, started to display a distinct anxiety for the company of at least one of the opposite sex, so I called on my good friend Bill Meuser, of the Anglican Mission, who had a herd of Brahman/Shorthorn cross cattle. I selected a young, roan, first-cross bull, which Bill delivered to me for the sum of £250. He was ceremoniously unloaded into my paddock and after a quick look at the females and a sniff and a promise, he lumbered off down the paddock and was quickly lost to sight in the long grass. The next morning, the lad who had been told to look after the cattle came to me with the bad news. The pidgin term for cattle is 'bulamacow', whether it be male or female.

'New fella bulamacow, 'e go finish.' (The new bull has gone.) I called the boss boy up and told him to take twenty cargo boys and find it. An hour later there was no result; I told him to take the whole line, about seventy or eighty boys. Unlike Aborigines, the New Guineans have no idea of tracking, and anyway it rains almost every night and tracks are quickly obliterated. I reckoned he would go back to his old home, and would follow the road back along which he was brought. I followed the road without any sign of him. By afternoon I was getting desperate. It was about four or half past in the afternoon I went to call on Doug McGraw, another missionary who flew a mission Cessna.

'Doug,' I said, 'I want to charter your aeroplane – I've lost a young bull I bought from Bill Meuser.'

'Goodness gracious me,' he said, 'you've lost a bull. Well, I never.'

This wasn't exactly what I thought. There was only an hour or so flying time left, but a lot of ground can be covered in an aeroplane in that time. I knew that it would cost me about £30 an hour, but I reckoned that we should locate him in half an hour and, once I knew where he was, I could take a few boys along who could bring him back.

The aeroplane was parked at the top of the Banz airstrip, not far from where Doug lived. We drove down and climbed in, Doug started the motor and we trundled down the strip and were soon airborne. We turned east and followed the road back along which Bill had travelled when he brought him to Sigri, which was the logical way for him to go. There was no sign of him. We turned back and flew low over Sigri house – the children waved as we went past. Standing round the yard were the half a dozen cows, placidly chewing their cud. Further down the paddock, comfortably curled up in the middle of a tall, matted patch of grass, was my roan bull. Doug made a low pass over him, banking steeply to enable me to have a good look – I swear the bastard winked at me as we thundered past.

The cattle proved to be more trouble than they were worth and I sold them all to Dick Hagen. I planted the paddock up with coffee. The kikuyu and molasses grass, which was now well established, was almost impossible to eradicate and proved a curse ever after.

Towards the end of August 1960, some startling news came over the radio. A young girl had been taken by a crocodile at a place called Marshall Lagoon, some distance south-east of Port Moresby. It seemed that the girl was in a canoe with a group of other villagers when the crocodile swam up from behind and placed its feet on the back of the canoe. It would have been a frightening experience for the people in the flimsy dugout with only two or three inches of freeboard. In the panic that followed, the canoe tipped over and they were all thrown into the water. The crocodile swam around, picked off the young girl and dived with her in its jaws. A few days later a part of the body was recovered and the villagers took it to the mission nearby, where, after a service was held, she was buried. From the reports that came through, this was not the first fatal attack. There had been quite a number and it surprised me that I hadn't heard of them before. But then it was only in recent years that Papua New Guinea had become newsworthy and had seen the establishment of a newspaper and the arrival of a flock of reporters from Australia.

A few days later I received a call from a young patrol officer, who was stationed at Minj on the other side of the valley. He brought a letter with him from the Director of District Services, Port Moresby, the gist of which was an instruction to contact me and ascertain whether I would be prepared to go to Marshall Lagoon and catch the man-eater and kill it, all expenses paid, of course. Naturally, I was delighted to receive the request. It would be a good break and I couldn't foresee any serious difficulties.

Although I had never been to Marshall Lagoon before, I couldn't see any reason why it shouldn't be a perfectly straightforward job. I anticipated that this lagoon was the same as any other dotted along the coastline – a stretch of water off the beach a mile or so long fringed with coconut palms – a piece of cake. I should have known better, of course. As I've been finding out all my life, the simpler something appears to be you can bet that tucked away somewhere or maybe hovering over- head, suspended by a slender thread, is a bloody great spanner poised to drop into the works.

In the meantime, I made my plans, having no doubt that I would be able to identify the man-eater. Almost all wild animals, when they reach maturity, take up a beat that they are more or less compelled to follow. To intrude into another creature's territory will almost always end up in savage fighting. It all revolves round that very basic first law of nature – the survival of the fittest.

Ian Parsons, of Nunga Plantation, got all enthusiastic about the forthcoming hunt and was keen to accompany me. I had no objection, he was good company and I had no doubt that the Administration would be unlikely to object to me taking an offsider – an extra air ticket wasn't going to amount to much. And so it turned out. A couple of days later we got a ride on a Government charter flight as far as Goroka, where I spent some of the time fossicking around one of the airport hangers in which a lot of maintenance work was done. I had no trouble finding what I wanted – a couple of lengths of discarded aileron cable.

Aileron cable is stainless steel, very, very strong, and extremely pliable, and would hold a very big crocodile easily. It was discarded from aeroplanes after a certain number of hours, regardless of its condition, which was usually close to perfect. If the worst came to the worst, I might have to trap the man-eater, which turned out to be sound thinking.

We went to Port Moresby the following day, where I called on Keith McCarthy, Director of District Services. McCarthy was a fine man who I got to know very well in later years. In his day as a patrol officer, he had really been through the mill. He still had at least one arrowhead embedded somewhere in his body, collected during a skirmish with some New Guinea tribesmen. I asked him if he couldn't get it out, but he said that he wanted to keep it as a souvenir. During the war he was one of that valiant band of Coastwatchers who worked behind the Japanese lines, relaying information of troop movements and shipping concentrations. For his exploits he was decorated with an MBE, Military Division, and an American citation. That day in his office he told me the Marshall Lagoon crocodile was causing him a lot of worry. He was not sure, but thought that it had taken at least ten people.

'You know what they are – when something like this starts they always reckon it's some kind of puri-puri that their enemies are working. Several of my POs have had a shot at him and they all reckon they've hit him, but the hide has turned the bullets. What do you think, Tom?' he asked anxiously.

'I suppose they'd have been using a .303.' I knew that ex-army .303s were standard issue. 'And I've not no doubt that they've hit him, but all this talk about the hide turning a bullet is a lot of nonsense. You must remember that it is not difficult to skin a crocodile. A sharp knife cuts through the skin easily. The fact of the matter is that your Patrol Officers have been hitting him, but not in the right place. They can take an awful lot of lead if they're not hit in a vital spot.'

He nodded, 'Do you think you can get him?'

'Yes,' I said confidently, 'I'll get him.'

He then told me that there was a Fisheries boat leaving for Marshall Lagoon in a couple of days. We could go on that.

'Dave Speakman is the PO at Marshall Lagoon. He's a good lad. I'll send him a signal to let him know you're coming.'

It was when I asked him how big the lagoon was that I got my first shock. 'Actually,' he said, 'it's not a lagoon in a true sense, it's really an estuary.'

'Oh, is that so?'

He picked up a ruler and walked over to a map of Papua New Guinea that occupied half of one wall of his office and pointed to a spot that looked to be about 100 miles south-east of Port Moresby. I think I went a bit goggle-eyed as I walked around his desk to get a closer look. It seemed to me to be about the size of Sydney Harbour, and there were several rivers feeding into it. I did my best to put on a brave face. 'It must be five or six miles to the back of it,' I said as casually as I could.

'Seven, I think, from memory. It's a good while since I was there. It would be three or four miles wide most of the way.'

I thought to myself, 'There's one crocodile in that estuary some-where and I've got to find him. I reckoned I must have been crazy when I jumped into this'. I made my way back to the Top Pub, where I found Ian in the bar engaged in earnest and enthusiastic conversation with a local newspaperman. 'Here's Tom now', he said, as I walked in and joined them.

I had known 'Steve' Stephens for some time and we had become very good friends. 'This sounds like a good story, Tom,' he said as we shook hands. But I wasn't so sure. I thought of that bloody great estu-ary and one solitary crocodile swimming around somewhere. I would have preferred to have the publicity after I had killed the brute. But knowing Steve, there was no way I would be able to stop him. Once he got his teeth into a story it was full steam ahead. Another couple of reporters joined us, one from the Sydney *Telegraph* and one from the *Sun*. After a few more rounds of drinks the situation didn't seem so bleak. They wanted photographs and I happily obliged, with the bar for a backdrop while they clicked merrily away.

The following morning we were advised that a Government 'K boat', the *Kauri*, belonging to the Fisheries Department, would be leaving for Marshall Lagoon that evening. Late that afternoon we went aboard. The skipper was Andy Quinlan, who greeted us with enthusiasm when he spotted a case of anti-seasickness medicine disguised as rum. At five o'clock we sailed, weaving our way through assorted craft and native canoes. We passed Paga Point and turned into a stinking south-easter and although we stayed inside the reef, it gave little protection; the seas broke over the whole length of the little ship. The only place where there was any protection was in the wheelhouse, where we braced ourselves as best we could. Visibility was almost nil because of the constant surge of the foaming waves.

Some time after sundown, the skipper pointed to a small island where we were to anchor for the night. It was a relief to sail into a small bay that provided a haven of clear, calm water. Next day we were away at first light. The sea had dropped considerably, and we turned into Marshall Lagoon just before midday, and tied up at a wharf below the District Office. From what I had seen of Administration outbuildings, the powers that be had gone overboard when approving the Marshall Lagoon buildings. The Kiap's house set on high stumps was a surprisingly substantial building with wide verandahs all round. The offices behind, over which the Australian flag flew, were a mix of native materials, timber and iron.

There was a small amount of cargo that was taken over by a corporal and a couple of prisoners, who also carried our luggage to the wharf. The corporal handed me a note from Dave Speakman in which he apologised for his absence from the station, explaining that he would be back in a few days. Judging by the date on the letter, he was due that evening. The cargo was carried to the station and the prisoners returned to collect our gear. I carried my rifle, the corporal eyeing it off with a good deal of interest. I told him that I had come to kill the crocodile that was taking the people, and he shook his head. Although Motu was the lingua franca, he spoke pidgin with which I was more familiar.

'No good true, 'im 'e masalai.'

Here we go, I thought, bloody masalai. When we got to the house, one of the servants appeared carrying a tray with two bottles of beer and glasses. Dave Speakman had a well trained staff. I picked a bunk on the verandah with a big mosquito net suspended over it, Parsons found himself a room, after which we settled down to enjoy the Patrol Officer's hospitality.

At sundown a cry went up, 'Kiap 'e come!' I looked over the verandah and saw the Patrol Officer at the head of a line of carriers. At the rear were a couple of policemen and some prisoners. He came into the house and greeted us warmly, apologising for his absence, explaining that he '...had to attend to a fight, nothing very serious'.

I asked him what he knew about the crocodile. 'Well,' he said, 'I've only been here six months and the girl that was taken last month is the only casualty since I've been here. But it's been going on for a long time, and it's difficult to get anything like an accurate figure, but I would say that he's gobbled up at least ten, and of course now they've got this bloody masalai fixation about it.'

'Have you ever seen him?'

'Yes, several times. In fact I've had a couple of shots at him.'

I asked him how big it was and he reckoned about fifteen feet, although he'd never seen it out of the water.

'Do you think you can get him?' he asked anxiously.

I tried to be frank and said with more confidence than I felt, 'I think so, but I expect that because he's been shot at so many times, it's going to be bloody difficult to get near him, and I reckon I'll have to trap him. Where's his beat?'

'Round about the Mission station, five miles or so each way. When do you want to go out?'

'I thought I might go out tonight, do you want to come?'

He laughed. 'There's no way you'll get away without me.'

I had seen a pair of canoes with an outboard motor mounted on them tied up at the wharf, and Dave confirmed that they were station canoes. Just then the *Kauri* captain walked in, announcing that he'd set his nets. 'We'll have a feed of barramundi tomorrow.'

Then, looking at me: 'When's the big crocodile hunt start, Tom?'

'About sundown,' I told him.

'Can I come?' Andy asked.

'If it's okay by Tom I don't mind.'

Dave had good canoes and I reckoned that they had a carrying capacity well in excess of us four plus a few paddlers. It was just on sundown when I buckled my cartridge belt on and said, 'Let's go'. We boarded the canoes. The corporal I had met when I arrived took charge of the motor. They were about thirty feet long, deep and wide, and rode well out of the water. I could see they were good weight carriers. Four prisoners with paddles were sitting cross-legged at the back, an emergency in case of engine trouble, which I thought was unlikely, but they would probably be needed to lift crocs out of the water, if I shot any.

It quickly got dark and I hooked the spotlight up to a battery. We were now getting close to where the man-eater was supposed to be. I was sitting in a patrol chair, Dave Speakman beside me. I warned everyone that there was to be no talking. As we approached the area, I could feel the tenseness. We turned into a channel, the Patrol Officer said we were getting close.

Then suddenly I saw it, the startlingly bright reflection of the eyes of a big crocodile, which I estimated to be at least a quarter of a mile away, swimming leisurely in mid-stream. I showed Dave, who whistled excitedly. The corporal, who had handed the steering to one of the prisoners, jabbered to his companions. I shot a cartridge into the breech of my rifle as he dived. I cursed and pushed the safety catch to the 'on' position and laid it down beside me. 'Do you think that was him?' I asked. 'I reckon', then turning to the corporal, Dave talked rapidly in Motu. The policeman nodded his head vigorously and spoke at some length, little of which I understood.

'The corporal's quite sure. He said there's only one big one round here' – I was sure, too. When I first picked up the reflection of his eyes, I got an immediate 'gut' feeling that it was the killer.

We turned into a wide creek and after travelling a short distance, I caught a glimpse of the lights of a settlement and asked Dave what it was. He informed me that it was a Mission station and as I swung the light around, I saw a cross on the bank. I steadied the light on the crude crucifix. The PO said it marked the grave that contained the remains of the girl, the crocodile's last victim. It looked so lonely and pathetic that I swore that somehow I would get the killer. We turned and returned to base. I shot two medium-sized crocodiles on the way home.

The aileron cable that I had picked up in Goroka for the express purpose of making a trap was the next thought, and in the morning I told Dave what I intended to do. He seemed very sceptical; obviously he didn't think it would work, but I had come to the conclusion that it was the only way, and was sure it would be successful. My confidence was largely fortified by the fact that I had caught one with a similar trap in the Norman River in Queensland some years earlier. I *knew* it would work. The next and most important item was suitable bait. I had used a wallaby in Queensland, but there were none in these parts. Fortunately, the problem was solved by Andy Quinlan. I was busy splicing the cables when he turned up after picking his nets up, saying that he had a good catch of fish the night before, also that he had unfortunately caught a porpoise in his nets and it had drowned. We were sorry to hear that one of these lovable creatures had died, but it is an ill wind... I immediately thought this will solve my bait problem for the trap. The best place for it was in the vicinity of where the girl had been taken, an important factor being the wind direction. It would need to be blowing off the bait, which by afternoon was beginning to get really high.

Eight prisoners with the corporal arrived from the calaboose, laughing and joking, obviously happy at the thought of some crocodile meat. We set off with half the stinking porpoise in the stern, smothered with copra sacks, which did little to disguise the stench. The prisoners were not unduly perturbed by the stink of the carcase, one of them sitting on it and appearing quite comfortable. When we turned into the creek where I proposed to set the trap, I noted that there was a steady breeze off the left-hand bank, which sloped gently down to the water's edge. It was a perfect place. I thought it unlikely that the wind would change, which was important. The prisoners set to with a will and soon had a large area cleared, the timber they felled being more than sufficient to construct the wings leading to the trap. When pegging it out, I took into consideration the likelihood of the wind veering, because it was now the south-east monsoon. It was most unlikely that it would change to any great extent. I made the opening about fifty yards wide. The walls didn't have to be high, a couple of feet was plenty, their purpose being to guide the creature to where the bait was, which would entice him into the noose.

The aileron cable was perfect for the job; it had a breaking strain of a couple of tons. There was a tree ideally placed where I could rig the walking beam, which would tighten the noose round its neck once it seized the bait and tripped it. Immediately the crocodile felt it tighten, he would struggle to get free, thus tightening the cable. It was nearly sundown when we finished and as we were leaving, I looked back on our handiwork with some satisfaction – I could see nothing wrong. When we got back to the station we were happy to have a night off, and settled down on the verandah to devote the rest of the evening to drinking to a successful capture. In the morning we were anxious to get back to the trap and, with great anticipation, boarded the canoes and took off for the site. We turned into the creek where we had worked with such enthusiasm.

The trap had been sprung, but there was no crocodile.

We went ashore and I looked at the wreckage where it had put its head inside the noose, grabbed at the bait and set it off. When it felt the noose tighten, the enraged creature managed to pull its head out. I could have wept with disappointment. To have got him in the trap and lost him was an unimaginable blow to me. And what made it worse was that it was all my fault – I had miscalculated the distance between the noose and the bait. When he got close enough to the bait to reach it and set it off, the noose would not have been past his forelegs, which was most important. It would have been somewhere round his neck or head and he was able to wrench his way out. It should have been round his shoulders. Surveying the wreckage, it must have been close to being caught or strangled – it had laid everything flat in its struggle to escape. I was very depressed when I said to David and Ian, 'I'll never get him now; he'll never go into the trap a second time'.

It was Sunday 18 September 1960. I had the wings of the trap straightened out, and examined the cable for any sign of a fracture, but it was in perfect condition. I reset it with the bait further away, so that if he went in again the noose would be halfway up his body. Actually, I didn't really think that he would be that stupid. I also was thinking about what the newspaper reporters would do to me if I didn't produce results. I thought of sitting up all night over the other half of the porpoise bait if necessary.

I set another trap further along the creek, thinking that perhaps he would be more likely to have another go in a different place. We went out shooting again that night and I killed three. We were all very tired when we flopped into our bunks and the sun was well up when I was woken by a commotion outside. I got up and peered over the verandah. A crowd of eight or ten natives were all talking at once in the Motu dialect, little of which I could understand. When they saw me they became more excited and called 'Taubada!' and I caught the word 'Huwala' frequently, the Motu word for crocodile, and 'Bada heria', which I knew meant very big.

I called David, who came from his bedroom half asleep, complaining at being roused. 'There's a mob of natives out there talking about a crocodile. I'm not sure what it's all about,' I told him. He called one of them up on to the verandah saying, 'Daharka?' (Well?). He then went into what appeared to me to be a long and convoluted conversation. David listened intently and then turned to me. 'He says that they were going past the trap and the man-eater was coming down the bank, and they ran ashore and killed it. Now what do you think of that Tom?'

'I think,' I replied, 'that they are exaggerating.'

He then turned to the man and, speaking in English, said, 'You're a bloody liar'. He hung his head, examining his feet for a few moments, then nodded his head. We both had to laugh. Ian Parson joined us, asking what was going on. 'I think we've trapped him,' I said and told him what had happened. David was questioning the man further. He turned to me and said, 'They've got the bloody croc in their canoe'. We all went down to the wharf and there, taking up the full length of a pair of canoes, was the killer, its head smashed in by axes.

I thought to myself that it wasn't a bad performance to have killed it with axes – it would have been pretty lively. They told David that some of them hung onto its tail while others got a big log, laid it on its neck and sat on it while another smashed its head in with an axe. Although it was a great relief to know that I had him, I was disappointed that we hadn't got there first. I had a movie camera with me and it would have made a great shot thrashing around. It was fourteen feet long. I took some photographs and then started them off skinning.

When we had finished our breakfast, I thought of the other trap. I didn't expect to catch anything in it, but we all wanted to have a look. Also there was the trap that had caught the big fellow: the gear had to be picked up. When we got there I wasn't surprised to see that it was a bigger wreck than the last time when he had wriggled out – I suppose because he was in it longer. We collected the rope, cable and gear and went to the other trap, which was about half a mile away. To my surprise there was a croc in this one, too. We could hear it roaring before we got there. It was about nine feet long, probably big enough to take someone, but every one of our lads were certain that the big fellow was the man-eater. It was all over now and although it had been quite an experience, I was relieved that it had been successful. We had a quiet celebration and farewell with David, and the next morning Andy Quinlan, who would be staying for some time longer, offered to take us to Cape Rodney, from where we could get a plane back to Moresby.

As I might have expected, the story of our success was well ahead of us in Port Moresby. Steve Stephens produced a number of newspaper cuttings, all of which gave varying imaginative accounts of how the killer had been captured. The one that I liked best said that in order to entice him within range, I might have to lie down in a canoe and pretend to be bait. I scoffed at that and told them that that was why I'd brought Ian Parsons.

The time was fast arriving when I had to have a factory for processing the coffee. I had a large, steel-framed building put up. Flying it in took up a full Bristol freighter charter. Next was a diesel engine, generator and pump, mainly for the huge volume of water needed to wash the coffee. The generator would supply power for lighting as well. It was a gala day when the house was wired up and the lights switched on. We were able to dispense with the kerosene lamps, which continually gave trouble with the mantles and glasses breaking and the closest replacement several hundred miles away by air.

Everything was now starting to pile up. Another planter, David Falconer, and I had started a coffee buying venture that was proving very successful. There was a good deal of native coffee growing out in the hills, which had been encouraged by the Department of Agriculture. What with Sigri Plantation and the coffee buying, I came to the conclusion that I could do with a manager, and so a house had to be built. My manager, Peter Warburton, was married and had two children, and a few months after he started he had occasion to visit friends for the weekend. He left his houseboy in charge, colloquially known as a 'manki masta'. His tasks were simple and undemanding, like feeding the fowls and perhaps sweeping a floor. But being of a particularly conscientious type, he decided to adjust the flame of the refrigerator, a popular country type that was operated by a kerosene lamp, and often used in this part of the world even when electricity was available. Of course, the lamp did not need any attention at all, but by applying himself industriously to the job, he managed to get it to explode and burn the house down. He managed to escape; at any rate I think he did. He no doubt thought that it was not worthwhile waiting to collect his pay – he was quite right there. I now had to get another house built. It took a month and this time I made sure it was well insured.

Coffee was starting to boom on world markets, the demand was insatiable and the aeroplanes were going out with full loads. The native coffee making being a substantial contribution, the Department of Agriculture had sent field men out in an endeavour to establish a kind of cottage industry, encouraging the natives to grow coffee. There were now hundreds of peasant farmers with little plots out in the hills. Although they lacked the expertise and equipment of the European planters, because of their numbers they made quite an impact on the market. Their equipment was of a very basic kind and although it was not the best coffee in the world, it was not the worst, although not far off it. But there was a market for it, which was important.

My coffee buying partner David Falconer, a Scotsman, had been planting in Malaysia and had come down to try his luck in the New Guinea Highlands. He bought Talu Plantation, and was one of the most competent and popular planters in the district. When he and I decided that the native coffee industry was well worth a close look, it seemed that we could, without a doubt, bring a ray of sunshine into the lives of the struggling peasant farmers and at the same time benefit from the warmth the exercise generated. Because of the state of the roads, it was necessarily a job for four-wheel drive vehicles with a trailer hitched on behind. The mountainous roads were somewhere between a hazard and a nightmare. As well as bridges being washed away at regular intervals, landslides were frequent. It also rained most of the time. We both had four-wheel drive vehicles and trailers; David's was a Land

Rover, mine was an ex-army jeep, and both had been tested to the limit from time to time and could stand up to almost any kind of battering.

At first we took it in turns to go out buying and it was rarely anything less than 100 miles there and back to the coffee growing villages. All sorts of things happened: bits used to break, generators burnt out, radiators boiled dry, headlamps broke all the time. As we became more affluent, we employed drivers. One of them, David Bennett, had a bad skid and the whole outfit went over the side. Fortunately, he managed to jump clear because it was a long way down; it took sixty natives to get it back up on the road, there was a load of coffee went with it and surprisingly there wasn't much damage done. What was bendable had already been bent some time previously. There had been only one headlight in the first place. We found that it was a good idea to keep things like headlights to a minimum; we never put an unnecessary strain on the battery with things like tail lights. It nearly always rained, mostly in the afternoons and evenings.

Our little company, Cole and Falconer, did very well. Whoever was buying had to carry a lot of coin, hundreds of pounds worth of marks; decimal currency had not come in. The natives would not accept notes because of the difficulty of recovering them when one of their houses went up, which was fairly often. The silver would fuse together in the intense heat, but it could be separated, although it took time, something they had plenty of. The name 'mark' went back to the days when it was German territory.

We had a change of District Commissioner. Tom Ellis was appointed and it was like a breath of fresh air. Of medium height, slight build and saturnine appearance, he had a reputation of getting things done; a man of few words and lots of action. He had a rejuvenating effect on the whole district. Behind his back he was almost reverently referred to as 'God'. He, too, had been a fighter pilot during the war and was decorated with a DFC. We became good friends.

When the Western Highlands had been first opened up, the kiaps supervised the road-making and, once put through, they were supposed to be maintained by the local people. Each clan was to be responsible for the section that traversed their territory, but there was little enthusiasm for the work.

Tom Ellis called a meeting of all the native policemen and 'Big Men', those with a strong influence in the native community. They gathered outside the District Office in Mt Hagen. Tom walked out onto the verandah and called for silence. He made an impressive speech, the gist being that the people were to work on the road every Monday morning; men, women and children; rain, hail or shine. Tom was a dedicated supporter of the British Raj; Empire building stuff it was. The response was remarkable: every Monday morning they came down from the hills in their hundreds, men, women and children; they carried tins, billycans, sheets of bark, and, in some cases, banana leaves. They streamed along the road like swarms of ants coming and going from the nearest creeks, which were an everlasting supply of gravel. On each side of the road were deep drains to carry away floodwaters, but these were clogged up and useless. Now they were cleaned out and deepened, while the flimsy bridges were strengthened with heavy bearers and sawn bridge decking.

Mt Hagen was officially declared a township and surveyors arrived and subdivided it up into industrial, commercial and residential areas. At the end of the airstrip was a site for a hotel. It was astonishing how rapidly it came to life. One minute the place was a stretch of grass interspersed with survey pegs, and next minute the place echoed with the sounds of hammers and saws. In no time there were a couple of garages, and Burns Philp and W. R. Carpenter stores. The island traders quickly established themselves. Joan Colman and Beth Parsons opened frock shops.

Mel Zebrovious, who had been running a passionfruit factory for Cottees, came to me and said that he had put in an application for the hotel and licence that automatically went with it. He didn't have enough capital, in fact, he didn't have any as far as I could make out. He asked me to come in with him. Without giving it much thought, I said that maybe I would; privately I thought that he wouldn't have a hope in the world, as I expected that there would be plenty of competition. To my astonishment, he was the only applicant, and it was quite a shock to wake up one morning and find that I was a partner in a prospective hotel. At this stage it was only a verbal agreement, but it sounded interesting and I did regard myself as committed. I just wondered where we would get the money.

I approached my old crocodile hunting mate Ian Parsons, 'Have you got any money, Ian?'

'Nope,' he said, 'why?'

I told him, and he immediately got all fired up. I think that we may have had £2000 between us. Two banks had opened their doors – the ANZ and the Commonwealth. I tackled the Commonwealth first.

'No trouble,' the amiable manager said, 'how much do you want?'

'Let's say £10,000 to start with.' I was surprised how easy it was.

It was six months to the first Mt Hagen show, and Tom Ellis promised the greatest spectacular of all times. 'And see that your bloody pub is ready,' he told me.

It was still three months to the show and Tom Ellis was running out of money. The Administration wasn't seeing eye to eye with him on the great spectacular he was visualising. One evening over dinner he said to me, 'I've given up on those miserable bastards in Moresby' – which may not have been strictly accurate – 'we've got to raise some money somehow, have you got any ideas?'

Before coming to New Guinea, I had been a keen clay pigeon shooter and I still had my gun and a trap that I had brought up from Sydney. I'd had vague ideas of installing it in the near future, but it was rusting away in a shed. The lawn in front of my house was plenty big enough for a trap shooting layout plus a few other activities. His enthusiasm was immediate and we got down to some intensive planning. Clay targets and cartridges had to be ordered, boat schedules were studied; we reckoned that we could put it on in two months' time. We also planned a gambling booth and, of course, a bar.

'What about a licence Tom?' I asked him.

'We won't worry too much about that,' he said.

'An honour system?' I suggested.

'Yes, that would be a good idea.'

The event turned out to be an outstanding success, and the enthusiasm it generated was tremendous. I didn't realise how many people were in the district until they accumulated on my lawn, and we raised nearly £1000.

'I ought to get a bloody knighthood out of this,' I said to Tom when we finished counting the money.

He laughed. 'Nothing under twenty thousand,' he said.

My visits to Mt Hagen were becoming more frequent as the opening date of the show drew closer. Tom Ellis was almost permanently surrounded by village policemen and 'Big Men'. There were going to be at least eight clans, each one putting on a sing-sing and each one trying to outdo the other with displays of blazing head-dresses made of exotic plumes. There was a competition for the best display, although I'd briefly puzzled over what the conditions would be, or how they'd work out the winner.

Tom said, 'You can be one of the judges'.

'No I bloody well can't,' I informed him. I'd visualised being chopped up by irate losers, a distinct possibility.

There were to be archery contests, and foot races for the youngsters. There was to be polocrosse, with Mt Hagen and Banz making up one team, one from Goroka and another from Port Moresby.

Then one day Tom said, 'I must get one of those smoked Kukukukus'. They are almost pygmies and the most savage fighters in all New Guinea; little men in bark cloaks who kill for the fun of it – and smoke their own dead. In his book *Plumes and Arrows*, Colin Simpson quoted ADO Lloyd Hurrell and his Patrol Officer Peter Maloney: 'Not all the dead are smoked, possibly fifty per cent are simply placed on stone ledges or specially built cages in the forest. The general rule is that battle victims, clan leaders, young warriors and young women are smoked. Children, elderly people who die from old age and illness, and known sorcerers are not smoked.'

It would seem that the distinction between the bodies that are smoked and those that are not is fairly flexible; they quote a case of a murder:

'In the case of a murder victim, the body was removed from the house after only three days and placed in the forest because the younger brother, whose job it was to carry out the ritual, had been negligent and let the fire die out and had left the house.

'Where there are extensive head injuries, the skin is sewn together, and in case where the wounds are large, the brain is removed.

'When death occurs the corpse is laid on leaves and covered with a bark cloth, the head only being left uncovered. Relatives and friends come from near and far to mourn. They beat their heads with stone implements until they draw blood. The women usually inflict worse wounds on themselves than the men. It is common to see scar tissue on the foreheads of the aged as a result of repeated mourning. There is a set wail of sorrow that is sung at all times of grief.'

The next stage is an important one. As the heat raises blisters on the skin, it must be peeled off by the mother or wife or the closest relative; as the process continues, the flesh is patted back into place. Hurrell writes that intestinal decomposition is drained off by a bamboo inserted rectally. He continues:

'The mourning lasts for four days after which the body is placed in a sitting position on a specially constructed platform. The platform is constructed of banana palm trunks. The arms and legs are bent, and a bark girdle is passed between the legs and firmly tied. The smoking fire is lit and the skin continues to blister and the peeling of the skin is continued by relatives who, in the course of their mourning, smear themselves with the juices!'

I said to Tom, 'They must smell pretty high'.

'Sweet as a side of bacon,' he told me.

As the big day approached, the tension and excitement mounted. Mt Hagen was swarming with warriors waving plumes day and night. Some of the clans lived only a few hours' walk away, while others were several days distant. To house these a Cadet Patrol Officer was instructed to supervise the building of an enormous thatched house at least a couple of hundred yards long. 'My instant Hilton,' he called it, and they gathered tons of kau-kau (sweet potato) and an abundance of firewood and water to satisfy the multitudes.

The hotel, which was fully booked several weeks in advance, was not without its problems. Ian Parsons came to me and said that he had to find a plumber, it was desperate. I asked him why. 'The only place we've got hot water,' he said, 'is in the toilets.' I couldn't help laughing. 'It's no bloody laughing matter,' he stormed.

The hotel was opened, and aeroplanes were beginning to arrive with visitors. Mel Zebrovious was looking increasingly worried: he'd never managed a hotel before, and was really in at the deep end. The hot water problem had been sorted out, but there was tension in the kitchen. The chief cook was a big chap from Madang, his offsider a much smaller fellow from Manus Island. As is often the case with people from different areas, there was some bad feeling. It all boiled over (I'm sure boiled is an appropriate expression) when the cook picked up his offsider and sat him on the red-hot stove. The hotel was immediately cookless, the result of that exercise being one in hospital and one in jail. A couple more cooks had to be found at very short notice. Although not exactly up to hotel standard, they got by surprisingly well, with Mel's wife helping out.

The big day arrived and everything went like a well-oiled machine. The Administrator, Sir Donald Cleland, arrived to open it to the accompaniment of military bands, naval bands and police bands. There must have been 2000 visitors, most arriving by air. There was no doubt it was a great spectacle, it would be impossible to calculate the number of natives taking part – perhaps 5000 would not be an excessive estimate – with their bird of paradise plumes; it was a colourful spectacle that would be unequalled anywhere. The sing-sing competitors were magnificent in their formations and control, and although there were no incidents, I was glad that I was not one of the judges, who had difficulty in deciding the winning clan. Eventually they were selected and there was no mayhem. They headed a parade of truly primitive magnificence. All other events paled into insignificance. The visitors who had chartered aeroplanes, some from Australia, could not complain that they didn't get their money's worth. The Administrator made an admirable speech and Tom Ellis promised that the next show would be better, which no one believed, but he was proved right.

N I N E

T O T A L   E C L I P S E

ON 1 FEBRUARY 1962, a phenomenon occurred that caused a good deal of excitement and not a little inconvenience – it was a full eclipse of the sun. The remarkable thing about it was the extent to which it affected the natives. They knew of its approach some weeks before it was due – this may have been because many of their legends and beliefs are associated with stellar bodies, the sun, moon and stars.

February was normally the wettest month of the year and 1962 was no exception. Consequently, my labour line was down to about forty and although none of them could read or write, I was surprised that they knew so much about the eclipse so long before it was due. However, I strongly suspect that a Highlands trader, Brian Heagney, had more than a little to do with it. I don't know how long it was since there was any kind of an eclipse, total or otherwise, but I cannot believe that an event of this nature would not be well embedded in their folklore and with accompanying legends.

Heagney was a very astute trader with a number of trade stores through the Highlands and was not one to miss an opportunity to make a quick quid, and I am quite sure that it was he who convinced the natives that during the period of the eclipse they were in great danger of losing their eyesight. I reckon that he must have imported at least 10,000 pairs of coloured spectacles – a week before it was due they all started to wear them in anticipation, men, women and most of the children, on the plantation and everywhere else.

For days before it was due, the boss boy was asking Peter Warburton about what they referred to in pidgin as 'time bilong too dark'! There was no doubt that they were all extremely concerned and although both Peter and I did our best to reassure them, it was obvious that they were really scared. In a case like this there is absolutely nothing one can do. No amount of talking would change their belief that this particular eclipse was fraught with some special danger.

When the big day dawned, the sun rose in a fairly clear sky shining perfectly normally, but before long a shadow started to appear. Immediately, every single worker disappeared into his house, the entire labour line. I can't remember how long it lasted. I suggested to Peter that we might as well have a day off, so we went to the Banz Club, where several other planters had come to the same conclusion.

Altogether it was an interesting experience as the shadow gradually crossed over. When the sun reappeared, my labour line, somewhat sheepishly, came out of their houses. They still wore their dark glasses, in fact, they kept them on, presumably as a safety precaution, for the next couple of days. Events such as this are an interesting exercise in the understanding of primitive people. For a layman like myself it is very difficult to properly explain such phenomena, more particularly when they affect their own beliefs and cut across old superstitions, therefore they are best left alone.

A few days after the eclipse, I had to go to Port Moresby on business, mainly connected with the hotel. The manager of the South Pacific Brewery was Bill Johns and when the business, which was simple and straightforward, was concluded, we repaired to the Papua Club. During the course of the evening Bill told me that he was leaving for a tour of the territory in a few days and his plans included driving to the Highlands from Lae over the recently completed highway. It was a rugged trip, but as I told him it was well worthwhile; some of the scenery was spectacular if a little hazardous in places. It might even be made more interesting, I told him, if he got caught up in the odd landslide. However, we were well into the dry season and if all went according to plan, he would be passing through Banz on the following

Tuesday. I asked him to be sure to call in to Sigri for lunch and a cold beer or two or three. He said that he would probably be accompanied by his accountant, who I assured him would be equally welcome.

On my return a couple of days later, I told my wife to expect visitors on the coming Tuesday, they would probably be arriving for lunch. The day arrived and Bill Johns and his accountant drove up to the house right on time. I was waiting to greet them on the verandah and as they got out of the car, I could see that they were in a state of considerable agitation. His first words were,

'Tom, we picked up an unconscious woman back along the road.'

'Good God! What happened to her?'

'She was laying in a ditch by the side of the road three or four miles back beside a car that was upside down.'

I went over to his car and peered in the back, she was deathly white but breathing evenly. She was an attractive young woman, in her mid-twenties, I thought. We carried her to the house and placed her on a spare bed. I turned to Bill and said, 'There's a plane due at Banz in about twenty minutes, a regular mail run, I'll race in and hold it up'.

I decided to leave the girl on the bed until I had intercepted the plane, I thought it better not to move her until we were sure that I had secured the plane; it might be late or it might be diverted. I raced into Banz, passing the car, a Volkswagen that was upside down in the ditch. I got to the airstrip a few minutes before the mail plane came into sight. It landed, taxied up the airstrip to a halt, and I called to the captain sitting up in the cockpit, busy filling in his flight plan. He came down and I explained to him what had happened. While we were talking the passengers gathered around, listening to the conversation. Suddenly one turned to me and said, 'Excuse me, but I'm a doctor'. I could hardly believe such good fortune, 'Is that a fact?' He nodded.

I turned to the captain, Tom Deegan, and said, 'You'd be going to Hagen from here I take it?' He nodded, it was a routine flight. I said to the doctor, 'Perhaps it's best that you come back with me and examine her and if it's okay, we'll bring her back and put her on board.' We drove back to Sigri and after a brief examination the doctor said that it was okay to move her. His pronouncement was that she was concussed, how badly he couldn't say. We drove back to Banz and she was placed aboard and the aeroplane took off. From the time that Bill Johns arrived at my place to the time the aeroplane left was just under two hours. It was, as Bill Johns said, a copybook rescue. A few days later the ADO from Minj came over and took her VW away. I often wondered who the girl was.

The following year, 1963, was a busy one. The Western Highlands had attained some kind of maturity, and Tom Ellis was instructed to form a District Advisory Council. 'I want you on it,' he told me, 'you will be the Minj/Banz representative'.

'One of those honour and glory jobs, I suppose?'

'Not even that,' he assured me, 'that bit's mine.'

'Ours is not to reason why... into the Valley of Death, sort of thing.'

'You're getting the idea.'

It had been agreed that Goroka and Mt Hagen would stage their shows on alternate years, which was a good idea, and it was now our turn again. We had a preliminary meeting and I found myself on the committee. Because of the expansion of Mt Hagen, the airstrip had been cut up into building blocks and a new aerodrome of international standard had been laid down at Kagamuga, five miles out. Close by, an area for a showgrounds was gazetted.

Mel Zebrovious, our hotel manager, had been getting restless. He was married and had two children, and his wife had been at him to return to Australia. We had a meeting and bought him out for £2/10 a share, which was a pretty good price. He must have got sidetracked because the next I heard, he had taken some kind of a job on a remote Pacific island. There was no difficulty getting a new manager, but I was beginning to think that maybe we should unload the hotel. It was never really my cup of tea – I wasn't even getting my booze wholesale! Every time it looked as though we were getting ahead, something important cropped up and gave our overdraft another nudge – it only went in one direction, of course.

At a District Advisory Council meeting, Tom Ellis started cracking the whip, telling us that this second Hagen Show was to be The Greatest Show on Earth, all of which we'd heard before. He paused for a moment to let it sink in and then played his trump card. 'Lord de L'Isle will be opening it.'

We looked at one another, it was quite a bombshell – the Governor-General! There was only one higher. I turned to Norman Camps sitting beside me, 'I s'pose the Queen's too busy'.

We were now the Western Highlands District Agricultural Society and the show was expanded to cover agricultural exhibits, which included cattle, pigs and horses, equestrian events and polocrosse.

The experience and success of the last show gave us a flying start and no doubt because we were getting the Governor-General to open it. This no doubt contributed to the Administration in Port Moresby loosening the purse strings. The new showgrounds close to the new Kagamuga airstrip was humming with activity. Tom Ellis was going round terrorising all his Patrol Officers, promising to have their balls on a toasting fork over a hot fire if they didn't perform miracles – it was unquestionably going to be The Greatest Show on Earth. It was also the kind of stuff on which Tom Ellis thrived.

The day before the show opened saw the arrival of the G-G. His flight consisted of two RAAF planes, as befits royalty; one with Lord de L'Isle and a few aide de camps and one presumably for the baggage. Tom Ellis asked me to the Residency, where His Excellency was staying, for drinks after dinner. A rather quiet, unassuming man, he was well versed in New Guinea affairs and very interested in the approaching self-government and independence. Both Tom and I expressed the opinion that it was being rushed; the natives themselves were very uneasy, especially the highlanders.

The next day was a tremendous success. The G-G, riding in an open Land Rover in full regalia, made an impressive figure, and first of the decorations on his breast, I noted, was the purple ribbon of the Victoria Cross. After circling the arena, he mounted a rostrum and the assembled bands played the national anthem. He then made a speech that I am sure few people heard, it being effectively drowned by the excited highlanders, who obviously loved the impressive panoply. There was no doubt that this show was better than the last one, and the show ball was a fitting finale. The invitations would have been a collector's item:

IN THE DISTINGUISHED PRESENCE OF

HIS EXCELLENCY THE RIGHT HONOURABLE LORD DE L'ISLE

V.C. P.C. G.C.M.G. K. ST JOHN

ETC. ETC.

When it was all over, we quietly went home with a feeling of satisfaction. Our eldest daughter, thirteen, was the proud recipient of a blue ribbon for best rider in the equestrian event, and Sigri Plantation won a commendation in the coffee section. The Western Highlands had reached maturity. The Mt Hagen Show really put it on the map.

The planters in the Banz area were a fairly close-knit mob; most weekends there was a convivial gathering at someone's place. On Saturday 6 April it was my turn. It was a jovial gathering of about twenty people, all of whom gave a good account of themselves so that by three o'clock in the afternoon refreshments were getting dangerously low, necessitating a quick trip to Banz to replenish stocks. It did not take me long to drive in to Ian Rutledge's store close to the Banz airstrip. I roused Ian out of a Sunday afternoon doze and when I had loaded a few cases of life-savers into the back of my truck, he invited me in for a drink, which I felt would be bad manners to refuse.

We had only been sitting down for a few minutes when Johnny Jones, a road worker who had been driving a bulldozer, burst in, dropped into a chair completely breathless and burst out with the news that he had been on the Wahgi River duck shooting with Peter Maxtone-Graham when their dinghy rammed a submerged log and capsized. Maxtone-Graham had his small son with him, and a half caste lad of perhaps five or six years old. The river was running strongly and although Peter couldn't swim, somehow he managed to push the boy in front of him towards the riverbank, which was only a few yards away, where the lad was able to hold onto some bushes and reach safety. In the meantime, Johnny Jones was trying, without much success, to recover the guns that had been tipped out in the capsize. He told us that when he looked across to where he had last seen Maxtone-Graham, there was no sign of him. The little boy, Mungo, was crying and when asked where his father was, he pointed downstream. There was no sign of Peter. Jones made several attempts to find him; the stream was running fast and the channel was very deep. In desperation he ran to Rutledge's house, a good five miles.

We all leapt into my ute and drove to Doug McGraw's place, which was a few minutes away, and explained the situation to him. We rushed down to his aeroplane parked at the top of the airstrip. A Cessna, it had two large doors to facilitate loading, which Doug quickly removed, enabling an unobstructed view. We strapped ourselves in and within a few minutes were airborne. We followed the winding river at tree-top level on the way downstream, then we turned to come back at a higher level. Their boat was settled against a sandbank, upside down. There was no sign of Peter. Thinking of the length of time that had elapsed between when the boat had turned over and when Jones reached Rutledge's place, it seemed a forlorn hope. Had he been able to swim he would have no doubt survived. It has always astonished me when someone tells me that they can't swim, especially men who choose to live in isolated places. We landed just after sundown, I drove back to Sigri to tell my guests the sad news. Peter Maxtone-Graham was well known and popular. Early the next morning the search got underway. A boat party found the body about eight miles downstream. It was the first fatality our little community had experienced, and we all felt it very much.

Shakespeare said, 'The evil that men do lives after them, the good is oft interred with their bones'. This is not true, of course, and at the inevitable wake after the funeral at Mt Hagen, many stories were told of Peter's wry sense of humour. I recalled not very long before the fatal accident when he and I were excelling ourselves at the Banz Club, and ruminating on some of life's injustices such as the excessive grants of lands made to missionaries.

We were undoubtedly in an advanced state of intoxication when we attempted to redress what we firmly believed was a gross imbalance of justice. Calling ourselves the Wahgi Evangelists, we concocted a letter to a Moresby barrister, Norman White, who we both knew very well. Bolstered by the knowledge that Norman had a quick wit and a lively sense of humour, we made him our Honorary Legal Adviser.

In the letter, we pointed out that we were anxious to obtain large acreages of land in the name of The Lord, Tom Cole and Peter Maxtone-Graham. Hallelujah! Norman entered into the spirit of the thing and replied as follows:

NORMAN   WHITE
BARRISTER & SOLICITOR

TELEPHONE 2660
REF. No.   M.24/14

P. O. BOX 21,
PORT MORESBY,
PAPUA.

23rd June, 1958.

T. E. Cole, Esq.,
President,
Wahgi Evangelists,
M I N J.   T.N.G.

Dear Sir,

      I received your letter of the 14th instant. There is no difficulty at all in forming the Wahgi Evangelists into an incorporated mission. It is simply necessary to prove to the Administrator-in-council that you have formed the mission for promoting religion, that it is your intention to apply the profits in promoting religion and that it is your intention to prohibit the payment of any dividend to the members of the mission. In order to persuade the Administrator to these points, it may be as well to change your names by deed poll and I would suggest that Mr. Maxtone-Graham change his to Robert Knox and that you change yours to Charles Wesley. Another selection of suitable pseudonyms for the two of you can be found in Book 1 of "Paradise Lost". The only difficulty is to know whether, having persuaded the Administrator that you do not intend to pay any dividends to members, you are still able to have the same fervour for the proposed mission work.

                     Yours to a cinder,

It was now harvest time once more. Every plantation was loaded with coffee. The blood-red cherries that always seemed to ripen overnight were a stimulating sight, to the owner at any rate. David Falconer and I were now employing several European coffee buyers on a regular basis and they brought in loads of native coffee. In May we picked for three weeks straight, then a couple of days' breather, and at it again.

In September we had another visitor of some importance, the Prime Minister of Australia, The Right Honourable R. G. Menzies, and his wife Dame Pattie. There was a reception at Mt Hagen to which most of us were invited. The following day, the Prime Minister and his party came to Banz where we entertained them at our club. I think that by now we were starting to get slightly blasé.

Then, quite suddenly, the year was gone again; it seemed to slip down a hole when no one was looking.

Nineteen sixty-four got away to a very quiet start: new coffee plantings were coming in to bearing, the coffee market was strong, and there was every indication of a good year. The only fly in the ointment was the hotel, which was becoming an increasing worry. I was never really at home with it. However, I had heard that some of the big companies were eyeing it off with interest, how strong I didn't know. I let a few hints drop here and there – the results were almost instantaneous with the New Guinea Company indicating an interest. They dithered around for a while, had a lot of enthusiasm for a start, but it gradually tapered off.

Steamships Trading Company was the next to become interested. Del Underwood, the general manager, got all worked up and finally some sort of a deal was hammered out; good enough for me to take a month off.

At this time both our daughters were at boarding school in Sydney and Kath had returned to be closer to them, and also with the object of establishing a home in Australia. She had been missing the children terribly. Unfortunately, Kath was never really home on the plantation. I loafed around Sydney for a week or so and then went up to the mountains for a week's trout fishing. Kiandra was marvellous, the fish were rising and there were no telephones. Then it was back to Sydney and down to earth to find that Steamships had changed their minds about buying our hotel; everything turned sour. I cursed my way back to New Guinea, and called on Steamships. Underwood was extraordinarily amiable; he could beat me hollow. A week later he sent me a telegram to say that at a directors' meeting a decision had been made to take up an option, I nearly told him to stick his option, but not quite. A month later, at the end of June, the deal was finalised. A couple of weeks later, the hotel sensibly caught fire and burnt down. But I didn't own it then, thank God!

The next year, 1965, started off quietly. Once the festivities were over, most planters concerned themselves with getting their labour line back together. A few years ago very few natives had ever heard of Christmas and New Year, but it hadn't taken them long to get the hang of it. I note that in my diary I started off with forty workers but, '...could do with 100'. Picking started early.

Tom Ellis had squeezed enough money out of a reluctant Administration to build a new suspension bridge over the Wahgi River. The existing one was in a pretty parlous state. Peter Harbeck's tractor and trailer had ended up in the river and by a miracle no one was hurt. The Government engineer who came over to inspect it didn't seem to think that it was serious. 'He got his tractor and trailer back didn't he?' he was heard to say. As Peter said, 'You'd think the bastard was spending his own money'. Some of these Government fellows ended up like that after a while.

Hornibrooks, who were building all sorts of things like airstrips and bridges, won the contract, and Mick Lloyd, their engineer, came over to inspect the site. I had known Mick for some time and invited him to stay with us, which he readily accepted. He was great company and a marvellous raconteur. Before he left, he more than repaid my hospitality by putting me on the company payroll as the Banz representative.

'What will I have to do, Mick?' I asked.

He laughed, 'I'm not too sure at the moment, but I'll think something up'.

At the club a couple of days later I mentioned as casually as I could my appointment, '...now "we" had the bridge contract'. It caused a mild sensation, and naturally someone asked, 'How come?'

'I'm the the only one with the qualifications,' I solemnly told them, which brought forth howls of laughter. A couple of months later a team arrived to start work and that was the day I went off the payroll.

In June I had to go to Madang to arrange a charter. Bristol freighters were giving a great service, they could lift ten tons. Out at the aerodrome all was bustle and hurry, engines roaring before take-off, trucks dodging around between aeroplanes looking for the right one.

I was looking for the New Guinea Company agent when a Department of Civil Aviation official approached me: 'Joe Walachy's lost, you go with Ivan Bennett.'

Father Joe was a well-loved Catholic Mission priest with hundreds of hours of flying experience, and knew the country like the back of his hand. I had flown with him a couple of times in my Sepik days. Not Joe, everyone said, he has landed somewhere, but with an uneasy sinking feeling just the same.

In a situation like this, everyone knew what to do. It wasn't a case of, 'Will you go with Ivan Bennett?' He pointed to a Cessna that was warming up, I ran over and climbed in, and Ivan took off with a chart on his knees. A spotter is very necessary, as a pilot has enough to do flying the aeroplane, usually at a low altitude, without looking for a grounded aeroplane. He pointed to the area we had been given to cover; two planes had already taken off in front of us. Ivan levelled off at 2000 feet – it was a bit dodgy, there was a fair bit of cloud about as we headed towards an escarpment.

We had been in the air for about two hours when Ivan got a call over his radio. I couldn't hear properly, but as he banked steeply and headed back towards Madang, he shook his head and turned a thumb down; I knew what that meant. Ivan had just heard that they'd found him: poor Joe had flown into the side of a mountain. Obviously, he had been in cloud at the time. Again, everybody felt the loss very much.

The following year our social activities started off with a visit from Australia by Ceb Barnes, the Minister for Territories. After a few rounds of drinks, we endeavoured to straighten him out on some of the more pressing problems of our district, to which he wasn't overly receptive – our problem was we didn't have any voting power. It makes a hell of a difference. The year was also notable for a spate of tea planting. The big companies were coming in and dazzling everyone with their high pressure activities, which resulted in an increased demand for labour, a logical consequence of which was a gradual rise in wages.

We had a visit from another Governor-General, Lord Casey this time, to officially open the first tea factory, which was enthusiastically supported, mainly because of the booze that was turned on. None of us could really be called dedicated supporters of Moet et Chandon, but it would have been bad manners to have refused; it didn't seem too bad after a while.

Clive Batten, the General Manager of Carpenters plantation division, called in at the end of the month and asked me if I would be prepared to sell Sigri. I told him I'd sell anything at a price, which seemed to scare him off. He left after getting through half a bottle of scotch – I thought, if he comes back I must remember to add it to the price.

August was the Mt Hagen Show again. There were no G-Gs to spare this year, but we got by very well, and there were more visitors than at any previous show. When it was all over, I dropped in at the club to steady my nerves for the forty-mile and three-hour drive home.

When I left I was in very good form and as I turned on to the main road that would take me home, I became aware of headlights behind me. Perhaps, I thought, one of my neighbours also was on his way home. He started to get uncomfortably close, his headlights blazing at me from my rear vision mirror. I put on a bit more pace, but I couldn't shake him off; I was starting to get annoyed. I twisted the rear vision mirror, I couldn't stand the glare, and settled down to keep ahead of him. I put on as much speed as I dare, crashing across creek crossings, slithering around bends, twisting and turning on a dirt track that was wet from recent rain. Suddenly, to my great relief, my tormentor disappeared and I was able to slow down to a reasonable speed.

It was several days later when a car drove up to the house and out stepped no less a person than the Superintendent of Police. I greeted him jovially and asked him inside. He appeared uncomfortable and embarrassed, excusing himself as he took an official-looking document from his briefcase. I took it from him and was astonished to find that it was a summons to appear in the Mt Hagen Court. The charge? Reckless and dangerous driving. The story emerged: a young and enthusiastic constable saw me leave the club and decided that I was in no fit state to drive, a decision that was to cost him dearly. I, of course, had no idea whatever that it was a police officer who had followed me that night. I naturally assumed that it was another enthusiastic planter, perhaps trying to scare me, decidedly a wrong line to take. The point where I'd shaken him off was where he had failed to negotiate a bend and had wrecked his Mini Moke. I imagine that walking back to Mt Hagen did nothing to improve his feelings towards me.

A few days later, with some trepidation, I faced the court. The magistrate took very little time to deal with the case: he unceremoniously threw it out of court and castigated the officer in no uncertain manner. In his summing up, he told the unfortunate policeman that if anyone should be on a dangerous driving charge it should be him. I felt a little bit sorry for him – just a little.

Cole and Falconer, coffee buyers, was by now going full blast. The road to Lae was in reasonable shape and David and I had invested in a five-ton International truck, the limit the road would carry. It was doing regular trips taking coffee down and returning with plantation supplies. Unfortunately, one day it went over the side going through Chimbu where, on most stretches, there is anything up to 1000 feet drop on either side. We got the bad news one Sunday at the club when another driver informed us that it was in a creek at the bottom of a 5000-foot gorge. I don't think it was anything like 5000, but anyway 1000 was plenty.

'There has been a lot of rain,' he told us cheerfully, 'it'll be washed away by now.' We asked about Charlie Ross and he told us that Charlie was in the Kundiawa 'haus sick' (hospital). 'He jumped out as it went over; he might have done a rib, nothing serious though. He was driving with his door open,' the driver explained, a practice followed by most drivers when going through the Chimbu. Charlie turned up a few days later. He had a broken rib but assured us he would be all right by the time we got another truck.

It was insured so we got all that straightened out and ordered another one. The second truck lasted until September when it too went over the side; not so far down this time but the result was the same. The insurance company was quite upset about this, which I suppose was predictable. They suggested that we stay out of the trucking business, with which we agreed. We thought that if it was going to go on like this we would probably lose a driver as well. Charlie's reflexes might be slowing down a bit, too; since breaking a rib, he might not be able to jump fast enough next time.

Peter Warburton, my plantation manager, suddenly gave notice to quit after receiving a better offer, which threw me into a temporary panic. He was a very good man and I was sorry to lose him. However, I was fortunate in getting Ken Godden as his replacement and everything settled down once more. Although coffee production was rising every year, expenses were doing the same, or faster it seemed. Ken Godden was doing an excellent job, and when picking started in February, he told me there was every indication it would be a good year.

In August, Clive Batten surfaced again with what seemed an anxious enquiry as to whether I was interested in selling the plantation. He left slightly sozzled, and I mentally chalked up another bottle of whisky. A month went by and he came back again. His company, he said, was quite serious and he had recommended that they make a firm offer. Now the real haggling started. We went through the business of clauses being changed and deleted, and finally got it all hammered out sufficiently to send to our respective solicitors.

The finalising of the sale of Sigri was spread over several months involving visits to Port Moresby and solicitors' offices. In the evenings, Clive and I usually dined at the Gateway Hotel, where quite a good floor show was run by Larry Danielson. He was a lively entertainer and, having known me for some time, was able to judge with reasonable accuracy at what stage he could confidently announce over the public address system, 'I am now going to call on Tom Cole to give us one of the monologues for which he is so justly famous'.

Being known to more than half the audience, this would be greeted with a great deal of enthusiasm and I would then proceed with gusto to deliver a slightly risqué piece dealing with a group of ladies whose competence in the field of flatulence was a never-ending source of delight. It was quite lengthy and verses such as this one rarely failed to bring a standing ovation:

> *And old Mrs Jones had a lovely backside*
> *With a bunch of red hair and a wart on each side*
> *And fancied her chances of winning with ease*
> *Having trained on a diet of cabbage and cheese*

Danielson was a man of many parts, and his engagement at the Gateway did not appear to be of a very substantial or permanent nature. So, it did not surprise me when he left the hotel, having acquired the management (I didn't imagine that it was the captaincy) of 110-foot Fairmile, an ex-naval patrol boat. They were powered with twin GM diesels and were very fast. In fact, it was one of these boats that brought General MacArthur out of Manila when the Philippines were overrun by the Japanese.

It was at the Port Moresby Yacht Club where I next saw Danielson. I was with a group that included Bryan Gray who, at the time, was managing Air Niugini. Danielson joined us and the talk turned to the Fairmile. He told us that he was planning to run the vessel on regular trips up and down the coast with tourists. Bryan was immediately interested and the discussion swung round to Air Niugini's interest in tourism, which they were endeavouring to develop. Danielson then suggested that he have a look at the boat, which was moored at the main wharf. We all drove down and went aboard, Larry giving us a guided tour of the boat. I was quite impressed with the quality of the fittings and so was Bryan. In the saloon the discussion became quite animated as they planned tours together. Danielson explained that there was only one proviso: the Queen was coming to Port Moresby later in the year and he would be taking her and her entourage out to the Trobriand Islands. It would have to be reserved for that week. No trouble, said Bryan. However, this venture never eventuated. Shortly after, it was chartered by an oil company to go up the Fly River, where it unfortunately ran onto a sand bank and is there to this day.

Danielson left Port Moresby and settled in Australia, where he endeavoured to apply his considerable talents to making a quick quid by scattering a few bombs indiscriminately in some of Woolworths' supermarkets. He became better known as the 'Woolworths Bomber'. I don't suppose the Queen of England ever heard about that. These events took place some time in the future, but I relate them here for the sake of continuity.

Clive Batten and I finalised our business and I went to the bank with a cheque with so many noughts on it, it reminded me of some of my more excessive overdrafts all added together.

Although this was not the end of my years in New Guinea, it was the end of an era that has gone forever: self-government and then independence overtook these people like a tidal wave.

A population of more than three and a half million had in turn been governed by Germans, Australians, Japanese, and Australians again (not to mention the Americans in the war). Here was a place with something like 700 different languages; the pressures of tribal laws, tribal thinking, and deep-seated superstitions – where cargo cult and cannibalism went hand in hand – and half a dozen missions fighting for their souls (something they didn't even know they possessed). Then into this confusion a 'Westminster-type government' was dropped into their laps by an Australian Administration. With a cheery pat on the back and a 'You'll be right, fellas', the rug was pulled from under them in 1975 and they were left to grope their way to a new destiny.

They were in the Big League now.

Under the circumstances, they were fortunate in having for their Prime Minister that very fine man Michael Somare, who steered them through their first turbulent years with the masterly touch of a polished politician, and also with a sympathy and understanding that is rare in any political world.

The teething troubles of this infant nation began on Bougainville in the Northern Solomons Province, where a group of militants with little or no knowledge of the ramifications of international business forced the closure of the copper and gold mine at Panguna, one of the biggest in the world. With a 'declaration of independence' they isolated themselves as effectively as though they were spinning dizzily on another planet.

There is much on the credit side. Papua New Guinea has immense mineral resources. The gold reserves at Lihir and Porgera are breathtakingly immense – billions on current values.

In the fulness of time, the Papua New Guineans will find their feet, but it will be a long, hard road.

ALSO PUBLISHED IN IMPRINT LIVES

HELL WEST AND CROOKED
TOM COLE

Hell West and Crooked is the autobiographical account of a young Englishman's life in the Outback during the 1920s and 1930s. It traces his life from his days as a drover and stationhand in the toughest country in Australia to his experiences as a buffalo shooter and crocodile hunter in the Northern Territory before the war. First published in 1988, it has now sold over 90 000 copies.

'Tom Cole is a living legend, a real-life Crocodile Dundee. His stories paint a vivid picture of wild and exciting times in the Australian Outback.'
MELBOURNE SUNDAY EXPRESS

'It's a real-life story of the pioneering days of the Top End that out-adventures anything fiction writers could hope to produce.'
THE WEST AUSTRALIAN

'It is a story of the Outback and cattlemen and women, stripped of glamour, that will become an Australian classic to rub covers with authors like Ion Idriess.'
GOLD COAST BULLETIN

'*Hell West and Crooked* is a valuable contribution to the preservation of the real history of Australia.'
THE CHRONICLE